Education
for an
Engaged Citizenry

The Hutchins School of Liberal Studies

D1739166

Edited By Debora Hammond, PhD

ISBN: 9781073871490

Education is a kind of continuing dialogue,
and a dialogue assumes different points of view.

It must be remembered that the purpose of education
is not to fill the minds of students with facts...
it is to teach them to think.

~ Robert Maynard Hutchins

Apart from inquiry, apart from the praxis,
individuals cannot be truly human.

Knowledge emerges only through the restless, impatient,
continuing, hopeful inquiry human beings pursue in the world,
with the world, and with each other.

~ Paulo Freire

DEDICATION AND ACKNOWLEDGEMENT

This anthology is dedicated to the visionary faculty who created and sustained the Hutchins School over the past 50 years, to the staff and administration for their continued support and, perhaps most of all, to the students who have provided the inspiration and motivation to keep the program alive. With sincere appreciation for the efforts of the faculty and alumni who took the time to share their thoughts; for the grant from the Emeritus and Retired Faculty and Staff Association to support publication costs; and for Debora Lewis and her patience and skill in formatting the cover and manuscript.

Note on the cover photos:
In celebrating the 50th anniversary of the founding of the Hutchins School, I wanted to honor the faculty who have served over the course of that half-century. Although I was not able to locate photos for all members of the faculty who have contributed their inspiration to this venture, and I apologize for any omissions, I think most are represented here.

Front cover – from top, left to right
Roshni Rustomji, River (Heidi) LaMoreaux, Stephanie Dyer, Lu Mattson
Janet Hess, Tony Mountain, Eric McGuckin, Nelson (Buzz) Kellogg
Wendy Ostroff, Warren Olson, Lou Miller
Les Adler, Jeannine Thompson, Barbara Lesch McCaffry, Francisco H. Vázquez
Ardath Lee, Debora Hammond, Mutombo M'Panya, Maurice Blaug

Back cover – from top, left to right
Lou Miller, Michael Coleman, Tony Mountain, Les Adler, Susan Barnes, Richard Zimmer
Tom Shaw, Rob Weiner
Justine Law, Margaret Anderson
Ajay Gehlewat, Ben Frymer
Wendy Ostroff, Ianthe Brautigan Swensen, Debora Hammond, Ajay Gehlewat, Russ Scarola, Donna Garbesi (Advisor), Stephanie Dyer, Eric McGuckin

Table of Contents

Introduction: On Education and Democracy

Debora Hammond

> Debora Hammond joined the Hutchins faculty full-time in 1997 after teaching for a year and a half while completing her PhD in the History of Science at the University of California at Berkeley. Her dissertation on the history of systems thinking was published in 2003 as *The Science of Synthesis: Exploring the Social Implications of General Systems Theory*. Systems thinking has informed her teaching, and resonates with the Hutchins approach to education in its emphasis on transdisciplinarity, collaboration, and inclusivity. Since her retirement in 2017 she has been working with local community groups on issues relating to climate change, public banking, and indigenous rights.

This anthology was inspired by the occasion of the 50th anniversary of the founding of the Hutchins School of Liberal Studies at Sonoma State University. Hutchins emerged during the tumultuous period of the late 1960s and, like other experimental programs established during that time, it sought to address what many saw as the limitations of the dominant approach to higher education. In an email exchange, as this project was just getting underway, Les Adler eloquently summed up the motivation for these initiatives:

> A strong drive for educational reform in the 1960s and early 1970s prompted the creation of a variety of experimental programs at colleges and universities across the nation. The majority had similar goals: crossing artificially restrictive disciplinary boundaries between fields of knowledge; bridging the gulf between teachers and learners; and enhancing the

process of active and collaborative learning in the context of what later became known as Learning Communities.

One of the most comprehensive and successful programs to emerge was the Hutchins School of Liberal Studies at the then Sonoma State College – later Sonoma State University – now in its fifth decade.

It is a testament to the vision and commitment of the founding faculty, and Warren Olson in particular, that the Hutchins School has survived, and even thrived, over the past half century. The Hutchins School is truly unique, particularly as a program within a large public university system, but also in comparison with many small private liberal arts colleges.

Robert Maynard Hutchins and the Great Conversation

In his chapter on "The Origin and Birth of the Hutchins School of Liberal Studies," Warren Olson describes his rationale for choosing to name the program after Robert Maynard Hutchins. As President and later Chancellor of the University of Chicago between 1929 and 1951, Hutchins was one of the most outspoken advocates of the need for innovation and reform in higher education. He promoted interdisciplinary initiatives in teaching and research, and emphasized the importance of active student engagement in the learning process, through Socratic dialogue and inquiry; both critical pedagogical commitments in the Hutchins School. He saw liberal education as an essential foundation for democratic society, inspiring his later work with the Center for the Study of Democratic Institutions, which he founded in 1959. His comments in the Preface to *The Great Conversation: The Substance of a Liberal Education* (1952) are more relevant today than ever:

> We believe that the reduction of the citizen to an object of propaganda, private and public, is one of the greatest dangers to democracy.... The reiteration of slogans, the distortion of the news, the great storm of propaganda that beats upon the citizen twenty-four hours a day all his life long mean either that democracy must fall prey to the loudest and most

persistent propagandists or that the people must save themselves by strengthening their minds so that they can appraise the issues for themselves. (xiii)

For Dr. Hutchins, the foundation of a liberal education was grounded in the "Great Books" of Western civilization, and he worked with Mortimer Adler to publish a 54 volume set including what they considered to be the most important works in this tradition. Their project grew out of a revival of interest in the liberal arts and a broader cross-disciplinary approach to learning. In *The Great Conversation,* which is the first volume of the series, Hutchins explains that they chose to leave out books published after 1900; and I was surprised to learn that they did not consider Emerson, Whitman, Thoreau, or Mark Twain to measure up to the other books in the set. However, while there are a few universities that continue to use the Great Books as the foundation of their curriculum, the Hutchins School is focused much more broadly on contemporary issues and draws on a variety of cultural traditions. Over the years, the readings selected in the lower division sequence have evolved significantly; indeed they change every year, as new faculty join the planning cadres. The list of thirty required texts for the first semester of LIBS 101, in the Appendix of Warren Olson's article, provides a sense of the breadth of the curriculum outlined by the founders that first year.

William Cronon (1998) echoes some of Dr. Hutchins's concerns in his discussion of the goals of a liberal education, which he describes as "an educational tradition that celebrates and nurtures human freedom." Rather than focusing on a particular curriculum, however, he highlights the personal qualities of individuals who embody the values of a liberal education. Some of these qualities reflect the more traditional academic skills, including the ability to listen and hear, to read and understand, and to write clearly, persuasively and movingly. In addition, however, Cronon lists qualities that are not normally considered part of a university curriculum, such as humility, tolerance, and self-criticism; as well as the capacity to nurture and empower the people around them. Finally, he suggests that, "more than anything else, being an educated person means being able to see connections that allow one to make sense of the world and act within it in creative ways," and further that "a liberal education is about gaining the power and the wisdom, the generosity and the freedom to connect" (76-79).

Generosity, humility, tolerance, self-criticism – these are the intangibles that are so difficult to measure on an objective test or to document in an assessment of educational effectiveness. And yet they are critical to our collective survival in these turbulent times. The Hutchins School seeks to cultivate these qualities through the process of collaborative inquiry embodied in the seminar. While we might challenge Dr. Hutchins's valorization of the West, which he describes as the "Civilization of the Dialogue," we would embrace his characterization of the spirit of inquiry so central to a democratic society: "Nothing is to remain un-discussed. Everybody is to speak his mind. No proposition is to be left unexamined" (1952: 1).

Henry Giroux (2006) offers another perspective on the importance of higher education in preserving a culture of democracy, in his discussion of the critical role of public intellectuals. Decrying the "ascendancy of cynicism and anti-democratic tendencies in the United States," he suggests that "defending the institutions and mechanisms that provide the pedagogical conditions for critical and engaged citizenship" is one of the most crucial tasks confronting educators (63). As the university has become increasingly corporatized, Giroux notes the tendency for some academics to retreat into a kind of moral indifference, severing the connection between learning and public life, "convinced that education is now about job training" (65). Instead he argues that the academic community should serve as the conscience of American society, and devote its energy to the creation of a more livable world:

> It is imperative that public intellectuals within and outside of the university defend higher education as a democratic public sphere, connect academic work to public life, and advance a notion of pedagogy that provides students with models of individual and social agency that enable them to be both engaged citizens and active participants in the struggle for global democracy. (66)

4

Paulo Freire and the Pedagogy of the Oppressed

If Robert Hutchins provided the name and the initial inspiration for the Hutchins School, Paulo Freire (1970) provided the pedagogical framework, offering a model of agency that empowers the students, both in the classroom and in the world at large. Most influential in the Hutchins community is his discussion of the "banking concept" of education, which our students are introduced to as they enter the program. In this approach, which characterizes the majority of our educational institutions from kindergarten through higher education, "education... becomes an act of depositing, in which the students are the depositories and the teacher is the depositor" (53). In contrast, Freire proposes what he calls the "liberatory" and "problem-posing" approach. Denouncing the system of oppression that is perpetuated in the dominant model of education, which he sees as dehumanizing, he argues instead for a model of education that nurtures freedom and the transformation of consciousness, supporting students young and old in their "ontological vocation to become fully human" (56). Education in this model is a partnership between students and teachers; knowledge an evolutionary process of inquiry.

So much of higher education involves taking notes in large lecture courses, and feeding back information from readings and lectures on the exam. There is very little opportunity for meaningful interaction or exploring alternative perspectives. This approach disempowers the student and reinforces passivity. Students are not able to develop their own ideas, or to learn from their peers as they engage in dialogue with each other. The dominant pedagogical approach is generally positivistic – "objective" and expert-based. As a result, students are trained to think that there are simple, pre-determined answers to complex problems, and they are less likely to question the simplistic, short-sighted, and self-serving presentations that pass for public discussion of challenging issues in most of today's media. If individuals are to become more actively engaged in the decisions that shape their lives, they need to have a sense of ownership in the process, instead of passively deferring to the "expertise" of those in leadership positions.

In its commitment to critical inquiry in the spirit of Freire, the Hutchins School offers an interactive, student-centered pedagogy, with a more constructivist and critical orientation. It is constructivist in the sense that it is concerned with the meaning that students themselves find in the material they are reading. It is dialectical, pluralistic, participatory, and seeks to cultivate mutual understanding. Students often report that they learn the most from hearing the various perspectives of their peers; at the end of her second year, one student in my section reported that the most important thing she had learned was to listen to something she disagreed with, without immediately reacting. The Hutchins pedagogy is critical, in that issues of power are not only an integral part of the curriculum, but are also addressed through the structure of the learning environment itself. By allowing students to share the power of the traditional authority figure, they learn to have confidence in their own ideas and to challenge received wisdom when their own perceptions support alternative views. Furthermore, this approach enhances skills in collaborative problem solving, as well as such values as mutual respect and inclusion, which are essential to the realization of a more equitable and sustainable future. During my tenure in Hutchins I have gained a tremendous appreciation for this unique and enduring experiment in integrative learning.

The Basic Scheme

There are three primary elements that distinguish the program: an interdisciplinary (or trans-disciplinary) curriculum, a seminar based pedagogy that fosters dialogue and critical inquiry, and an integrated general education program, which could be seen as the hallmark of Hutchins. These various dimensions of the program will be described throughout the chapters that follow, but a brief overview of the structure of the program might serve as a helpful orientation for the reader.

General education requirements are designed to provide students with a comprehensive academic background, and to lay the foundation for specialization in an upper division major. These requirements are usually met through a smorgasbord approach where students take a sampling of courses across a prescribed range of disciplines; normally these courses are large lecture courses, often taught by adjunct faculty. In most cases these courses are accorded a kind of secondary status; faculty prefer to focus on their academic specialty, and students see these requirements as something to "get through." If students have an opportunity to enroll in a small seminar, it is generally not until their junior or senior year, and it will be narrowly focused on a specialized area of study. While many universities are beginning to incorporate more interactive courses in the lower division, such as the Freshman Year Experience at Sonoma State, these courses lack the depth and breadth of the integrated general education program offered in Hutchins.

When students enroll in Hutchins as freshmen, they are signing up for a sequence of four 12-unit seminars that together complete their lower division general education requirements, with the exception of mathematics (which would have been challenging to integrate into the seminar format). Each of the four seminars is organized around a particular theme, integrating natural science, social science, and the humanities in relation to that theme: LIBS 101: The Human Enigma; LIBS 102: In Search of Self; LIBS 201: Exploring the Unknown; and LIBS 202: Challenge and Response in the Modern World. Currently there are five sections of each seminar, with roughly 15 students and one member of the faculty assigned to each section. Those five faculty form the "cadre" for that seminar and work together to plan the curriculum for that semester. Due to both internal and external pressures, the weekly schedule is changing, but traditionally each seminar met three times a week for two to three hours, and all five seminars came together once a week for lectures, films, field trips, guest speakers and other activities.

Although the upper division program has evolved considerably over the years, the basic framework remains. In order to complete the requirements for the Hutchins major, students enroll in an upper division seminar in each of four different core areas: Core A: Society and Self; Core B: The Individual and the Material World; Core C: The

Arts and Human Experience; and Core D: Consciousness and Reality. For students who transfer into the program as juniors, there is an additional seminar, LIBS 302: Introduction to Liberal Studies, which provides an orientation to the program. These seminars are broadly interdisciplinary, and faculty have considerable freedom to create courses that reflect their personal interests. I generally taught courses in the Core B area, which included "The Global Food Web"; "Water Matters"; "Health and Healing"; and "Ecology and Economics." During the final semester, students enroll in LIBS 402: Senior Synthesis in which they compile a portfolio of their work throughout the program, write an intellectual autobiography, and complete a senior project to be presented to the Hutchins community.

The remainder of the upper division curriculum depends upon whether the student is planning to pursue a teaching career, in which case the program includes courses that meet the requirements for admission to the credential program; or, alternatively, is interested in pursuing a more general liberal arts education. Students in the latter category are able to create their own area of interest and can apply courses from other departments toward their major requirements in Hutchins. Often these students will complete a Minor or a second Major, in another field. In addition to the residential program, an on-line Degree Completion Program (DCP) was designed by Ardath Lee and established in 1997 under the Hutchins umbrella for working adults seeking to complete their education. The 40 unit Major is modeled after the integrated lower division program, with a sequence of four ten-unit courses that meet once a month on Saturdays, with weekly online assignments in between.

The Hutchins School is a very demanding program, for both students and faculty. While the smaller class size is an advantage, facilitating a seminar can be far more challenging than presenting a lecture, and the number of contact hours is substantial. However, I feel tremendously fortunate to have stumbled across the program as I was completing my doctorate, and to have spent the remainder of my career as a member of the faculty. I believe it embodies a model of

education that effectively addresses the most ɪ
increasingly global social order: for mutua
compassion, and for collaborative efforts to ɾ
and articulate common goals. The skills t
through the program, which include the
conflicting points of view in a non-adversarial manner, and the
willingness to suspend judgment and to examine their own beliefs
and assumptions, are absolutely critical in a democratic society.

Brief Overview of the Chapters to Follow

The book opens with a "Declaration of Interdependence," which was
written by students in Tony Mountain's Fall 1988 freshman seminar.
It embodies the spirit of Hutchins, and provides a great example of
the creativity and initiative that the program nurtures. The
remaining chapters are organized more or less chronologically.

The five chapters in the first section are written by faculty who joined
the Hutchins School in the first two or three years of the program. In
his chapter about the founding of Hutchins, Warren Olson
introduces the theme of the dialectic between Apollonian structure
and Dionysian freedom, which is echoed throughout this collection;
as for example, in Maurice Blaug's drawing illustrating the tension
between order and disorder. Warren's account has often been
assigned to students as an introduction to the program, along with
Les Adler's article, "Uncommon Sense," on the kind of
transformative learning that is possible in a learning community.
Both Les's article and Richard Zimmer's discussion of the
anthropologist's role were previously published and are included
with permission from the publishers. And Tony Mountain offers a
delightful account of the way in which literature can inspire
reflection.

The second section includes perspectives from faculty who joined the
program beginning in 1990, twenty years after its initial launch.
Francisco Vazquez and Buzz Kellogg joined in 1990 and 1991
respectively; then between 1997 and 2017 several new faculty became
part of the Hutchins family, as the founding faculty retired. Francisco

on a conversation between Robert Maynard Hutchins and
on Fadiman about whether or not a liberal education is still
elevant in a technological society; augmenting the
Apollonian/Dionysian dichotomy with his discussion of the Aztec
myth of the struggle between the gods of creation and destruction,
Tezcatlipoca and Quetzalcoatl. In his Reminiscence, Buzz highlights
the importance of collegial relationships among the faculty, as well as
the kinds of creative initiatives that can emerge from the freedom to
design innovative courses in one's areas of interest. Eric McGuckin
elaborates on the Apollonian/Dionysian dynamic in the context of
increased standardization and regimentation of higher education,
while River (formerly Heidi) LaMoreaux celebrates the ways in which
Hutchins nurtures creativity, for both students and faculty. Wendy
Ostroff provides a thoughtful exploration of the art and science of the
seminar – the inexplicable magic that can be so transformative for
students and teachers alike. Janet Hess brings a passion for art and
social justice to her reflection on the limitations of the traditional
canon, and shares her personal conversion from the competitive
culture of graduate school (and academia in general) to what she
calls the "joy of collaboration." Finally, Ben Frymer has transcribed
an interview he conducted with Margaret Anderson on her
perceptions of Hutchins in her experience as both student and
faculty member.

The next section provides a glimpse into the Hybrid Degree
Completion Program (DCP). Ardath Lee reflects on her motivations
for establishing a distance learning program for working adults and
the importance of preserving the "social dimension of learning" so
central to the Hutchins pedagogy. Jack Wikse, who became the
faculty coordinator of the program in 2010, reiterates the Hutchins
commitment to an integrative, interactive and inclusive educational
model. Echoing Janet, he rejects the competitive approach that
characterizes most higher education, which he suggests, "enhances
the privatization of consciousness." And Beth Warner offers a
whimsical orientation to incoming DCP students, comparing
Hutchins with the technicolor reality of Oz, in contrast with the drab
black-and-white reality of the traditional classroom.

The final section includes reflections from Hutchins alumni, beginning with John Esterle, who graduated in 1979, and concluding with AnnMarie Miller, who completed her degree in 2016. John takes us on a walk through the gallery of his memories of Hutchins, painting a picture of meaningful moments that have inspired a life-long career nurturing dialogue through the Whitman Institute, which has supported Margaret Anderson in establishing the Hutchins Dialogue Center. Meredith Caplan, whom I met through a Hutchins book club that I established in 2001, shares an inspiring account of the ways in which she has incorporated the seminar and student-centered learning, first in her teaching in public schools and, more recently, in her home school science classes. Owen Laws wrote his "Introduction to Seminaring in Hutchins" during his senior year in Hutchins, and it is still being used today to orient our students to the program. He is currently living in Sweden, and I was delighted to find him (on Facebook no less) in order to get his permission to include it in this collection. Lena McQuade describes how the opportunity to teach her own course during her senior year inspired her interest in queer theory, which she pursued in graduate school, leading to her tenured position in the Women's and Gender Studies Department at SSU, where she received the Excellence in Teaching Award in 2016. Building on his interest in sustainable food systems, Kevin Cody recounts the ways in which Hutchins has informed his journey through grad school, then as a faculty member in Environmental and Sustainability Studies at the University of Northern Colorado, and currently as Program Manager for Farmer Training at New Entry Sustainable Farming Project. Finn Menzies shares a poem about how Hutchins taught him to listen, perhaps one of the most important skills of all. And AnnMarie Miller gave me her permission to include her essay, "Amazing Grace," which she wrote as she completed her senior year. It has often been part of the curriculum in the Introduction to Liberal Studies seminar, and provides an insightful reflection on her own evolution from a stance of judgment and intellectual superiority to one of engaging collaboratively with others.

It has been a joy to work with faculty and alumni over the past couple of years as I have been compiling these chapters, and I have been inspired anew by the magic that is Hutchins. Several of the authors express concerns about the future survival of Hutchins in the current climate. I hope this collection attests to the value of the kind of learning that this interdisciplinary, interactive, creative and liberating approach to education can engender. In my perpetual quest for the right words to adequately express what I want to say, I stumbled upon an entry in the Collins English Dictionary for the word "regimentation," which they define as "very strict control over the way a group of people behave or the way something is done," and then go on to suggest that "Democracy is incompatible with excessive, bureaucratic regimentation of social life." Amen to that.

References

Cronon, William. 1998. "'Only Connect...': The Goals of a Liberal Education." *The American Scholar 67:4.* 73-80.

Freire, Paulo. 1970. *Pedagogy of the Oppressed.*

Giroux, Henri A. 2006. "Higher Education Under Siege: Implications for Public Intellectuals. *Thought and Action.* 63-78.

Hutchins, Robert Maynard. 1952. *The Great Conversation: The Substance of a Liberal Education.* Encyclopædia Britannica, Inc.

A Declaration of Interdependence

Hutchins Freshman Seminar

Fall 1988

This Declaration, written in Tony Mountain's freshman seminar, embodies the spirit of Hutchins and provides a fitting opening to this anthology. When asked about the document, he explained, "We were doing some American history reading (including at one point the Declaration of Independence) and the students, as I remember, got really interested in the power of a declaration and how it can be a statement of fundamental values. I recall that this led to a great discussion about what fundamental values they collectively could agree on. This document is the product of their thinking about 'interdependence.' It was a fabulous group of students and a great example of the sometimes extraordinary things that happened in Hutchins seminars. By the way, I was simply the seminar facilitator, I wrote not a word of the document though I loved its prose and believed every word of it."

Given that the Human Being is by nature a social being, living in mutual interdependence with all Humankind; that equality among people does not end at national borders; that humanity as a whole is driven by not only self-interested but altruistic motives; that we are not only physical but spiritual beings;

Given that governments are instituted within a society to secure the welfare of the people in that society; that the proper function of a government is not to control but to serve the people; that it is therefore not sufficient for a government simply to prevent people from doing harm to one another, but that it shall also take responsibility for ensuring their basic needs;

Given that mankind is by nature inseparable from the environment; that the environment is therefore possessed of rights of an importance equal to that of Human Beings; that these rights must be given due and proper consideration in all events, concerns, and activities of Mankind;

We, the undersigned, being in large degree dissatisfied with our present governmental, social and ecological course, find ourselves ethically compelled to recognize and address the natural rights of all beings in the following Declaration of Interdependence.

Inasmuch as the health and welfare of society, the individual, and the environment are understood to be mutually interdependent, our primary requirement is a shift of emphasis from divisiveness to unity and the great good.

In view of the existing threat to all forms of life due to the rapid deterioration of the global environment, we recognize the need to establish the rights of the environment as our highest priority. To ensure this priority, the existing Environmental Protection Agency must be upgraded to an environmental conservation and education agency whose primary focus will derive from the understanding of our dependence on, and interdependence with, our environment. It will be the responsibility of this agency to preserve, protect, and replenish the environment, with due regard for our society's proper role and place in the global natural order.

From the fact of our mutual interdependence naturally follows the inherent equality of all people, irrespective of superficial differences such as gender, ethnic origin, or religion. It is therefore essential for us to understand the nature of this interdependence, and in light of this understanding to re-evaluate and redefine the rights and responsibilities of the individual within society, and our collective role in the world community.

In the awareness of the futility of war, and of the basic equality of all persons regardless of national boundaries, and underscoring the shift of emphasis from separateness to unity, a Department of Peace is to be established, to be funded equality with the Department of Defense.

Given that the fragmentation and alienation which have become our common experience in today's society can be directly traced to upbringing and education; understanding that a healthy, rational and intelligent society can only come from healthy, rational, and intelligent individuals; it must therefore be made a high priority to ensure to all persons a complete and comprehensive education. To these ends, the highest standards shall be required for teachers, teacher training, and teaching systems. Emphasis shall be placed, within a sound curriculum, on the teaching of the essential equality of all people, on our inseparability from and responsibility to the environment, on responsible social interaction, and on the free and creative development of the individual, with regard for the unique makeup and psychology of each person. This education must be firmly based on the understanding of the interdependence of all life, and on the original meaning of the work "education": to "draw out" rather than to "put in."

Given that the multitude of social ills we face cannot be adequately addressed in a piecemeal fashion, a fundamental shift in approach is required, reflecting the awareness of our mutually interdependent Human needs and values. This will naturally result in the proper and adequate care of all persons, regardless of individual needs and resources, and will include the basic requirements of food and shelter, health care, and care of the very young, the very old, and the physically and mentally handicapped.

In order to provide society with the necessary resources to meet these needs, many of which are currently going unmet, and as an alternative to military service, all people shall have the opportunity and experience of giving service to their society. Each person shall be required to give service for a specified time, to the society or the environment. Additionally, recognizing that the problem of crime may best be solved through the approach of prevention and true rehabilitation rather than punishment, which only increases the alienation of those punished, many or most persons convicted of crimes may be required to do service for the society as an alternative to incarceration.

It shall be the responsibility of the people to ensure that the government responds to and implements the public will. Special emphasis is to be placed on ensuring the freedom of dissemination of all information that concerns the public, and on ensuring that the people are being truly heard and properly represented. In light of the awareness of worldwide Human interdependence, a high priority is also to be given to international cooperation and the welfare of the world community.

We, the undersigned, firmly believe that there is no principle higher than this: that all life springs from the same source, and that the good of one is therefore to be found in the good of the many, and the good of the many in the good of each; and that there is not cause greater than the reunification of Humankind, for which purpose we do make this Declaration.

Markus Bennett

Graham Lawler

Stacey Kaufman

Matthew S. Jones

Darrel Dean

Yvette Schnoeker-Shorb

Josh E. Lynn

Bonny O'Neal

Deirdre Hamilton

Margaret Reynolds

Christina Nichol

Perspectives

from the

Founding Faculty

Warren Olson

Les Adler

Anthony Mountain

Richard Zimmer

Maurice Blaug

The Origin and Birth of the Hutchins School of Liberal Studies

Warren E. Olson

Warren Olson joined the faculty of what was then Sonoma State College in 1962 as its first professor of philosophy and humanities. As the College was still in its infancy, having just been founded the previous year, Warren was in a position to help guide the direction of the brand new campus. Coming from Chico State College, where he had taught in the philosophy department, he was particularly interested in developing an integrated general education program. This is an account written in 1992 of the initial vision and ultimate implementation of his dream. Embedded in the larger social and cultural context of the mid to late 1960s, his story documents the first tumultuous year of the Hutchins School of Liberal Studies, caught in the creative tension between Apollonian structure and Dionysian chaos.

Reminiscing about the conception and parturition of a twenty-three year-old innovative program in higher education is a privilege few academics have enjoyed. Even fewer have had the temerity to commit those reminiscences to the printed page. Indeed, simply contemplating writing that narrative awakens ancient fears that naming something will lead to its destruction. Shouldering aside such superstitions as an outcropping of post-modernism, I shall plunge into the stream of memory and attempt to describe, and account for, the coming into being of the Hutchins School of Liberal Studies at Sonoma State University. Telling that story may prove interesting at several levels. It may contribute in a small way to the reader's understanding of what had gone awry in undergraduate education by the 1960s and it will exemplify the clash of competing remedies current at that time. The tale will also clarify the assumptions, values, and goals, which brought the Hutchins School into being. Not to be ignored is the additional possibility that this story may have some utility for those idealistic academics who secretly pant to discover how undergraduate education might be rescued from its present malaise.

Setting the Stage

As with all things human, the Hutchins School was conceived and birthed in a context, that of Sonoma State College. Founded in spring of 1961, Sonoma State was the latest addition to the California State College system. Situated 45 miles north of the Golden Gate in a semi-rural area, the college's mission was that of teaching the liberal arts and sciences. Its first faculty consisted of eight persons who had constituted the Santa Rosa Center of San Francisco State College; their spirit and views were an important influence on the early development of SSC. Subsequent growth of the faculty and student body was slow, but steady; curricular planning was conventional and congruent with norms of the 1950's. An important exception was the Psychology Department whose members were openly and proudly "humanistic," and in rebellion against the regnant "behaviorism" of the day. Student-centered, concerned with process, and committed to allowing the affective realm a central place in their teaching, the psychologists soon found allies and critics among the newly hired faculty. A majority were critical, often derisive, but the psychologists had an interestingly subversive effect on many of their critics who began to see their own students differently and who found that their teaching objectives and styles needed overhauling. I believe that the influence of the psychologists (who had been at the Santa Rosa Center) was an important factor in creating faculty willingness to consider the possibility of radical change at Sonoma State.

In considering the context into which the Hutchins School was born, one must factor in the prevalent mood of the mid and late sixties, a time of noisy dissatisfaction with many institutions and practices; everyone wanted change. Within higher education the area most needful of change was the undergraduate level; indeed, the journal most-read by academics interested in revamping their practices was entitled "Change". Articles in the magazine reported on a wide variety of experiments and possible institutional structures. Writers offered advice and models to be emulated by hopeful innovators. Change helped to create a nationwide constituency of professors anxious to transform the educational process; the magazine also gave innovation a kind of legitimacy it otherwise might have lacked.

The ailment sapping the strength and effectiveness of higher education, for which innovation was the antidote, was generally recognized as consisting of: 1) Passivity, 2) Fragmentation, and 3) Alienation. Passivity was bred into students as a consequence of large lecture classes (or small ones, for that matter) in which they were charged with remembering what the lecturer had said and being able to reproduce that content on exams. Objective exams seldom asked the student to integrate what he had learned, thus requiring that he take an active role in his own learning. Students rarely had the opportunity to engage in dialogue, thus losing vital chances to do something with course content. Put another way, innovators believed that genuine learning occurs only when the learner makes material his own through his own activity. Since few colleges and university required that of students, passivity was the name of the academic game.

The second part of the ailment afflicting higher education was fragmentation. Because the American university adopted as its model the nineteenth-century German university with its disciplinary organization and enshrinement of the academic department, the curriculum was divided into neat little specialties, each owning its own portion of human knowledge. As specialization became ever-finer and more exotic, as specialists developed their own languages and were thus disinclined to build linguistic and conceptual bridges between their academic worlds, students were left in the lurch; they were seldom asked to integrate what they had painstakingly learned in their separate courses, thus their education failed to help them make sense of the world they lived in and learned about. No wonder, then, that students of the sixties complained that their collegiate work was irrelevant to their lives. Furthermore, fragmentation reinforces passivity, for being active presupposes that one has a sense of direction. In turn, knowing where one is going presupposes a sense of how one's efforts fit into the scheme of things.

The third villain, alienation, follows close on the heels of passivity and fragmentation, for both contribute to a lessened sense of self and loss of meaningfulness of one's experience. By adding the anonymity imposed on students condemned to spending four years in large, impersonal institutions, the result seems to be a human product which has not only escaped being educated, but which emerges having lost much of its ability to act purposively and intelligently.

The foregoing description of the malaise present in higher education in the 1960's is reasonably close to what many academics had come to believe about the house they lived in. To them, working to change the structures and practices which bred Passivity, Fragmentation, and Alienation seemed eminently reasonable and, therefore, possible.

Meanwhile, Sonoma State College was taking shape: the faculty and administration were busily planning majors, hiring new faculty, working up new courses, instituting faculty governance structures, and planning a brand new campus. Classes were small, relations between faculty and students were close; in brief, the malaise of passivity, fragmentation, and alienation did not exist on our small campus. However, the seeds of education sickness had been sown: while eschewing large lecture rooms, classes of 40 to 50 could easily be accommodated in the new building, thus keeping the lecture mode of teaching alive and well. In addition, academic planning presupposed that the academic department would be the programmatic building block, thus assuring that when the campus had reached its ultimate size of 13,000 students the fragmentation of the "multiversity" and the alienation of students would be solidly in place. Put another way, the inertia of conventionality and the failure to imagine better ways of doing undergraduate education bid fair to consign Sonoma State College to the fate of "clone-ism."

Beating Ideas into Institutions

At this point the narrative and my own story merge, for I had joined the faculty of SSC in 1962 as its first teacher of philosophy and humanities, hoping that a vital integrative general education program could be developed at this collegiate tabula rasa and that my experience in interdisciplinary studies and as the initiator of an Honors program at Chico State College would be of some use in building a model General Education program. Alas, I was to discover that few of my colleagues shared my vision or understood that something could be wrong with the status quo. Obviously, they had priorities, interests and ambitions different from mine, for my rhetoric had little effect. However, I had learned that finding help outside one's home turf can stimulate attentiveness and awaken neighbors to the need for change.

Quite by chance I happened to have lunch one autumn day in 1965 with Mervyn Cadwallader and five colleagues who were just beginning the Tutorial Program at San Jose State College. (Its twin at U.C., Berkeley, Joseph Tussman's Experimental College, had also just begun.) As they explained the goals and nature of their program my excitement mounted, for it was clear that their game was the one I wanted to play; furthermore, the structure of the Tutorial Program could be replicated at Sonoma State! As I learned later, Cadwallader's innovative General Education program was inspired by Alexander Meiklejohn' Experimental College at the University of Wisconsin which existed from 1927-33.

Meiklejohn (1872-1964), a philosopher and former president of Amherst College, was a bold innovator who developed a program for the Freshman-Sophomore years which cut across disciplinary lines by concentrating on ideas and themes which would nurture the intelligence and awareness necessary if students were to become fully engaged citizens of a democracy. Small seminars replaced the usual lecture-discussion classes and student wring rather than exams were the test of learning. Meiklejohn's Experimental College was a resounding success and is generally regarded as the most daring innovation in higher education that this century has witnessed. Clearly the San Jose Tutorial Program had a most distinguished ancestor. Since the goals, structure, and teaching-learning practices of Cadwallader's program were intended to combat passivity, fragmentation, and alienation, it was evident to me that my colleagues might well be awakened from their slumber were they to know that such daring innovations were afoot.

Hibernation characterized the next eighteen months; one might aver that I lay in wait for an opportunity to ring the tocsin. That occurred in 1967 when an Accreditation Team from WASC visited Sonoma State to determine its fitness to educate Californian youth. Its report took the faculty to task for not embracing innovation, especially since long-standing traditions and well-defined territory had not been established. Quite fortuitously, I had been elected Chair of the Faculty of 1967-8 and as a consequence of the WASC critique was charged with organizing a Faculty Conference for Fall, 1967 devoted to innovation and experimentation. By that time many faculty had manifested interest in learning about such matters; after all, University of the Pacific had begun to develop cluster colleges, as had U.C. Santa Cruz; innovative ideas for teaching and learning seemed to emerge from every academic corner and, of course, we had our very own humanistic psychologists as local models of how to innovate. At the other end of various spectrums Robert Maynard Hutchins, in his weekly syndicated column, maintained a steady barrage of criticism directed at the failure of the academy to educate for citizenship in a presumably democratic state. As ever, he argued the case for the importance of liberal education in a highly technologized society and for the necessity of trying new approaches. The time was ripe for changing the old order.

The conference went splendidly: a wide variety of reforms were discussed by interest groups which then formulated proposals to be considered by the whole faculty. The reforms considered ranged from cross-disciplinary courses, which would focus on a single era, event, or movement to breaking up the calendar so that a student could concentrate on one course at a time. Three of my colleagues (from Political Science, History, and English) and I settled on nothing less than proposing a Tutorial Program similar to the one at San Jose State. The conferees were most interested in our proposal, perhaps

23

because it had worked elsewhere, but also because it addressed the problem of how best to do general education, an ever-present academic concern. On the strength of that encouragement our small committee drafted a formal proposal to be presented to the Academic Senate.

At this point I must say a word about the colleagues who joined forces with me. The political scientist and the historian were new to the faculty and were both eager to reform the College's General Education Program. The man from English, also a poet, had joined the faculty when I did; we had become good friends and had often discussed how we might adapt the San Jose innovation to our situation. We four were of one mind at the time of the conference and were ready to engage in heavy persuasion. On January 5, 1968 the Senate approved the plan for Tutorials in the Liberal Arts and Sciences on a two-year trial basis. We described it as a two-year program of:

> reading, writing, seminar discussions and occasional lectures organized around central problems and general themes... [which] will meet all the General Education requirements of the College.... Typically, the student will spend from four to six hours in seminar discussion, two hours in lecture, and an hour in individual conferences every week. Writing assignments are expected to be heavy and the student's own responsibility for doing the work of the program will be heavy.

Rather than teaching his own specialty, each tutor would facilitate the learning of all the material; in most cases he would be an "advanced learner." A common core of readings would be used and one morning each week would be devoted to the faculty's own seminar on the material. The goals of the Tutorial Program were not understated. We saw it as a means whereby:

> students will make considerable strides toward intellectual and emotional liberation and as a two-year occasion in which they will have a much better than average chance to become engaged with various worlds each of us lives in. We would hope to develop skills of analysis and criticism which would allow

students to grapple with the persistent problems of man and society, to support students' growth toward lives of integrity and principle by studying the relationship of values to action, and of the significance of the individual in history, to improve the quality of their lives by adding the usable past to their experience, including cultural and aesthetic achievements, and to provide them with the tools and motivation for continual self education.

Despite the proffered riches of the Tutorial Program, its inauguration had to be postponed until Fall 1969, for the simple reason that additional faculty positions would not be available until that time.

During the Spring 1968 term, the Appeals and Administrative Appointments Committee startled the campus by presenting a proposal that Sonoma State grow smaller as it grew larger by reorganizing as a "cluster" of semi-autonomous schools none of which would exceed 750 students and 50 faculty. The already-present collection of departments and the appropriate administrative structure would constitute School #1 whose student population would be limited to 7500. The intent of the plan was to preserve the best features of Sonoma State: the accessibility of faculty and administration to students, small to moderate-sized classes, relatively small departments in which the faculty know each other, ability to innovate without threatening fiefdoms and long-established programs, and ability to participate meaningfully in college and school governance. The faculty responded readily and positively to the proposal. An Ad Hoc Committee was formed and charged with presenting a plan for Cluster School reorganization by March 1, 1969.

Composed of faculty, administrators, and students the committee met throughout the Fall semester of 1968, worked zealously and productively, and presented its recommendations for faculty approval in January, 1969. Basically, the plan stipulated that the present college be named Cluster School #1 and that all subsequent "schools" join in federation with it. Included was a proposal to establish Cluster School #2 as a four-year program which would grant a B.A. in Liberal Studies and whose "primary aim will be that of affording students an educational experience which is liberalizing and liberating; it will mark a significant departure from traditional liberal arts degrees, for this college will be experimental in both subject matter and educational methods."

The reader should not be astonished to find that the previously approved Tutorial Program was to constitute the first two, general education, years of this new Cluster School. The Junior and Senior years would allow students to pursue their own interests through a combination of seminars, tutorials, independent study and relevant classes in Cluster School #1 (later to be known as "Olde School"). The faculty approved the entire proposal, though not without misgivings on the part of some traditionalists, and the Fearless Four found themselves facing the daunting task of making abstract, idealized concepts real in concrete, particular ways, for Cluster School #2 was to be born in early September, 1969! It should be noted that the historian had defected from our quartet and was replaced by a member of the Psychology Department.

Early in our deliberations we decided that "Cluster School #2" had decidedly little sex appeal as a name for the institution we were about to fabricate. Sufficient to our ends would be a name that suggested something about the nature of our enterprise and the tradition we wished to embody. I suggested that if we wanted s name that would confer upon us instant recognition and success, we should call our school the Robert Maynard Hutchins School of Liberal Studies. Chuckling good-naturedly, my colleagues pressed me to justify my suggestion. I told them of a speech on liberal education Hutchins had given in 1942 at my high school in Evanston, Illinois and of the major impact it had on my thinking about education. Too, I pointed out, his current writing on the need for educational innovation was congruent with our intentions, that he had become famous for enabling important educational innovations at the University of Chicago when he was its president, and that, most important of all, Hutchins had engaged in a lifelong attempt to convince Americans that democracy will not be realized unless its citizens are liberally educated; a belief with which we were in complete accord. In addition, Robert M. Hutchins represented that intellectual tradition associated with Socrates which we sought to embody in our school.

To my delight both my colleagues and the College's president, Ambrose R. Nichols, endorsed calling Cluster School #2 the Hutchins School of Liberal Studies. But, would Robert Hutchins agree? In a longish letter I make our pitch to him; in a very brief letter he replied:

> I am deeply honored by your suggestion regarding lending my name to your new experimental school. I hope you will not feel bound to adhere to it if you find the name does you more harm than good. The idea of the college is one with which I am happy to be associated.

Several months later Hutchins responded to another of my missives:

> I only hope that the name doesn't do you harm. What will happen when Governor Reagan finds out what you have done? I am deeply honored. I hope you will let me know if there is ever anything I can do for you. And I authorize you in advance to drop the name whenever it becomes embarrassing!

How satisfying! Now that we had a good, solid, recognizable name, we could get about the work of school building!

At that point we (a philosopher, a political scientist, a poet, and a psychologist) were faced with the difficult task of translating noble rhetoric into real structures and educational substance. We had a near-encyclopedic knowledge of what was wrong with higher education and had a solid grounding in most of the slogans then extant, but was that a sufficient basis for building an exemplary four-year liberal education? For example, we had been impressed by the Hazen Foundation's booklet, which called for the "education of persons" and a balance between cognitive and affective education; however, getting clear about those issues alone would have taken time we did not have. Clarity about goals and pedagogy, however, was sorely needed, as this narrative will demonstrate.

We did, however, have a structure for the lower division of seminars, tutorials and weekly lectures, thanks to the San Jose State Tutorials Program; thus, we had at least one foot hovering over reality. Our plan called for seminars of ten persons each led by a faculty member who would set aside his disciplinary habits and become an "advanced learner" in an interdisciplinary, or integrative, consideration of various themes and ideas. Since the seminar was to be the major pedagogical feature of the program, and because none of us had conducted seminars wherein students bear great responsibility for the seminar's success, we were understandably anxious, though convinced, that we were on the right track. Tutorial sessions would focus on the individual student's writing, while weekly lectures would combine actual lectures on the subject matter with something approaching a "town meeting." The faculty would have its own weekly seminar at which problems and prospects of the program would be discussed and whoever had a keen grasp of the week's reading would seek to enlighten his colleagues and lead a discussion.

Having settled on the structural format of the Hutchins School's lower division, the four faculty planners turned to the curriculum. Since each seminar would account for four-fifths of a student's normal load, we could afford to be ambitious in building seminar content. "Images of Man" was the title of the first semester's seminar; that involved exploring a variety of conceptions of man's nature drawn from ethnographic materials through works in literature, philosophy, psychology and the social sciences. Semester two would examine "Man in Civilization," focusing on American values and their expression in a variety of institutions. The third seminar (twelve units of credit, remember) was to examine "Change and Continuity in Civilization" as witnessed in the various intellectual and social revolutions of the Nineteenth Century, while Semester four would concentrate on "Alternatives for the Future," in some sense a response to the previous term's work.

Given that thematic framework we proceeded to flesh-out the first term's academic content. (By that time we had hired a young theoretical physicist, fresh from graduate school, whose presence would justify our including natural science in the curriculum and who suggested readings for the Fall term.) Having no particular insight into how much reading should be required, I suggested that since students in my humanities courses generally plowed through ten to twelve books per semester, we could hardly ask less of our bright-eyed charges than four times that number, that is, forty! After all, they would have to earn those twelve units of credit! We finally agreed that thirty books would be preferable. Whom did they read? Beckett, Feynman, Schrodinger, Gamow, Weiner, five ethnographies, Malcom X, Lorca, Eliade, Kafka, Jung, Hess, Fromm, Joyce, Tillich, Buber, and a few others! (See Appendix) Having accomplished that much, we turned to other, more mundane matters, the chief one being recruitment of a student body. Consideration of the upper division program was postponed until the next year.

Slightly more than 200 daring souls applied for admission to the Hutchins School, but only the first hundred could be accommodated. We did not intend to become an Honors program, hence first-come-first-served was the only criterion for admission. They were invited to the campus for an orientation meeting in early May of 1969. It was difficult to discern whether the soon-to-be freshmen were as excited as we were. Here, at last, was hirsute and rumpled teenagers eager to participate in Sonoma State's entry in the Cluster College Sweepstakes. Everyone wore grins of delight, the speeches were short, the question period long, and a sense of bonding pervaded the room. Ah! How sweet it was!

A Tragicomedy in two Acts:

Act I

Little did we realize that characterizing the Hutchins School as "free" and "experimental" would have near-cataclysmic consequences. Those emblematic slogans of the 1960's had a power no one interested in changing higher education could resist, especially in the context of educational institutions grown rigid and insensitive to individual needs and desires. Agreement on what those slogans meant, however, was not easily attained. As a rule, interpretations of those meanings fell into two basic clusters, or perspectives (described in terms of a distinction between "innovation" and "experimentation" by Warren Bryan Martin, the first Provost of Old School), which separated faculty rather fundamentally, as we were to discover. Inhabiting one major perspective was the innovator who sought new means in order to achieve old goals: placing reliance on the seminar

29

in order to work toward the traditional goals of liberal education, for example. The other notable point of view was that of the experimenter who sought new means to reach new goals. That more adventuresome fellow would change higher education's priorities, for example, by attempting to improve the student's mental health through the use of encounter groups, a favorite tool of psychologists during the 1960's. Innovators and experimenters fought often and noisily over that issue, particularly when the mental health enthusiasts attempted to blend the encounter group with the subject matter seminar. Perhaps the contrast between the two dominant camps might be clarified through yet another distinction.

In the late nineteenth century, Friedrich Nietzsche distinguished two principles lying at the heart of Greek tragedy: The Apollonian and the Dionysian. The contest between them, the agon, is what makes tragedy dynamic, for it corresponds to the eternal struggle within the human personality and in society as well. The Greek god, Apollo, represented reason, the rational impulse, which was conscious and form-giving; indeed, reason is man's chief defense and bulwark against the chaos which threatens him on all sides, and... rom within. Dionysus, on the other hand, represented the irrational principle which beckons man to embrace chaos, to enter a realm of emotional frenzy in which he is utterly isolated from his fellows, free of all fetters and ties, including all bonds to his community. These antithetic principles/myths are in perpetual struggle with each other, in a dialectical tension. Like Odysseus, each of us negotiates passage between the chaos of Scylla and the stultified order of Charybdis. Each of us, then, charts for himself a "worldline" in virtue of his choosing where he will stand between Apollo and Dionysus. Much of the anxiety which attends our existence must arise from this dialectical tension.

Imagine, then, the impact on a faculty member of reading Rousseau's *Emile*, A. S. Neill's *Summerhill*, or the latest issue of *Change*! If he had been chafing at the frustrations endemic to the bureaucratized university or hungering for the vaunted satisfactions of genuine community, not to mention the joys of working with students who were eager to learn, he probably felt the pull of Dionysus away from the ossified, hallowed forms and practices of the Apollonian multiversity. Enlisting in the service of Dionysus meant experiencing real freedom, throwing off the spirit-killing formalisms of the academy, divesting oneself of burdensome, inauthentic roles, and turning to the really important issues of human existence. Some faculty joined the Dionysian revels, some liked the music and danced a few steps, other chose to observe and learn, while the true Apollonians dismissed the revelry as meaningless, ugly, and evil. Except for the latter, all responded to the arrival of the "stranger-god" and were changed by the event, each in his own way. Differences in degree, however, often appear to be differences in kind, particularly when disagreements arise. Therefore, those faculty who chose to stand closer to Apollo than to Dionysus were viewed by their Dionysus-leaning colleagues as rigid, rule-encrusted bureaucrats enamored of a stale rationality which was chiefly responsible for the various crises peculiar to Western Civilization; those within the ambit of Apollo judged their opponents as loose, permissive, irrational and anti-intellectual fools besotted by the cult of youth and suspicious of all authority. When both camps found themselves separated only by a seminar table and pledged to undertake a common endeavor, which required mutuality, disaster hovered in the wings.

The first meeting of the miniscule, five-person, faculty of the Hutchins School occurred in early September, 1969. Our agenda consisted of a discussion of Camus' *The Stranger*, the first book on our reading list, as well as working out details for the next day's Hutchins School Retreat for our hundred eager freshmen at a nearby, appropriately funky resort. Expecting to participate in a scintillating discussion of the novel, I was astonished when the poet and the newly-hired young physicist announced, separately and without collusion, that each had decided not to use the book list because he wished to embrace "freedom" rather than "structure" and to take seriously our proclamation that faculty should be "co-learners." When reminded of our prior agreement on the book list, they countered that we had also subscribed to "experimentalism," whose banner they would hold high. To that end they would plump for participatory democracy by letting their seminars decide which books should be read, if any! Well, the glove hit the table with a genuine "thump." Apollo and Dionysus had squared off; Act I suddenly became Round I.

What was the lineup of forces? Dionysus claimed the poet and the physicist, while Apollo could count on a philosopher and a political scientist. In between stood the psychologist who attempted to be a mediator and referee; his recent experience working in a mental hospital promised to be of great value. We might think of him as Hephaistos, the lame god of Homer's *Iliad* who sought to maintain order among Olympians.

The Apollonians, also known as the Innovators, responded to the Dionysians, or Experimenters, by arguing that our conception of the lower-division seminars was a far cry from the unstructured model in which faculty and students had complete latitude to "do their own thing," an au courant slogan of the times. Rather, our plan committed us to conducting seminars in which students would be able to develop their own styles of learning in the context of a cooperative community of inquirers. Who, we said, could ask for an innovation more far-reaching than that? Further, the interdisciplinary (or, transdisciplinary) approach to subject matter would derail the rigid boundaries between academic disciplines which, we believed, undercut a comprehensive general education for undergraduates. The seminars could not function without a center, something studied in common, for they were to be cooperative. In an academic setting that focal point is a text. Put succinctly, we held that the learning experience must be structured, in an elastic and flexible fashion, in order for personal and intellectual development to take place.

Not so, flashed back the Dionysians, you are simply adopting the tired old goals of liberal education and pumping life into them by using new pedagogical techniques, thereby deceiving yourselves that any real changes have been made. Rather, they said, we aim to achieve true liberation for students by letting them decide what will be discussed and studied, whether singly or as a group; indeed, we will scrap all requirements, thus removing any punitive motivators.

Well, the Apollonians, light-headed and somewhat giddy from being exposed to the real Dionysus, rallied in time to aver that even if the Dionysians' intentions were desirable and "do-able," it was clear to any rational person that the college had approved a plan which could not be reconciled with the unstructured model of education our more radical colleagues wished to promulgate. To no avail we argued that unless we tried the approved plan, we could never determine whether it would work; only by following through could we discover, after two years, whether our "experiment" was successful. Not being in vogue that year, reason did not prevail.

Our meeting ended in a dissonance which affected the subsequent retreat: each contingent subtly sought to enlist student support for its conception of the academic program. I could see that students were likely to become unwitting pawns and the do-or-die conflict could wound us all. On the other hand, I thought, perhaps we could learn from each other, thus crafting an eventual synthesis of Apollo and Dionysus, an outcome superior to what each faction originally intended. Such was not to be, however; the schism widened with each passing week. Cadre meetings were a brim with scarcely concealed acrimony; agreement on most anything was impossible to achieve. As a consequence, the faculty found themselves isolated in a structure designed for collaboration; the knowledge and talents of colleagues were not available, a fact which severely hampered the interdisciplinary nature of our endeavor. Too, our fragmentation deprived us of information about what was happening in other seminars, thus precluding our gaining insight from each other's experience. In addition, where mutual respect and caring might have existed, rancor and loathing took their place.

As the Apollonians and Dionysians avoided each other (each encounter increased the flow of stomach acid), the students began to suspect that something had gone awry, that vast disparities existed among the faculty concerning the goals and pedagogy of the school, not to mention faculty expectations regarding the level of student accomplishment and to what extent they should participate in the academic program. The "stodgy" faculty kept faith with their interpretation of academic integrity, as well as with the original agreement, while the "swingers" used the seminar as a meeting place (attendance optional) where students could "interact" in order to discover what they were interested in learning and whether it would be "fun" to do so. Though there was no direct evidence (we *really* didn't communicate) of the Dionysians' divergence from the curriculum, an occasion arose which made the hiatus clear.

Early in our discussion of "Alternative Ways of Being Human," perhaps while considering Newman's *Knowing the Gururumba*, a student in one of my seminars (each of us had two ten-student seminars) suggested that we might all learn more were each seminar to construct an imaginative account of a culture which would be presented at one of the three-hour Monday meetings. I liked the idea, presented it to my colleagues as a possibility, found it warmly received by my ally and the psychologist, but stonewalled by the Dionysians on the grounds that it would force students to do something that did not originate with them. The Apollonians agreed to implement the idea. What followed not only created a stark contrast between the two conceptions of our educational enterprise, but also illustrates vividly how collaborative learning functions. The following account deals only with my seminars.

Composed of stalwart, serious folk, most of whom seemed satisfied with reading and discussing books and ideas (at least none of them were in open rebellion), my morning seminar quickly embraced the plan to create and present a fictive culture. One fellow, having a strong reality-orientation, opined that we really must find an actual place for the culture before getting about the task of imagining it. So, one fine autumn morning we journeyed to a nearby state park, hiked up to a promontory overlooking a lovely valley and held a seminar crowded round a picnic table. Inspired by their surroundings the students did a fine job of sketching out the distinguishing features of the Native American culture which well might have lived there. Each student took responsibility for describing a specific aspect of the culture, for example, the land and economy, mythology, rites of passage, kinship and family structure. Seminar time was devoted in part to progress reports.

My afternoon seminar accepted the task with delight and verve. A "place" didn't matter much to this bunch: they had a ready store of ideas about what culture ought to be and that's what they designed. Basic to their culture was "androgyny;" that is, everyone in the society was physically able to have sex with any other member of the society, male or female. That pleasant capability gave rise to an appropriate mythology and highly unusual art. Interpersonal relations took precedence over economics while self-actualization stole the privileged position of politics. Our seminar sessions were often laced with exuberant mirth.

When the "Day of Telling" arrived the only seminars participating were those of the Apollonians. My morning group did a fine, solid job of reading descriptions of their culture: I was inordinately proud of them. My ally's two seminars did equally well. However, the final act of the morning was my afternoon seminar: the androgynous ones. One young lady and her boyfriend baked a five-foot-long, whole wheat, androgynous human (a totem?) which was placed on a grand piano, ready to be cannibalized. Rather than reading their descriptions they chose to present a modified tableau; "modified" in the sense that the local canons of decency were respected... despite the spirit of the times. The "native" danced and pranced accompanied by a bongo drummer and their seminar leader who improvised on a soprano recorder. They managed to convey the essence of their fictive culture rather well in the process of raising everyone's spirits.

The Creating A Culture game worked well because every member of each seminar developed a specific aspect of an imagined culture, but always in relation to what everyone else was doing. Their work was guided by the principle that all aspects of a culture are internally related, thus whatever anyone imagined had to be checked with their fellows for consistency and integration. One might aver that the development of each participant was a condition for the development of all. Their work was collaborative and productive of self-esteem. In fact, this exercise became a standard part of each year's freshman seminar for about ten years. Dropping it was largely a result of changes in student motivation and of faculty ennui.

That morning's demonstration of the power of collaborative learning was immensely gratifying to the Apollonians, for it underscored our claim that students working together in a structure which rewards collaboration are able to learn more than if they embrace a decentralized, "do your own thing" ethos. Feeling vindicated, the Apollonians hoped that their Dionysian colleagues (and their students) would see the error of their ways, thus bringing us back to the harmony of mutual intention and act which was to have obtained from the outset.

The state of utopian bliss was not to be; the contending forces remained divided on just about every issue. Indeed, one might infer that the Creating A Culture game served to deepen, as well as illustrate, the gulf which separated us.

Another, rather upsetting, development occurred somewhat later when the parents of a student in one of the poet's seminars asked to meet with him and me concerning their son's progress. The mother, an alert, attractive and socially adept Berkeleyite took the initiative by asserting that her son was depressed, possibly suicidal, because he wasn't learning and had nothing to show for two months of being in my colleague's seminar. The boy's older brother was finishing a Ph.D. at Yale and was a role model for the younger brother whose spinning in the void could best be explained by lack of accomplishment. The father, a Harvard Ph.D., seconded his wife's analysis and asked my Dionysian colleague if he would please require the young man to at least write some essays. The poet responded by thoroughly explaining why such a requirement would contradict the experiment he was conducting. He could have quoted Nietzsche (in *Thus spoke Zarathustra*) who said: "One must still have chaos in oneself to be able to give birth to a dancing star." It is not clear that Nietzsche had college freshmen in mind, but there was no doubt that the elder Dionysian was acting in harmony with his own version of what the Hutchins School was about. The concerned parents left dissatisfied while I concluded that if the Hutchins School were to last more than a year, faculty agreement on goals and pedagogy would be necessary.

Since every day brought further evidence of factional digging-in, the hope that we might effect a grand synthesis of Apollonian structure and rationality with Dionysian individualism and affectivity was decisively negated. Toward the close of the Fall semester recommendations for renewal of faculty appointments had to be made. Having been appointed Provost of the Hutchins School by the President of the College, I recommended that the poet be returned to the English Department at the end of the academic year. My justification was that he was not in agreement with the goals and minimal structure of the Hutchins School and that his continued presence would be destructive of the school itself. A similar fate was meted out to the young physicist, except that his employment at the college was terminated in June, 1970. The President and various intermediate faculty committees concurred.

A harsh decision, undoubtedly, but one that was necessary were the school to continue. In the best of circumstances a new educational program largely founded on a rejection of the academic status quo is risky, for it appears as a statement to other faculty that their craft is suspect and mediocre. Our civil war, therefore, gave the real Apollonians on campus possible ammunition for a battle to do us in. Not being willing to give up our school, we had no choice but to part ways with the Dionysians, and to live with the decision.

NOTE: I have decided not to provide the names of the principal actors in this small drama with one exception: I must recognize the truly important role of Professor Jerry L. Tucker, the political scientist. He was a staunch ally, a fast friend, and fellow-sufferer during the year of our travail. In every way imaginable, he was the cofounder of the Hutchins School.

Act II

Knowing that many of our students would be seriously angered and upset by the "firing" of the Dionysians, I addressed a letter to the returnees which emphasized the fact that the Hutchins School had a constitutional status and authority to which all of us must be committed if we were to be tolerated, let alone allowed to exist. I also pointed out that most innovative programs have had a stormy first year and that the issue over which controversy usually boiled was structure vs. non-structure. Obviously I hoped that the students would see that much more was at stake than personal differences between faculty members.

A goodly number of the students were infuriated by the decision to terminate the poet and physicist: they held a few rallies, wrote letters to the editor of the campus newspaper denouncing me as a "fascistic dictator" and vented their displeasure in various forms of behavior. The physicist urged his students to fight the recommendations, while the poet remained fairly passive. Another clustering of students was in basic agreement with the Apollonians; yet another group was indifferent to the fracas.

To understand more adequately the student reactions to the "firings" and the polarization within the faculty, one must take into account the sociopolitical climate of 1969-70. As one of those students (Richard Mahler, in a letter dated January 27, 1992) recently reminded me:

> For me, as a student, things like the Vietnam War (from Golden Gate park anti-war rallies to the Kent State killings) were very much "in my face." I had no intention of going to 'Nam and the student deferment available via Hutchins was an enormous incentive to stick around for another year. That was the year of the Altamount Rock Festival, open dope smoking on the Sonoma State campus, along with sweat lodges and skinny-dipping. The college was at the height of its Granola U period. Many students showed up for Hutchins seminars stoned, even at 9 am. Others were emotionally overwrought by the social turmoil around them. Don't forget, Eva Blau died of a drug overdose that year, and Stacy Gleason's father, Ralph, was flying high as the guru of Rolling Stone magazine. LSD was a very popular recreational drug, along with other psychedelics. Cotati's Inn of the Beginning was as popular a hangout as the classroom. We were experimenting with free love, "living together" and brand new causes like Earth Day.

Small wonder, then, that my entreaty during the holidays fell on deaf ears. We Apollonians three (the psychologist had clearly committed himself to our cause) had to face the possibility that our "bold innovation" might succumb. However, we found comfort and strength in realizing that our endeavor had an importance transcending our own ambitions or academic fantasies: that the Hutchins School was really an attempt to find a more effective way of transmuting the intellectual tradition of the West. That meant that we defined ourselves in relation to that tradition and saw the intellectual life as a good in itself. Not the only good, but that one to which higher education is dedicated. In failing to attract American youth to intellectual pursuits, higher education was in need of alternative pedagogies. That, after all, was our charge and goal: to see whether California students could become intellectually engaged as a consequence of learning in a collaborative fashion and of learning how to become life-long learners. Believing that gave our efforts a significance sufficient to carry us through whatever traumas the Spring term might bring.

Many of the returning students sensed our renewed seriousness and commitment to making the Hutchins School work as intended. My only seminar was composed of young people who were eager to participate and to learn, who did the reading and writing required of them, and who appeared to enjoy the entire process. One young woman, very rational and critical, enjoyed a brief period of rebellion against rationality, but evidently found no rational grounds for her temporary departure. While some students did not return, presumably because of the controversy or because the program did not meet their expectations, a significant number of returnees sought to effect a reconciliation with the faculty. A student advisory committee was established (the first incarnation of an Academic Council) which met with the faculty to plan curriculum and to advise us on other matters. (The lame-duck Dionysians did not, of course, participate in any of these activities.) The rapprochement was very successful; for the first time students had a say in important matters. There were probably fewer jokes about "Warren's little acre" than in the past, as a sense of communal purpose began to emerge.

Our growing feeling of hope for the future was reinforced by our being given five additional faculty positions to accommodate an expected increase of one hundred students in the Fall of 1970. Since our psychologist ally had decided to return to his department and because the poet and physicist were to be replaced, we had eight faculty positions to fill! Much of my non-teaching time during the spring was devoted to the hiring process. Applicants were many; indeed, an impressive number of new Ph.D.'s were very eager to join us. Given that our troubles of the Fall term were very much on our minds, we sought to avoid even a minimal repetition of that misery. Accordingly, each candidate was provided with a "Statement of Instructional Responsibilities," which tersely stated what would be expected of a faculty member regarding seminars, curriculum, independent study and staff conferences. A "Cautionary Note" was appended:

> The Hutchins School is not a "free university" or a collegiate level Summerhill. Our primary aim is to enable students to become self-motivated and responsible for their own learning, and, to that end, students are freed from many of the traditional academic pressures and requirements. However, such an increase in student freedom does not imply abandoning intellectual standards or a lessening of rigor in the pursuit of knowledge.

Conformity of thought was hardly our goal; rather, we hoped to weed-out applicants whose presence on the faculty of our struggling school would lead to dissension and conflict known to us all too well. We wanted candidates who chose to teach with us because our goals and pedagogy appealed to them, not because they believed the Hutchins School would give them a chance to devise their own educational utopias.

Our recruiting was very successful: the six men and two women we hired were quite aware of the dangerous waters we negotiated in Fall 1969. Most of them joined us for an orientation meeting in May, 1970 at which all manner of topics were hashed over, including the recent town gown clash over nude bathing in the campus lake. The meeting was often punctuated by roars of laughter, a phenomenon in short supply during our brief history. As our students would have observed, we shared a "high" on humor. The new academic year looked promising indeed!

Our physical quarters then consisted of a "temporary" building made up of fairly adequate administrative space and a number of faculty office seminar rooms. While fine in the short run, our housing would not allow for growth; hence, we worked with the architects charged with designing the Cluster School buildings. They responded positively to our suggestions that the complex consist of small one-story buildings dispersed around a number of piazza, as in medieval towns, and that one should be able to get lost while wandering through the area. In essence, these requirements were aimed at keeping the building within human scale as well as introducing a complexity of arrangement in contract to the simplicity of the structures. Happily our suggestions carried the day. Clearly, the prospect of an aesthetically pleasing and functional "home" helped dissipate the darkness of our birthing process.

The natal year of the Hutchins School of Liberal Studies ended on notes of hope, celebration, relief, and exhaustion. Much had been accomplished regarding the next year's curriculum, thanks to the efforts of the new faculty, and a faculty-student committee had labored many hours designing models for school governance, thus creating the mutuality we had desired from the outset. Not everyone, of course, had experienced the spirit of community; however, its promise must have affected those who were not severely disaffected, for 55 out of the original 100 students returned for the sophomore year, a statistic which compared favorably with traditional rates of return. (Ultimately, 25 of the pioneers graduated with degrees in Liberal Studies.) [Editor's note: current rates of retention and graduation are significantly higher; in fact they are higher than the University average. Between 2010 and 2017 an average of 93% returned for the second year, and for the first five of those years an average of 65% graduated from the program.]

Any Enlightenment

Any dramatic episode darkened by elements of the tragic should provide its characters (and audience) with insights and knowledge. Did we learn anything as a result of our experiences? Yes, a fair amount.

As we had hoped and expected, the seminar proved to be a powerful tool for learning, if its members prepare for and participate in the discussions. Given the overwhelming fallibility of college freshmen, one cannot count on their devoted participation. However, if the faculty seminar leader is patient and helps his charges discover their responsibility for the seminar's success, they will likely make genuine progress. As one student put it: "Your job is to get a hook into us during the freshman year, but you can't yank us out of the water, else you'll break the leader. You must play us throughout the year and by the time we are sophomores we'll be ready to net." The trout-fishing metaphor is apt: "landing" the student is the ultimate goal. However, from a faculty perspective the highly personal situation which a seminar creates allows one to experience and appreciate intellectual and affective changes in students which traditional pedagogies seldom make possible. That is why faculty become ecstatic when seminars really work.

Another item: utopian assumptions about students who select an innovative college are counter-productive. About a fifth of our first-year students found the Hutchins School to be exactly what they wanted: time to follow their own interests and to explore new areas, an integrated course of study, and opportunities to develop their own standard and styles of learning. Another 20% were "floaters," the opposite of those just described; uninterested in learning and not motivated to do much of anything, these students dropped out after a semester. They remaining 60% lacked customary faculty direction. They were the trout for whom we fished. Accustomed to academic passivity, these students floundered and flailed about, but usually came to have confidence in their abilities as learners. They also came to understand what our fledgling innovation was about and how it could satisfy their educational needs.

An innovative educational program owes the students who select it an accurate description of what goes on there. Much of our misery during that first year was caused by the variety of conceptions of the school brought by both faculty and students. We discovered that we could not be all things to all people. Indeed that principle was implicit in the Cluster College Plan of 1968. Thus, a careful description of the program, agreed upon by the school's faculty, is of prime importance.

We also learned that those entering upon the perilous path of institutional change require an ideal to light the way and to provide energy for their quest; however, they must not be possessed by the ideal, for in that direction lies rigidity and tunnel vision. Avoiding single-mindedness is not an easy task, however, when one's creation is being assaulted from without or undermined from within, or both. It is likely that we Apollonians did suffer from possession and possessiveness during the 1969-70 year, but in semi-consciousness of what we were doing. Had we not held fast to our vision of what the Hutchins School ought to be, its life would have been short indeed.

Were we to need justification for holding the line, it occurred in early November 1991, when the first graduating class held a reunion to which everyone who had participated in the turbulent first year was invited. Some sixty-five brave souls returned to Sonoma State for the celebration. One feature was a yearbook which contained responses to a questionnaire circulated prior to the reunion. Those comments amply demonstrated that almost all of the responding student-veterans felt positively about their experiences in the school, praising many elements of the curriculum and pedagogy which they had experienced 22 years before.

Veterans of educational experiments often claim that the early years were the most exciting and rewarding. That is true of the Hutchins School generally for the first five years, but the initial year stands alone. The teaching and one-to-one work with students was immensely rewarding: I can recall those seminars and students with greater clarity than more recent ones. However, the emotional and psychological toll of our internal warfare was considerably less than productive. As I often have said of my experience as a combat infantryman in World War II, "I am glad that I went through it, but, please... not again!" The following four years were a different matter. We hired strong faculty who were committed to the Hutchins School, its goals and its pedagogy. They knew that the real building of the program was in their hands. They brought much energy and intelligence to that task, and although a somewhat subliminal Apollonian/Dionysian dialectic was in evidence, they used that agon positively rather than be destroyed by it. They learned from our initial mistakes and made some of their own; none of the latter were critically serious to the well being of the school.

In its twenty-three years of existence the Hutchins School has become an accepted and valued part of Sonoma State University. The road has often been rocky, but always negotiable. Our school has institutional rigidities of its own which deserve scrutiny, yet the inclination to innovate remains alive and well. The first, explosive year is seldom mentioned now; after all, who remembers his own birth process? Perhaps the principal reason for this exercise of putting memories in order is to let future faculty and students know what vision inspired the school's founders and what the founding faculty and students experienced during the trauma of birth. Perhaps they will conclude that Nietzsche's aphorism applies to institutions as well as to persons: One must still have chaos in oneself to be able to give birth to a dancing star.

APPENDIX: Liberal Studies 101

A. Man and the Absurd
    1. Samuel Beckett, *Waiting for Godot*
    2. Albert Camus, *The Stranger* and *The Myth of Sisyphus*
    3. Sophocles, *Oedipus Rex*
    4. Friedrich Nietzsche, *Thus Spoke Zarathustra*

B. Man and the Cosmos
    1. Hermann Bondi, *Cosmology*
    2. Richard Feynman, *The Character of Physical Law*
    3. Banesh Hoffmann, *The Strange Story of the Quantum*
    4. Erwin Schrödinger, *What is Life?* and *Mind and Matter*

5. George Gamow, *One, Two, Three... Infinity*
6. Norbert Weiner, *The Human Use of Human Beings*

C. Alternate Ways of Being Human
   1. Alfred Kroeber, *Ishi*
   2. Philip Newman, *Knowing the Gururumba*
   3. Leo Simmons [also Don Talayesva], *Sun Chief: The Autobiography of a Hopi Indian*
   4. Elizabeth Marshall Thomas, *The Harmless People*
   5. Malcolm X, *Autobiography*
   6. Frederico Garcia Lorca, *Blood Wedding*

D. Alternate Systems of Belief
   1. Robert Heinlein, *Stranger in a Strange Land*
   2. *Book of Job*
   3. Huston Smith, *The Religions of Man*
   4. Mircea Eliade, *The Sacred and the Profane*
   5. Franz Kafka, *The Castle*

E. The Self: Images, Concepts
   1. Karl Jung, *Memories, Dreams, and Reflections*
   2. Hermann Hesse, *Steppenwolf*
   3. Erich Fromm, *Man for Himself*
   4. Stanley Coopersmith, ed., *Frontiers of Psychological Research*
   5. James Joyce, *Portrait of the Artist as a Young Man*
   6. Paul Tillich, *Courage to Be*
   7. Nikos Kazantzakis, *Zorba the Greek*
   8. Eugen Herrigel, *Zen and the Art of Archery*
   9. Martin Buber, *I and Thou*

Uncommon Sense:

Liberal Education, Learning Communities and the Transformative Quest

Les K. Adler

> *"Midway this way of life we're bound upon*
> *I woke to find myself in a dark wood,*
> *Where the right road was wholly lost and gone."*
>
> ~ Dante, The Divine Comedy

> *"We must always follow somebody looking for truth,*
> *and we must always run away from anyone who finds it."*
>
> ~ Andre Gide

Les Adler was one of eight new faculty members representing seven different disciplines hired in 1970 to join the two founders in completing the creation of the new School. A specialist in Russian and American studies, with additional background in psychology and literature, he earned both his M.A. and Ph.D. degrees in history from the University of California at Berkeley. While developing and teaching multiple interdisciplinary courses in Hutchins over more than four decades, and also lecturing as a Fulbright Scholar at the National University of Singapore, he served Sonoma State as Provost of the Hutchins School and Dean of the School of Extended Education.

"Uncommon Sense" is his attempt to describe the program's evolutionary development while defining its most salient and lasting qualities. It makes the case that the interdisciplinary undergraduate seminar was and has remained the core of Hutchins powerful and innovative pedagogy, empowering students, energizing faculty and ultimately leading to the development of a truly transformative Liberal Education.

This article was previously published in Barbara Leigh Smith and John McCann, eds. *Reinventing Ourselves: Interdisciplinary Education, Collaborative Learning, and Experimentation in Higher Education*, Jossey-Bass, 2001.

Defining the elusive quality of a Liberal Education has challenged educators since the modern university began its slow rise to prominence nearly 800 years ago. Where once mastery of a particular body of knowledge and the possession of certain moral and intellectual traits were the recognized hallmarks of a liberally educated person, modern educational systems now offer only statistical variations of what might be called the Mass Educated Being.

For all practical purposes, the MEB is basically defined as one who has collected a specified number of units across a Whitman's Sampler of introductory classes ranging from sociology to statistics, along with a specialized major where, presumably, s/he would have acquired the real tools necessary for a successful life and career. What is happily avoided in such a scenario, of course, is any discussion of what a liberal education actually consists of or what the liberally educated student has or should have become in his or her four or more years at college. To paraphrase Descartes, *I count therefore I am!*

Recognizing that modern universities must serve a variety of socially useful purposes including preparing students for careers and advancing the cutting edge of knowledge through basic research – purposes which at the moment need no advocates – I want to address, however, the institution's most ancient and basic purpose which in far too many cases is reflected all-too-often in name only. Rooted in the Greek *holon* or whole, or its Latin translation *universum*, the university was originally organized as a society of teachers and students where the whole, or the meaning of the whole could be studied.

Certainly, we are long past believing either that there is a single nameable whole to be grasped, or that anyone can seriously claim to achieve the necessary breadth of knowledge to do so in one or more lifetimes, or even that there is a specific methodology for doing so. Yet in fact Western societies have maintained the university as the principle institution devoted to teaching and learning on the highest level, entrusting, and even requiring, in most cases, that its leaders in virtually every field of endeavor gain its mark of approval. Whatever its limitations, society evidently agrees there is no better place than the university for the educating process to take place. Perhaps the question to pose at this point is: what is it that we believe goes on in a university to warrant this trust?

Does society merely want the assurance that our graduated artists and architects will be able to draw, our accountants count, our engineers build and our doctors heal? For these skills, and most others, high-level trade or professional schools might –and often do– suffice. Obviously there is some more basic quality or transformation of mind we deem vital, especially in our experts and leaders, but more and more inherently in a democracy, in our people themselves. Granted that the meaning of the whole may never be entirely understood, the foundation stone of modern thought is that through the gradual application of human reason, important connections and relationships within that whole can be known and brought to benefit humankind. Indeed, the entire premise of democratic government rests on the assumption that self-governing individuals can grasp the complex dimensions of the vital issues of their times in order to make essential judgments as citizens.

The role of higher education in this process appears to be two-fold. To act responsibly, individuals must first be capable of making accurate judgments about the islands of purported truth constantly being discovered, claimed and mapped by others in the vast, oceanic unknown surrounding them. Critical thinking skills and a highly developed "crap detector" coupled with breadth of knowledge and exposure to the wide variety and elasticity of the human experience are essential ingredients here. Educated in such a fashion, a citizen, presumably, is less likely to be swept-up in the passions of the moment and more likely to substitute reason for prejudice in making essential judgments.

A second level of educational achievement rests on the attainment of that harder-to-define attribute of mind which we call wisdom. Building on that solid base of knowledge and mastery of critical reasoning skills, wisdom also implies a high degree of self knowledge coupled with a greatly enhanced ability to evaluate complex issues and determine courses of action based on the application of the deepest perceptions and highest ideals of the individual or group involved.

Important as these achievements are, there is yet an even more basic transformative task for liberal education to perform, one which is certainly the hardest of all both to articulate and achieve in the academy as it is presently structured. Like all of us, students are invariably shaped by the increasing fragmentation characteristic of our world on virtually every level. It is hardly a new idea that the anguished, often frantic search for belonging, meaning and belief in our powerfully individualistic and rapidly changing society contributes to many of its most destructive excesses.

Conditioned to the separateness of existence, prey to the reflexive divisions of psyche and self, mind/body, good/evil, us/them/, male/female, human and animal, and myriad consequent sub-distinctions, including the specialization and fragmentation of knowledge, our students come to us at a time of fundamental challenge to most of these rigid lines. A new universum of knowledge is emerging in which the rule appears to be wholeness and integration, interconnection and relatedness, rather than separation. It is here, in the service of healing the divisive and limiting breaches within and between ourselves, as well as between the human and natural worlds that the contribution of a contemporary liberal education is potentially the greatest. For this to happen, however, a substantial re-thinking of both the methods and goals of the educational process itself may be required. Whether a fragmented system of education can in any effective way produce integrated beings is perhaps the most significant question confronting practitioners of liberal education today.

In order to discuss what an alternative *holistic* model of education might look like, it is useful to define the term itself. More than 25 years ago, the late Arthur Koestler (1967, 1979) proposed the word "holon," combining the Greek word for "whole" with the suffix which suggests a particle or part. A holon, as Koestler defined it, thus has the two seemingly contradictory properties of being both a whole and a part of larger wholes. A holon exists as a self-contained functional unit, independent and self-regulating within its environment; yet it simultaneously exists as a subordinated part of larger holons which themselves exists as part of a larger holarchy or hierarchy of self-regulating holons. Theorists such as Ken Wilbur (1996) have since applied the concept to an enormous range of phenomena from biological organisms, to mental processes to the organization of knowledge."

To make sense of this conception within an education setting, one might think of the university *holon* itself. Within it, individual students take individual courses in individual departments which are themselves parts of individual schools or divisions within the campus structure. Autonomous, self-regulating holons (students, courses, departments, divisions, campuses) clearly exist at each level within the larger system. Yet each unit simultaneously exists in supra-ordination to its own parts, and as a dependent part in sub-ordination to controls on higher level –that is, each holon is at all times both independent and relational. Finally, it is essential to recognize that each holon in this system exists, as well, as an information-carrying or cognitive representative of numerous other systems (students as parts of families, social and cultural groups, departments as representatives of disciplines and sub-disciplines and made-up of individual faculty members, universities as parts of larger public or private political, economic and social structures, etc.) As Koestler expresses it, "No man is an island; he is a holon."

Looked at closely, the dominant educational model as practiced from public schools to colleges and universities, rests on several basic assumptions. First among these is that exposure to introductory level, discipline-based courses followed by a graduated exposure to a specific discipline, will produce the liberally educated individual who is capable of making the critical and decisive judgments required of an educated citizen and a future societal leader in this day and age. While this is a model which has grown up under the guidance of the modern university, whose rules and boundaries it reflects, I suggest that it is based on the confusion of the powerful research tools of the disciplines, of which faculty are justifiably proud and to which they are deeply attached, with those best designed to bring about the personal and intellectual transformation which is actually at the heart of a liberal education.

In addition, the model most often rests on the beguilingly efficient and seemingly cost-effective method of a one-pointed system of information transmission which may actually work directly against the desired personal transformation discussed above by reinforcing both individual fragmentation and the habit of intellectual passivity while further confusing the act of absorbing information with the essence of education.

Finally, the model's deepest and most rarely-challenged message is that specialized learning is somehow "higher" and of greater value than more "generalized" education, which for most students is perceived as something to get through as quickly as possible. The act of integrating and relating disparate bits of knowledge –making sense of it – for the most part, is left entirely to the individual student, busy as s/he is competing for grades, collecting units and preparing for the job market. It is a task analogous to expecting each assembly-line worker to collect and assemble enough individual parts to create a functioning automobile, while simultaneously installing spark plugs as the line speeds by.

It is hardly surprising that from somewhat different perspectives, major national reviews of higher education in America beginning in the 1980's all concluded that undergraduate education was suffering from a serious malaise brought on by just such factors as over-specialization and professionalization. David Kennedy, then President of Stanford University, publically called for serious reconsideration of the relative place of research and teaching on his own prestigious campus, admitting that undergraduates at what have been considered the "best" universities were being cheated of an essential part of their education because of an increasing imbalance in favor of research. Despite strong criticism of the existing model, however, neither Kennedy's report nor other critical studies went very far in specifying either the viable alternatives available or the underlying educational or philosophical rational necessary to support a liberal education outside of the framework that has traditionally existed. While suggesting that the answers may lie in smaller classes and closer contact between faculty and students, most critics stopped short of confronting two of the most basic issues of all: whether discipline-based, highly specialized education may itself be a barrier to the stated goals of a truly liberal education; and whether the almost universally-practiced methods of transmitting knowledge are adequate to the task at hand.

It is here, I would suggest, that the theory and practice of Learning Communities-as they have been evolving at campuses across the nation –can best contribute to educational reform efforts. Let me draw on two sources to illustrate the point: one, the educational implications of Koestler's concept of the holon; and the other, nearly thirty years of Learning Community experience in the Hutchins School of Liberal Studies at Sonoma State University.

Koestler's "nested" conception offers a radically different educational vision largely because it shifts the focus to the hierarchical multiplicity of relationships implicit at each holarchic level and point-of-intersection of knowledge. The process of education is conceived of less as a narrowing, two-dimensional ladder than as an expanding three dimensional web where the learner's growing mastery of an area of knowledge depends on his/her ability to integrate, connect and define both the area's own patterns and relationships as well as its reciprocal and relational meaning relative to the larger patterns of which it is a part. Significantly, the model re-conceives of the student as the active patternmaker at the center of the web, making and applying connections, rather than as the mountaineer scaling the peak of one specific body of knowledge.

The holarchic model recognizes that students at every educational level are involved in what my colleague, Nelson Kellogg, has called the "co-creation of wisdom," a necessarily collective and interactive process which requires profound engagement with questions, ideas and problems, as well as effective personal and intellectual interaction with others engaged in similar processes.

Most importantly, the holarchic model suggests that just as the transformative vision of Earth from space has changed forever our perspectives on our home planet, an "aerial" view of knowledge, looking across, beyond and through the disciplines to discover and explore the fundamental questions and deepest connections underlying them, may similarly alter our vision of education. It is within this framework that the experiment carried out in the Hutchins School can best be understood.

Despite its choice of name, the Hutchins School is, in fact, more a spiritual than a direct descendant of the undergraduate college created by Robert Hutchins and Mortimer Adler at the established and well-endowed University of Chicago in the 1930's. Created by a small group of interdisciplinary-minded faculty at a young, rural and highly innovative branch of the California State University in northern California, the Hutchins School first opened its doors to a freshman class of 100 in the fall of 1969. Of the five founding faculty drawn from existing departments, only two survived the turmoil of the School's first year.

As was the case in numerous other experimental programs at the time, bitter differences rapidly surfaced over the program's philosophy and structure. In the Hutchins case, the "structuralists" won, establishing the principle that at the bare minimum, college classes –even experimental ones –required reading lists, regular meeting times and recourse to traditional academic requirements and standards. One has to recall the extremely radical anti-establishment feeling pervading much of higher education (as well as most other aspects of national life) in the late 1960's and early 1970's to appreciate the utter sincerity and passion of those on both sides of such arguments. Any number of well-meaning experimental programs at universities and colleges across the nation foundered on just such disputes.

In outlining the principle features of the Hutchins School, two in particular seem significant for this discussion: the process of curriculum-building and the undergraduate seminar. In contrast to the top-down evolution of courses and programs in every academic discipline, in which undergraduate education is conceived of as a series of graduated introductions to specialized fields, the Hutchins program evolved, as it were, from below. No specialized graduate-level liberal studies curriculum existed to drive undergraduate preparation. The surviving faculty, joined over the next two years by eleven new recruits hired directly into the Hutchins School, were in the enviable position of being charged with creating a meaningful undergraduate education from the ground up, and in the process with rethinking virtually all standard educational beliefs and formulas.

As in similar innovative programs, the evolution of the curriculum in large part reflected the growth and evolving interests of the faculty members themselves as they expanded outward from their original areas of specialization to address the issues central to interdisciplinary, liberal education . Initially sharing a common commitment to little more than the ideal of interdisciplinarity and the belief in education as a community process, the faculty eventually self-organized into teams, or what in those more radical days we called "cadres," to work out the large thematic units that gradually allowed us to overcome the gravitational force of our own academic disciplines as well as the temptation to fall back upon an established canon of 'great books' at the core of the curriculum. Keeping the larger focus on questions and issues we took to be essential for educated individuals to ask and encounter in the modem age, we gradually developed a sequence of integrated courses: "The Human Enigma," "In Search of Self," "Exploring the Unknown," and "Challenge and Response in the Modern World" as the program's fundamental building blocks –though with constantly evolving content and changing faculty.

At the risk of imposing the artificial harmony of theory on what was experienced most often as an organic, evolutionary and at times highly contentious human process, I would propose, however, that the evolution of both the structure and content of the Hutchins Learning Community can be best understood as the emergence of a new and more comprehensive holistic form of learning. Using Koestler's formula once again, the act of stepping back from the sharp edge of discipline-based structures of knowledge in order to permit the emergence of less differentiated but more highly integrated holarchic forms –a paradoxical "regression" in order to progress – effectively opened the way for the evolution of new and more comprehensive ways of organizing learning and teaching.

Beyond the nature of the curriculum, the most distinctive feature of the Hutchins School itself has been its undergraduate seminar. Typically consisting of 12 to 14 students and a faculty member, the seminar has been the crucible in which the variety of ingredients available in the Hutchins Learning Community have been mixed. Unlike research-oriented seminars familiar to many who have attended graduate school, or presentation seminars common in the sciences in which experts share their specialized work, or highly directive seminars in which the more-or-less Socratic instructor asks and the students answer the relevant questions which move the discussion from predetermined point to point, the Hutchins seminar involves students from freshmen to seniors in a highly interactive process in which both instructors and students conduct a joint exploration of the topics and materials at hand.

While in almost all cases an individual faculty member or a faculty cadre will have planned the course, selected the readings and designed the basic topics and issues of study, the open-ended nature of the Hutchins seminar mandates active student participation in shaping the interior structure of the course. As one senior described her learning experience, " we were given basic requirements and encouraged to fly. There is something elemental about being behind the wheel of your own education; it is liberating, empowering and inspiring." Within the seminar, the issues raised by students are explored as seriously as those raised by the instructor, and in the process all participants are challenged to question their own personal and intellectual assumptions on every level. The seminar's very nature as a deliberately collective and non-competitive exploration of truth provides a relatively safe testing-ground in which students are encouraged to try out ideas and risk asking their own questions rather than continually relying on or responding to those of others. Refining their thoughts and judgments while confronting respectfully those of both other seminar members and accepted authorities, students gain an enormously empowering sense of their own intellectual power and responsibility. In the process they encounter a stimulating and evolving mixture of the best of classical and current thought, all of which is to be discussed, analyzed, written about and employed in the context of many of the major issues and problems facing both the students and the contemporary world.

What is unique is less the specific curricular material, much if not all of which is used in a variety of combinations in other higher educational institutions, than the way in which it is used within the seminar itself. As a form of a learning community, the seminar's goal is decidedly not to showcase the brilliance and knowledge of either individual faculty or individual students. Instead, moving toward the more elemental meaning of the term "community of scholars," its aim is to involve all participants in a common process of active inquiry and shared insight leading to intellectual growth and personal transformation. Coming from a traditionally competitive educational background, a student spoke of her dawning realization that "being a 'good' seminar participant required more than preparing my own analysis of the text," adding that, "a 'good' seminar is one where each person is both participant and facilitator. The responsibility of the seminar is shared and becomes a truly rich experience."

Faculty and students become co-learners in a process which vastly revises the traditional relationship between the two, requiring an often ego-threatening abandonment by the faculty member of the protective barriers provided by his or her professional expertise and status. The seminar format itself removes the physical support of podium and lectern. Wide-ranging and often unpredictable discussions render obsolete carefully crafted notes and a planned "coverage" schedule of material. Excursions outside the faculty member's syllabus or even original areas of specialization demand a constant process of reading, thinking and exploring, akin to, but more advanced than that being undergone by the students themselves. This does not mean, however, that the instructor's hard-earned expertise is useless or abandoned, only that it is used in a very different fashion and for significantly different goals. One newer faculty member likens the facilitator's role in a Hutchins seminar to that of an artist whose trained "viewfinder" and carefully refined sensibilities are most powerfully employed in enabling others see reality in new ways and aiding them in "framing the gems" of their own visions more effectively.

Essential to any faculty member's transformation from purveyor of specialized knowledge to facilitator of interdisciplinary learning is his or her active participation in faculty cadres where courses and themes are formulated and through which the process of continuing interdisciplinary faculty education occurs. Ideally providing faculty members with a learning community of their own, in which pedagogical strategies, knowledge and insight are shared, the cadre serves likewise as a primary vehicle for the creation of new and unique course syntheses.

For the student, the format poses a series of immediate challenges. Since virtually all of his or her previous education occurred within the context of individual competition (for grades, attention, standardized test scores, etc.) effectively depicted by Paulo Freire's (1970) "banking" model of knowledge accumulation, the collective model of the seminar initiates a serious process of unlearning deeply entrenched behavioral patterns and assumptions. Reflecting back at the end of her Hutchins experience, one student admitted frankly that "I did not enter the program to become educated. I entered it to become an educator." Yet the seminar experience of being part of a team of "twelve to fourteen students and one professor working together to solve a problem..." raising and attempting to answer "some of the truly puzzling questions of our time..." gradually led to her recognition "that my education has now just begun."

Functioning in the seminar likewise requires a combination of both active and interactive learning skills which often are neither taught nor tolerated in the traditional classroom. Though critical thought and rigorous analysis of texts and ideas are required, it is equally essential that the seminar become what one proponent calls "a hospitable environment" in which "every attempt at truth, no matter how off the mark, is a contribution to the larger search for corporate and consensual truth" (Palmer, 1989, p. 25). This does not imply absence of conflict and disagreement, only that these exciting and inevitable differences in individual perception and levels of understanding be treated as part of a larger process of personal and intellectual community-building. Assessing the workings of the seminar process itself, one student described the task as one of developing, "a vocabulary to give voice to the intricate processes which constitute the keystone of meaningful dialogue." Her recognition that the seminar's goal is to increase understanding rather than win a game of intellectual hand-to-hand combat is of critical importance in defining the meaning of both a true learning community and a *holistic* liberal education today.

Underlying this model of learning is indeed an alternative epistemology, one in which, as Parker J. Palmer has written, "the relational nature of reality" supersedes a previously-held vision of separation, fragmentation, individualism and simple objectivism. Here we move to "juxtapose analysis with synthesis, integration, and the creative act" (1989, p. 24). For this to occur effectively in the classroom, a radical shift in emphasis is essential. What may be appropriate training for specialized research in the disciplines should be recognized as counterproductive in creating the conditions for liberal learning, particularly when we are faced with questions which fall outside the boundaries of any single field or collection of disciplines.

We are increasingly being confronted with the fact that the important issues regarding human life, our coexistence with nature and the planet, the proper allocation of natural, social and human resources, and our judgments about the uses of our immensely powerful technological tools cannot and should not be left to specialists alone.

While we necessarily concern ourselves with the seemingly mundane requirements and activities of our individual lives, we are now inevitably faced with the larger consequences and broader relational web of those actions.

In many ways the seminar models for students an alternative method of dealing with the complex issues which face all of us. A learning community which supports the individual in exploring both his or her own ignorance and knowledge enhances not only external but internal learning. The variety of perspectives, observations and experiences readily available on any topic provide a healthy antidote to the typical isolation of traditional learning experiences, contributing to a deep understanding of alternative ways of seeing reality. The fact that the "right road" alluded to in Dante's classic lines has always been "wholly lost and gone," can serve symbolically as a starting-point for the collective search which has always been central to a liberal education.

Gide's warning that our greatest enemy may be the persistent human tendency to accept answers —our own or those of others —and to stop asking questions is the paradoxical meat and drink of the seminar process.

If the real value of the liberal education process is that through it students will learn how to live successfully in the vast middle ground between attachment to absolute truths and surrender to powerlessness and personal despair, and to make accurate, creative and wise judgments about the important issues confronting them as individuals who are also part of a social community, then a serious reconsideration of current educational structures is essential. Just as the eternal questions of good, evil, beauty, truth, love, justice and meaning cannot be answered on a scantron sheet, so the academy cannot pretend to confront them adequately without providing an interactive, relational and assessable structure in which students and teachers can search for their own answers together.

Wholeness will not be found either in isolation or absolutes, but by individuals who have confronted and challenged their own definitions and limitations, using all the tools universities have to offer, and who have also developed their own identities within true learning communities.

References

Freire, Paulo. 1970. *Pedagogy of the Oppressed*. Herder and Herder.

Koestler, Arthur. 1967. *The Ghost in the Machine*. Hutchinson of London. 1979. *Janus: A Summing Up*. Vintage.

Palmer, Parker J. 1989. "Community, Conflict, and Ways of Knowing: Ways to Deepen Our Educational Agenda." *Change*. September/October.

Wilbur, Ken. 1996. *A Brief History of Everything*. Shambhala.

HUTCHINS AND THE FA CUP

Anthony Mountain

Tony Mountain received a BA from Columbia University and a PhD in Comparative Literature from the University of Washington. He was one of the first faculty members to join the Hutchins School in 1970 and continued to teach there for his entire career. He always taught in the lower division General Education seminar program and in the upper division Liberal Studies major. Because the Hutchins School participates in the University's elementary teacher credential program, Tony took a great interest in the quality of the education given to potential teachers, insisting on its breadth and depth quite apart from classroom teacher training. In this regard, for years he taught the broad course LIBS 327: The English Language. His favorite upper division seminars were "Themes in the Literary Humanities" and "The Moral Imagination." He reluctantly retired in 2011.

Before I retired from The Hutchins School of Liberal Studies the faculty agreed to have a seminar on a book of my choosing. I chose *A Month in the Country* by the lovely and eccentric English author J.L. Carr (now deceased). *A Month in the Country* is, in my opinion, a quiet and in its own way magnificent novel. We had a good time with it.

I mention Carr's novel entirely because of the small possibility that someone reading this might, out of curiosity, hunt up a copy and – what else? – fall in love with it. That done, I want to move on to another Carr novel with the beguiling title *How Steeple Sinderby Wanderers Won the FA Cup*. I invite readers to investigate this novel, too. It's much funnier than the first book and I occasionally choose (perhaps rashly) to believe its every word. Why not? It's full of lovely sentences. For example, once Sinderby is on its wondrous football (soccer) national winning streak, there's this: "Mrs Fangfoss [ah, Mrs Fangfoss!], taking the tide at its flood, had circulated a list of grievances to the village people, urging that they should air these when approached by Press or TV, so that, greatly to the annoyance of Authority, the World learnt that our school's toilets were still at the bottom of the playground and froze up in winter, that Sinderby's dustbins were emptied only once a fortnight compared to once a week in Barchester although we paid exactly the same rates, and that the County library wouldn't stock easy-to-read love stories including her own novels."

We are not to ask where in the depths of rural England a place with the name of Steeple Sinderby might be, but we must believe how shocked England's population was to learn that Sinderby's football team won the coveted FA Cup. However, I quote Carr's sentence not just for its prose (which itself is worth the price), but also for somewhat more serious reasons which I think Carr has in mind. The above sentence is followed by this: "And, when our member of Parliament, normally glimpsed only once each five years, turned up with a glad smile for his meed of publicity, aglow with solutions to the world's crises, all he got was nationwide pictures showing him surrounded by dissatisfied consumers of government demanding why he didn't get off his backside and do something for Steeple Sinderby."

All this is fine fun but Carr is never just an entertainer. His next paragraph (in the narrator's voice) begins thus: "But the great and abiding Truth I learned these weeks was how many people in this world have no Purpose in life, people who live second-hand, sitting all the hours God gives them free of drudgery, staring at either picture papers or TV, waiting like little kids for just another story or for Guidance." think it possible to argue that the point of the book is enclosed in that sentence.

With the reader's indulgence I have taken some time to get to Carr's phrase about the "second-hand" life. From his point of view, people living the second-hand life – and one wonders who isn't – do not and are taught not to expect to win the FA Cup (to speak metaphorically). And I might add that the best way to assure this is to arrange things so that, finally, no one has any interest in the road to Wembley Stadium much less winning the FA Cup. Let me anticipate myself by saying that the Hutchins School was dedicated to trying to make sure that that doesn't happen.

One can argue that the second-hand life is not worldwide, that it is largely a product of the richly endowed and high-consuming West. And one can argue that there are consequences for all of this, consequences that may seem far from but are not unrelated to the second-hand life. In a 2017 review of Pankaj Mishra's *Age of Anger: A History of the Present*, Franklin Foer begins by saying, "Across the world, a spirit of anarchy is in bloom – an aimless desire to smash the liberal order, with only the distant, inchoate hope that a better world will emerge from the wreckage." He suggests that this destructive impulse – spurred by, among other things, fearful poverty and a near-wild Nietzschean "resentment" – is behind the recent upending of traditional American politics and the radicalization of the multitudes who follow ISIS. We are not here talking about people "with no Purpose in life." How is one to respond to Carr's "second-hand life" or Foer's "spirit of anarchy"? Well, I'm sure by this time the reader suspects that all this is a shameless setup for a plug for the kind of education offered by the Hutchins School. It is.

J.L. Carr was himself a teacher and school principal, much beloved. He explored the boundaries (if there are any) of quirkiness, impulsive and imaginative pedagogy, and the inciting and remembering of spontaneous responses – and all of it with no tolerance for smart-mouthery. Hutchins isn't like that but it is moved, as was Carr's school, by the desire to make learning important, desirable, and even transformative and a joy. This was not a simple thing; often our students came to us having thoroughly learned the general if unconscious cultural proposition that thinking is unpleasant labor.

The approach Hutchins takes is to try to involve the students directly in their own learning. This largely takes the form of seminars or discussion groups, though other more traditionally didactic approaches are also used. Materials from traditional disciplines are used but courses are thematically oriented. (For years I offered – perhaps "facilitated" is a better word – a seminar called "The Moral Imagination" that used literature and philosophy. I loved it; for fifteen weeks a semester we were learners and teachers together.)

Of course, education is not single-handedly going to awaken the second-hand life or end the stupefying brutality that is currently infesting our planet. But it can help. If it can assist in showing and practicing the process of critical thinking, if it can nurture and nudge students to their own best thinking, if it can develop a taste for learning such that people leave with a desire to continue their own education throughout their lives and have a sense how to do that, then it can help.

A large impediment to this is the impulse to accept false limitations. When I was much younger I sometimes heard the phrase, "You can't beat city hall." Then one day I heard this: When someone used that phrase someone else said, "Why not?" I was transfixed. And the person went on to say, "After all, who built city hall? City hall isn't an act of God." An education involving critical thinking is an education that questions false limitations and encourages reaching. I give an example: There is no doubt that we would recover our democracy if we put into law the requirement that campaigns for all federal high offices must be publicly funded. Now nothing like that will remotely happen if we accept false limitations. Again, good critical thinking can result in what used to be call "consciousness raising." Currently many men are being called to account for their past dreadful behavior toward women; and for many of them this must come as a shock because at least some of their behavior was quite possibly not ill intended, the men were simply acting on the deep sexism of the male culture. To go against that sexism – to critically examine it – didn't come to mind at the time and hence wasn't a possibility. There was need of a critical "consciousness raising." Education can help with that.

I can hardly claim that the Hutchins School was and is everywhere and always a success in all of this, but I do (and did during all of my

41 years there) think it was going in the right direction. And so in defiance of all false and disempowering limitations, I declare that there should be many more schools like the Hutchins School. None have to be duplicates of it, of course; suggestions for new and inspired approaches must be encouraged. But I insist that everyone in our country should have access to such schools. To say otherwise is a false limitation (and an attempt to hide the possibility that we really don't believe our own high-sounding statements about quality education and access to it for everyone). If Hutchins or something like it were everywhere it would change everything.

I fear that this is sounding too general, high-minded, and abstract. So I will close with a couple of descriptions of educational moments that have stayed with me as examples of education that counts. In the first I am thinking of a seminar some years ago that had a large focus on environmental problems and what could be done about them. As a simple project, I asked the students each to take something they commonly used (soap, pencil graphite, etc.) and find out everything they could about it, including possible environmental problems it caused and possible solutions. I asked the students to make brief reports to the group about what they discovered. One student came to me for a topic suggestion; she said she couldn't think of one not already taken. I suggested she look into what she might find about the small batteries used in watches and all sorts of other products. She said she would. In time her turn came to give her report and as she started to do so she became visibly upset. "You don't want to hear this," she said, and she began to cry. But she then reversed herself. "You have to hear this, everyone does." Pulling herself together, she outlined what she had found. Her research had led from the tiny batteries – discarded by the hundred million – to the plastic Sargasso Sea floating in the Pacific. We were stunned. I tell this story because that day that student won the FA Cup.

Another memory. I asked a class of students to submit substantive questions and issues, one of which they would prepare each week and be ready to discuss. I had done this several times before and it had worked well. On one occasion when the students were settling down and reviewing their notes for the discussion, one of the students happened to ask if any of the others had seen the TV pictures the night before of drought-stricken Ethiopia and of its many starving children. Most of the students had. Then another student asked how many of the students would give ten percent of their income to help alleviate such a situation if they were certain all their money would reach its intended destination. No hands went up. Five percent? No hands. Another student said, "Maybe we should talk about *this*." So they put away their notes and began. Among those students there was always at least one (and often many) who knew something – sometimes a lot – about every issue they took up. International responsibilities. Capitalism, profit and greed. Empathy and distance. Who is whose brother and sister's keeper? There was much more, because the deeper they got the more need there was for further questions and more clarity. Eventually students outside began to look in the window; there was polite knocking on the door. "We have to give up the room," someone said, but they clearly didn't want to leave. During the entire session I had not uttered a single word. As they finally rose and gathered up their books and papers, someone said, "This is the kind of class I came to college for." On that day and in that classroom those students won the FA Cup.

Postscript

J.L. Carr and the FA Cup aside, I have a Hutchins anecdote that I want to share. Here it is.

I often go to a beach near where I live to get some exercise. Last summer as I was getting off the beach one afternoon, a group of seniors, tourists, asked me for some directions and some recommendations about places to eat. We got to talking and eventually they asked where I worked. I told them that I had retired from the faculty of the Hutchins School of Liberal Studies at Sonoma State University. They wanted to know all about the Hutchins School so I went into some detail (small seminars, a thematic curriculum, etc.). At one point I said that my own background was in literature but that over the years I had — and in some sense the whole program had — taken a greater and greater interest in and concern about critical thinking.

What a bombshell the phrase "critical thinking" had on the group! At first they all started talking at once. To paraphrase, it went like this: "No! I thought critical thinking was long dead." "Does anyone talk about it in school anymore?" Then one woman said, "Your Hutchins School needs to behave like rabbits, breed all over the place." Another added that we might start that project in Washington. They were laughing uproariously by then: "Think critically. Start a revolution." But then one of the men said that it was in fact a dreadfully serious matter. "Sometimes I feel like I'm losing my own country." Then he looked hard at me and added, "You put in all those years, you and your colleagues, in that program. You all must feel enormously dedicated. Given what's going on in the country, do you sometimes feel disappointed?"

So far as the country is concerned, I often feel that the most patriotic citizens are the most disappointed citizens these days. So far as critical thinking is concerned, may the Hutchins School never give up. To that I'm sure that that group of tourists would say, "Amen."

References

Carr, J.L. 1975. *How Steeple Sinderby Wanderers Won the FA Cup.* Penguin. 1980. *A Month in the Country,* New York Review Book.

Foer, Franklin. 2017. *The New York Times: Book Review,* February 19. Rogers, Byron. 2003. *The Last Englishman: The Life of J.L. Carr.* Aurum Press.

Note: Carr founded The Quince Tree Press and published all his novels and a good deal more.

Interdisciplinary Innovative Education and an Anthropologist's Role

Richard Zimmer

Richard Zimmer, Professor Emeritus, Hutchins School. Sonoma State University. BA, History, University of Michigan. MA, History, U California, Berkeley. PhD Anthropology, UCLA. PhD Psychology, Center for Psychological Studies. Licensed Psychologist. Previously taught at Los Angeles Valley College. Continues to teach at the Eisner Institute for Professional Studies and at the Older Adults Program at Santa Rosa Junior College.

This chapter was previously published in the November 1975 issue of the *Anthropology and Education Quarterly.*

The Hutchins School of Liberal Studies is one of the many innovative programs established in higher education during the 1960s. It followed some of the line of earlier experiments at New College at California State University, San Jose and St. John's at Annapolis and Santa Fe. These programs have certain common characteristics – they are innovative, experimental, and interdisciplinary. Students are expected to develop their education from their personal sources, using both the instructor and the community as "resources."

For those of us who had previously taught in "traditional" departments, the "lessons" learned have been exciting and significant. I have taught at Hutchins for the last four years as the "house" anthropologist, and I would like to share some of these lessons with those interested in developing new programs or finding new ways of teaching traditional material.

Hutchins School is part of [what was then] California State College Sonoma. The College is located 50 miles north of San Francisco in a somewhat rural setting, now being invaded by tract housing. Students are drawn to the school from all over California, particularly from Los Angeles. It has an "experimental" flavor to it, and its Humanistic Psychology Institute is well known. There are two main divisions to the College: the "Old School" of traditional departments, and three cluster colleges. Hutchins is one of these three; it emphasizes liberal arts and has an enrollment of 250 lower and upper division students. The Expressive Arts School emphasizes creative arts and enrolls 125 upper division students, and the Environmental Studies School focuses on ecology and urban planning and enrolls 75 upper division majors. The total college enrollment is 5500 and is growing slowly. Each cluster school is autonomous in curriculum and promotion, retention, and tenure. The faculty is drawn from all the disciplines including natural sciences. All professors have return rights, by state law, to their respective departments, even though these departments were not necessarily consulted on hiring. The significance of this cannot be understated and will be discussed below.

Hutchins School maintains both a lower division and an upper division program. The lower division places students into seminars of 10 people. Each student is enrolled for 12 units except for 1st-semester freshmen; they take 15 units. Lower division students are randomly assigned to classes after they are admitted to the program. They fulfill their general education requirements by meeting in seminars several times a week for two-hour sessions. The curriculum they follow is decided upon by a "cadre" of faculty members who agree to teach 50% of the same material around a given "theme"~ e.g., Man the Knower or Order and Disorder. The material changes somewhat depending upon the faculty assigned. The 50% rule gives the teachers sufficient latitude to pursue their own interests and to take on new material spontaneously. As students progress through the lower division, they are allowed - and encouraged - to take more units of independent study. Seminars stress writing and interdisciplinary thinking and prepare students for independent learning.

The upper division is more open-ended. Continuing students are free to take 10 units of independent study; transfer students must take a lecture course that focuses on an interdisciplinary theme, and a "home-room" type of seminar in which 10 students and an instructor discuss the lecture and other material. In lower and upper division, the students meet in the instructor's office, designed to hold 12 people. Students can then take any one of a series of courses offered by the faculty, or can develop a project or series of projects with one or several instructors, as they see fit. They are encouraged to take on more independent study through the remaining three semesters, and culminate with a final senior project supervised by several faculty members. Originally the school was on a pass-fail system; Board of Trustees rulings have made most classes graded.

Students are evaluated by instructors in addition to receiving a grade. Files are open, and students are often consulted on the evaluation procedure. Following the recent shifts in the nature of students nationally, Hutchins students have become more grade-conscious and more eager to take specifically-focused classes rather than engage in creative projects in independent study. This is true of older students as well as the new teaching credential students. At the same time, there is an increasing interest in "nostalgia" courses such as The Renaissance Mind. The program caters to many tastes and many levels of students, yet it has done well placing those who wish to go to graduate and professional school.

The program is ambitious and it requires the continual working together of 14 teachers from very different fields. Lower-division cadres must agree to share the same booklist, team teachers must constantly work together, and all faculty must agree on the nature of the program. Unlike traditional departments, where teachers are left to do their specialty and only occasionally meet with colleagues on matters of departmental concern, Hutchins faculty meet constantly - planning courses, evaluating students, and evaluating the program. There is thus a special pressure within the department for those people who work well together.

Faculty members must also be competent to teach in several different fields. This, of course, is a sensitive point: what is "competence" in another person's field? Faculty in Hutchins have varied backgrounds; I, for example, have taught history and political science as well as anthropology in traditional departments. Cadre meetings and informal consultations among faculty help to bring about this competency. Yet, competency must be of a somewhat different sort from traditional departments. All of us had done our own specialized research, but we must be able to teach as generalists. A consensus on what this competency is has developed in the school – a focus on good writing, critical thinking, imaginative projects, and tackling any project inter-disciplinarily. What we try to teach is, for lack of a better term, a critical approach to material. A Hutchins student who wants a body of specialized knowledge on a particular subject is encouraged to take that class in the Old School, if it is available. At Hutchins, that student must use that specialized knowledge to reach general theoretical or critical concerns.

An example may make this point more clearly. One student of mine first began a project comparing Sonoma County's free and public schools. He visited several schools, read some of their current books on educational philosophy such as Holt, and interviewed both students and staff. He then went on to work in a school for children with severe psychological issues. Initially, he did an ethnography of the school, while doing extensive reading in abnormal psychology. His final project was a rough attempt to understand why certain children preferred various ways of acting out their problems. He used data from his previous studies and readings as well as interviews and students' files. He did most of that work with me, though he was asked to take Abnormal Psychology in the Psychology Department.

Projects like this require faculty to move across fields as well as be flexible in dealing with students. In some ways, it is a particularly demanding process. Not all faculty in all departments are eager or able to move in these directions, both for personal and professional reasons. That is why curriculum and tenure decisions must be made by the school; competence is on Hutchins' terms, not on traditional terms. This often leads to Old School distrust and suspicion of innovation. Teaching effectiveness is measured at Hutchins in terms of cross-disciplinary competency, personal flexibility, and ability to work well with others. These criteria are not the ones found in traditional departments. In addition, curricula must be innovative and easily changed; colleges and universities that require elaborate bureaucratic procedures for course approval are likely to stifle creativity.

Faculty members in Hutchins work closely with small groups of students, both in seminars and individually. With a focus on experiential, personal learning, the nature of this interaction is emotionally charged. A Hutchins teacher is, in effect, a resource person, a group leader, and a counselor all rolled into one. That is an emotionally demanding role for which academicians are rarely trained. Those of us in the social sciences, particularly anthropologists, sociologists, and psychologists, are more readily attuned to interpersonal dynamics. These dynamics must be dealt with both creatively and ethically. The situation requires closeness yet distance, and demands considerable skill to manage. Colleges and universities are legally withdrawing from the in loco parentis role; consequently, the responsibilities of teachers are becoming more demanding as they deal with students' problems. In simple terms, there is no easy way out of the dilemma caused by process's effects in the classroom.

Often, interpersonal dynamics may serve as the content of a class, or at least part of the content. Non-verbal language, for example, can be taught by having students focus on seating arrangements, hand positions, and eye contact in each session. Prejudice themes can be taught by having students take an F-Scale test [a test designed by Theodor Adorno to measure receptivity to authoritarian/fascist beliefs; published in *The Authoritarian Personality* in 1950] and then using their answers to stimulate discussions. Law, in sociological terms, can be explored by the ways a class initiates rules to effectively focus discussion on material. The instructor must be able to draw a fine line so the classes do not turn into therapy groups.

Not all faculty members prefer teaching in this style or on these subjects. They may choose more content structured courses; nevertheless, they always find that they must handle this class process. A few examples should make this clear: breaks in curriculum are planned for, spontaneity is encouraged, and students are often asked to hold additional seminars without instructors to "straighten out" process conflicts. The rapid change in student character and preparation in the last few years has left us with one maxim: be flexible!

There are some personal dilemmas in being the house anthropologist, which have larger curricular application. I must be the professional advocate for ending culture-bound points of view. Colleagues deeply embedded in the Western philosophical tradition must be carefully educated to get a sense of cultural differences and culture-bound statements. Levels of trust must be built up. I hear such statements as, "You're just doing another idealist trip." For colleagues originally trained to teach their own courses in specialized fields, this is indeed a difficult process.

Professionally, I watch people. Like the psychologist on the faculty, I am "suspect." I first see things in social rather than philosophical terms. I must sensitize my colleagues to these kinds of issues in a cautious manner. It is a taxing position, and I have learned that time is necessary for me to communicate these perspectives as well as to learn those of others. We are only too well socialized in graduate schools and in departmental teaching into narrow thinking. When questions of promotion and tenure are involved in this learning process, the stakes become very high.

The experience of teaching in Hutchins is exciting. I have learned to learn faster than I did in undergraduate and graduate school. I have learned much from my colleagues, and I will continue to learn. Moreover, I have learned some basics about working in this kind of educational format. The most important basic, obviously, is that the faculty dynamics are of crucial, if not primary, importance. Faculty members must trust one another and respect what their colleagues are trying to do; they must learn to work closely with one another; that takes time. The traditional models of one-semester, one-time courses must be set aside. Our lower-division program took five years to achieve reasonable shape. The faculty had to be satisfied, and that required skillful negotiation. Students, incidentally, had to be satisfied and made part of the process also. That, too, is difficult. It is quite easy to arrange "touchy-feely" programs, but we have definitely not taken that course. It is difficult to learn to work with students in quasi-clinical terms and yet retain an academic focus to the program. It may mean incurring student displeasure, not giving them what they want or think they deserve. Trust must be brought about, not assumed. "Students learning to take the control of classes away from instructors and to become self motivated learners" is often a complex process.

Working in this fashion has prepared us to meet some of the challenges of extended education and still retain an academic focus. We are in the process of developing programs for returning and retired students as well as for students with technical backgrounds. Programs like this go beyond the base of the college, they require increasing use of the community resources. We haven't done all we want perfectly because we are very aware of faculty "burnout" as well as jealousy and resentment from the Old School for our experiments with closeness and new forms of competence. However, I feel we are succeeding, earning the respect of colleagues throughout our college, and, most of all, doing a good job with the students.

If it is possible, I would like to invite a more extended discussion on the problems of process content courses. Such courses appear to be effective in teaching certain basic concepts in social science in meaningful, experiential terms. I would also invite discussion on the effects of process on teaching at the college level. Too often, the subject is de-emphasized or not considered suitable for academic discussion. As colleges and universities reach out to new categories of students, such concerns are of primary importance.

ORDER/UNTITLED/DISORDER

Maurice Blaug

Maurice Blaug came to Hutchins for the Fall 1970 term a freshly-minted Ph.D. in Zoology along with several other new faculty to put the program together after the chaotic first year. Over the next few years he helped to develop the curriculum for LIBS 101 and LIBS 202, and even ran a human biology lab for a while. His passion for the sciences, art, literature and history led him to create upper division, interdisciplinary courses on human nature and the human body, an interdisciplinary science course for prospective teachers, a hands-on course in making art of all kinds, and a spring term course called "Seeing Nature Whole" in which the class spent a lot of time in the Fairfield Osborn Preserve working on natural history and arts projects. He painted and showed his work when he could.

When I was teaching at Hutchins and painting after hours, so to speak, I became aware that the tension between ordered (geometric) and disordered (biomorphic) forms interested me and has played a part in my work ever since. The idea of that tension is evident in Freud's id and superego, in Marx's and other German philosophies of the dialectic, in recent art history and more lately in 'disruption,' not to leave out the theory of evolution. In the political/social realm we've lived through momentous struggles between revolution and the status quo. In my next lifetime I shall teach a course on this.

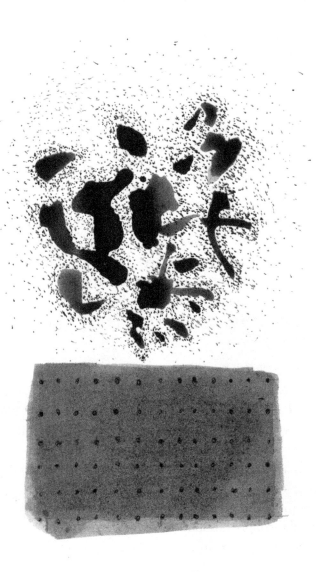

Insights
from the
Second Generation

Francisco Vázquez

Nelson (Buzz) Kellogg

Eric McGuckin

Riversteadt LaMoreaux

Wendy Ostroff

Janet Hess

Ben Frymer

A CRITICAL GAZE THROUGH MY HUTCHINS KALEIDOSCOPE

Francisco H. Vázquez, Ph.D.

Dr. Francisco H. Vázquez first joined the Hutchins School in 1990, with a focus on the History of Ideas. Among his publications are two editions of *Latino/Latina Thought: Culture, Politics and Society,* and a recently completed book-length manuscript on *Continental Americans: Quest for Human Dignity.* He attended the Claremont Colleges, for both his Bachelor's Degree in philosophy and his Doctorate in European Intellectual History. He was a Ford Fellow 1972-1977 and a Post-Doctoral Southern Fellowship Fund Fellow 1981-82. For over four decades he has taught at Claremont, Cal Poly Pomona, Loyola Marymount University, World College West, and for the last 30 years, at SSU.

I agonize over the task of choosing the words to deploy in a text that marks the momentous occasion of the 50th Anniversary of the Hutchins School. Words, furthermore, that symbolize my farewell to four decades of my teaching profession. Though I remind myself that discourse, like time, is a thread with no beginning and no end, I still agonize because I am greedy. Like Caden Cotard, the character in the film *Synecdoche: New York,* I desire to capture and convey an entire lifetime of *vivencias* (lived experiences). Not only mine but those of the Hutchins founders, new faculty, supporters and fellow learners for the last half-century. And like all writers I want readers to commune with my words and *feel* my *vivencias* at such an honorable institution as the Hutchins School. This *agonía,* however, gives way to a humbling and sobering realization: that the desire to convey experiences and feelings, and even knowledge and wisdom, is detained at the border of the reader's own sentiments. Surrendering to the limitations of words and the theory of minds, and taking my cue from the fact that my most popular class *ever* is my *Values and Power in the Twilight Zone* course, I present here a kaleidoscope of reflections that I hope resonate with some readers.

Genesis and Evolution in a Mythological Context

"The first principle of value that we need to rediscover is this: that all reality hinges on moral foundations. In other words, that this is a moral universe, and that there are moral laws of the universe just as abiding as the physical laws."

~ Martin Luther King Jr.

In the beginning it was the archetype, and the archetype was based on the Greek gods Dionysius and Apollo. Or so says the lore started by the Hutchins School founder Dr. Warren Olson. Some of the initial faculty, the Dionysians, wanted pure Creativity in the process with no restraints whatsoever: on the first day of class the professor would co-create the syllabus with the students, and together make it up as we went along. The Apollonians would not hear of it. They demanded Structure and Order: well defined courses, syllabi, and curricula. Apparently the latter won the initial struggle. To this day, in the maze-like halls of Carson Hall one sometimes hears the Greek chorus chanting that, thanks to the Apollonians, this 1960's "experimental" program survived the heyday of the Cultural Revolution. Nevertheless, in human affairs the Dionysian spirit never really goes away because as humans we embody emotion as well as reason and the quixotic goal is to maintain a healthy balance between the two. It is no surprise that after fifty years we still refer to "Apollonian" and "Dionysian" qualities when we discuss the Hutchins School.

Focusing my kaleidoscope on the evolution of the Hutchins School up to the present tumultuous start of a new millennium, I see two additional mythological archetypes. One of them is the myth of the struggle between the Aztec gods Tezcatlipoca and Quetzalcoatl that leads to the recurrent creation and destruction of the human world. Quetzalcoatl and Tezcatlipoca are twins and they are both creators and destroyers. Analogous to Friedrich Nietzsche's *The Birth of Tragedy*, rather than standing in direct opposition with each other, each one of them embodies positive and negative qualities and they are engaged in a cosmic dance where the human world is created and destroyed. As the Aztec Calendar indicates, this has happened four times and we are now in the *Quinto Sol* (the Fifth Sun or World), which is destined to end by earthquakes in due time. In each new world humankind is brought back to life but in different forms. This Eternal Return is of course a universal concept, which incidentally also resonates with the contemporary scientific theory of recurring Big Bangs. At any rate, adding this mythological evolutionary dimension to our discussion may give us a more comprehensive assessment of the nature of challenges the Hutchins School may be confronting.

I was led to this analogy while reading "The Intellectual Community," a short article written in 1977 by Robert Maynard Hutchins who includes a response by his long-time friend Mr. Clifton "Kip" Fadiman, an Associate at the Center for the Study of Democratic Institutions. Dr. Hutchins, who would agree with Dr. Martin Luther King Jr. that, "The first principle of value... is that this is a moral universe...," places his bet on the side of the human spirit, virtue, and the intellectual community. Fadiman, on the contrary, challenges this assumption and argues that in the upcoming new world there is no room for virtue, an intellectual community or a democratic society. According to Fadiman, we are caught in a paradigm shift, "between worlds, one dying, one crying to be born" (Hutchins, 11). Presently, many people are aware of (or feel) our *being-between-worlds* and its possible consequences for Homo sapiens. Among them is Yuval Noah Harari who, in *Homo Deus: A Brief History of Tomorrow,* points to evidence that seems to support Fadiman's contention. This is, of course, more than an academic debate; there are serious implications for the future of the Hutchins School and for all of humanity. Now, perceptions that the world is drastically changing are not new. Some people have experienced an apocalypse, like the indigenous people slaughtered by the Europeans, black people taken as slaves, and those exposed to a series of holocausts in the 20th century. And all humans have experienced stunning shift of values through the agricultural, industrial, information, and digital revolutions and increasingly every generation feels like they are going through some kind of Cultural Revolution.

This debate is manifested today in the disintegration of the concept of common good and the emergence of ethnic and ideological tribalism. And this directs our gaze towards another Greek tragedy, one that used to be a staple in the Hutchins' curriculum: Aeschylus' trilogy of plays, *The Oresteia*. Here we witness the struggle between the Furies (protectors of the integrity of the human body, Justice and Memory) and Apollo (defender of the State, the Law and Historical Amnesia). When the polis (State, government) does not take care of the wellbeing of the human bodies, or human blood has been shed unjustly, the Furies come out to avenge those who have been wronged. This archetype points to a historical tension between two sources of Justice: the ethnos (the clans, tribes, we the people) and the polis (the government). In other words, justice as carried out by one's own hand when there is a perception that the Law itself is unjust and justice as carried out by Law.

A moving discussion of the notion of resistance to unjust laws can be found in King's 1963 "Letter from a Birmingham Jail." And it was during the tumultuous period of the 1960's that we witness the genesis of the Hutchins School. In 1968 student demonstration took center stage all over the world to signal the need for social change. With the cry of "No Justice, No Peace!" people who had been marginalized because of their skin color, nationality or gender rose up in a Civil Rights movement to demand the same rights as U.S. Americans "who call themselves white" (Ta-Nehisi Coates). In the current emerging postmodern new world the latter are now claiming that they are the ones who are getting no justice and therefore, there will be no peace until they "Make America Great." The inclusion of *The Oresteia* in the lower division is a testament of the efforts of the faculty to educate students about this particular human predicament and I personally found it very useful in understanding the struggles of oppressed peoples in the Americas and in the world.

Referencing archetypical mythologies to help us frame the fifty-year-old evolution and future prospects of the Hutchins School, can also lead us into sensitive areas that, if not fully relegated to historical amnesia, are seldom discussed openly. Turning our gaze inward we see that, as much as we love this successful, venerable institution, it too has a shadow. In the spirit of critical inquiry, and uncomfortable and impolitic as it may be, one must take a look at the evolutionary struggles for social and racial equity *within* the Hutchins School.

In terms of gender equity, for example, the first of four-12-unit-course sequence Hutchins course was initially titled *Man's Enigma* and at some point changed to *The Human Enigma*. I don't know how long that first title lasted because the women in the Hutchins faculty exercised a strong presence; they insisted on gender parity in the hiring process and held equal footing with men on departmental affairs. In terms of what goes by the name "cultural diversity," the story is a bit more complicated. In the upper division curriculum there was a two-course sequence: 304A We Hold These Truths, a course about U.S. American Culture, and the untitled sequel 304B, which focused on a country of the faculty member's choice. In effect, the first course I ever taught in Hutchins, as an adjunct, was 304B: México. After I was hired in a tenure-track position I asked the faculty (half-jokingly) if the implied counterpart of "We Hold These Truths" was meant to be "And They Hold Theirs."

Borrowing from my previous intercultural experience at World College West, I proposed that 304B become a course on comparative, global cross-cultural studies. The faculty quickly agreed and it became "The Practice of Culture." And just so that it would not be an appendage of "304A" it got its own number: LIBS 308. As with the introductory upper division course, LIBS 302 Introduction to Liberal Studies, we agreed on a number of topics that had to be included in each course and then left it up to the individual faculty members to choose the way they wanted to teach it. This creative freedom is, by the way, the kind of academic freedom that makes teaching in Hutchins such a sheer delight. A few years ago this course was changed to a lower division course with an enrollment capacity of

200 students and now it is back to whatever content each faculty choses.

Another aspect of diversity is reflected in the racial make up of the Hutchins School student body and faculty. While there are many factors involved here, one must face the painful reality of unconscious bias, which is so deeply imbedded in all humans. While there is undoubtedly a conscious effort to include multicultural perspectives in all Hutchins School courses, the struggle with lack of ethnic diversity continues to this day. In half a century there have only been a handful of faculty of color. This lack of diversity, it must be noted occurs not only in Hutchins, but also in the entire University. It has not been easy to bring in faculty from underrepresented groups such as Latinx, African, Native and Asian Americans, but there is promise in the current SSU administration's efforts to remedy this situation.

A shadow can only be cast by a strong light. And the Hutchins School has been a strong light for all of us who have had the fortune of being illumed by it. As we celebrate the many and notable accomplishments of the Hutchins School in the last fifty years, my hope is that these critical recollections lead to a discussion of the questions and challenges that are facing this remarkable institution and the whole of humanity in the near and far future. For as we transition from the old to the new world led by bio- and digital technology, the question of the balance among the diverse antagonistic human qualities remains as urgent as it was in ancient times.

From this brief review of the genesis and evolution of the Hutchins School several questions arise that have direct implications for its future. In the balancing act between chaos and order, process and form, will the fulcrum move irremediably towards the Apollonian side? More specific to the task at hand, what are the implications of a new world for the future of what we currently define as "human nature"? Are virtue, morality and justice a social construction? Are we humans destined to become cyborgs?

Before we turn the Hutchins kaleidoscope towards a critical assessment of these questions, I need to disclose my own biases and prejudices via a short biographical detour.

A Curriculum for a Nomad Scholar

"The starting-point of critical elaboration is the consciousness of what one really is, and is 'knowing thyself' as a product of the historical processes to date, which has deposited in you an infinity of traces, without leaving an inventory; therefore it is imperative at the outset to compile such an inventory."

~ Antonio Gramsci, *Prison Notebooks* (1929-1935)

I came to Hutchins with a particular personal history of struggles with a variety of institutions. Having an extended family split throughout Guadalajara, Mexico, and Cheyenne, Wyoming, my family moved between the two countries from 1954 until 1964 when we finally settled in Los Angeles. Our nomadic life was due to the 1930's Repatriation Program, which deported 1.8 million Mexicans and their U.S.-born children (like my mother) to Mexico. I grew up witnessing the relativity of the truths held as sacred by the political and social customs of each new locality. Consequently my *vivencias* were in a constant dialectical struggle with the *prepotencia* (arrogance, abuse of authority) at play in the many cultures I encountered. Cultural norms and institutional policies (like at the variety of schools that I attended) always seemed to be out of sync with the people's experiences of everyday life. I always felt uncomfortable with people who demanded respect but did not practice what they preached.

It's the contradictions, stupid!

In México, I saw the contradictions between a) the ideals of human dignity we learned in the Catholic Church regarding the love for God and our fellow beings and the civic lessons we learned at the public school regarding our civil and human rights, and b) the gross *prepotencia* (abuse of authority) by people in authority in the treatment of women and people that were considered to be from an inferior social class, or who had a darker skin or indigenous features.

Once we settled in the Los Angeles, my life encountered another set of contradictions. As a student in Dana Junior High in San Pedro, California I challenged the boring ESL curriculum that assumed (and does to this day) that all immigrants are illiterate. Around that time my identity was challenged by the corrosive realization that Mexicans in the United States were (and still are in the Trump era) considered an inferior people. In two different High Schools I argued for academic courses I wanted to take instead of the "shop" ones I was assigned to (because I spoke with an accent). At Claremont Men's College I joined the student Chicano movement, which challenged the claim that there were no qualified Chicano students and demanded the establishment of Chicano Studies Program at the Claremont Colleges. This experience formed my identity as a community organizer and public scholar (or what Gramsci calls "an organic intellectual." In Graduate School I had to patch together my own interdisciplinary program in European Intellectual History to be able to study Latin American Philosophy which I was told "did not exist."

By this time, I had a clear understanding of the difference between learning as a personal quest and learning as an institutional process. It was acquired through realization that I had had to learn both *with the help of* and *despite of* the institutions of learning. In fact, my first published letter to the editor as a graduate student was titled "The Choice of Education or *Educación*: For Chicanos the Real Issue is Minority Rights" (*Los Angeles Times,* February 28, 1975), in which I refer to this difference from a Chicano perspective.

Once I received my doctorate and became Department Chair of Chicano Studies) at Loyola Marymount University, I struggled with the Jesuit administration to get graduation credit for Chicano Studies Courses. Four years later at World College West I enjoyed taking students to Mexico and creating my own curricula there, but back at the campus in Petaluma, California I spoke against the unconscious bias on the part of some of the administrators. In 1989 at the Mexican American Studies Department at Sonoma State I challenged the Department Chair's dictatorial management style risking (and losing) the opportunity to get a tenure-track position. But this opened the door for me to teach in the Hutchins School for which I am eternally grateful.

(I was born under the sign of Gemini so it is makes sense that my inner child seems to be a set of twins: Dionysius/Apollo and Quetzalcoatl/Tezcatlipoca.)

In retrospect my own shadow seems to be channeling Don Quixote. I became totally seduced by the childhood stories I was told and read about truth and justice and naively embarked in a lifelong battle against the windmills of contradiction I encountered. And blindly and impatiently ignored the fact that these contradictions and complexities along with contingency are the very fabric of existence, not something that can be overcome. I am just now barely coming to understand that this is probably what the Spanish philosopher Miguel de Unamuno means by "the tragic sense of life."

I Found a Home in the Hutchins School But Change is the Only Constant

It was a serendipitous path that led me to the Hutchins School. Although I would continue challenging the status quo, I knew I had finally found the intellectual home I had been looking for in a lifetime of being a nomad scholar and insisting on my identity as a citizen of the world. Being interdisciplinary and issue/problem oriented, I found the curriculum to be similar to those at World College West and the various Chicano Studies Departments where I taught before. There was the added benefit of the intellectual stimulation of the cadre discussions every week on the many texts from the collective syllabus we use in lower division courses. I learned so much that it was like getting another Ph.D. with fellow learners instead of professors. I'd say at that time we came close to fulfilling Dr. Hutchins' ideal of "The Intellectual Community."

I felt at home with the founding faculty with whom I shared the 1960's spirit of optimism about changing the world for the better. Some of them I only knew for a short while. I had the pleasure of meeting and having long conversations with the founder of the Hutchins School, the unforgettable Warren Olson. Roshni Rustomji retired early but she, like many others, remains a friend to this day. Jeannine Thompson, Lu Mattson, and Lou Miller unfortunately passed away at an early age. Too many to acknowledge here, they all were and their successors continue to be a vibrant, passionate, intellectual, and artistic group of individuals. Then as now we constantly motivated each other to do our best for the students, the campus and the community. The indefatigable Debora Hammond deserves special mention for her many contributions and especially for her efforts to preserve the Hutchins legacy via the publication of a book for 50th Anniversary among the myriad projects she takes on. And the same goes for the members of the committee planning the actual event, Margaret Anderson, Wendy Ostroff, and Ianthe Brautigan Swanson who invested much of their time and energy in the planning.

Looking back on my three decades in Hutchins I realize how fortunate I have been to work with all my colleagues throughout those years and am especially grateful for those that have become my role models. Dr. Anthony (Tony) Mountain who, to this day is known as "the soul of Hutchins," continues to be an inspiration to all of us who know him. Dr. Ardath Lee invited me to teach my first course in Hutchins, and years later to direct the Master's Program Action for a Viable Future that she created after she retired (as a follow up to her previous contribution: the Hutchins Degree Completion program). She mentored me first in Hutchins and, for the past 15 years, in the practice of Qigong. My *compañero de armas* Dr. Mutombo M'Panya whom I first met at World College West, a wise man and kindred soul has become the older brother I never had.

I was the first Latinx in the Hutchins faculty, but the cultural differences that arose seemed mostly due to my and Dr. Susan Gevirtz' (a simultaneous new hire) postmodernist views. Of course my colleagues had their cultural and racial blind spots, as we all do, and there were times during my career when I wondered if a colleague was being arrogant or prejudiced. As a community my Hutchins colleagues were conscious of their biases and would act to address them. Their intentions seemed sincere and for the most part they were very supportive of my proposals for new courses and my activities in the community, which took much of my time. The only time the faculty asked me to curtail my community organizing was when it was my turn to be the Provost (as the Hutchins chair used to be titled, until one SSU VP-Provost said there could only be one Sheriff in town).

During my one term as Provost I tried to address a contradiction between policies and their actual implementation. I emphasized continuity in the lower division and the upper division required courses, formalization of evaluation procedures and accountability in cadre participation. My Apollonian spirit, however, was kept in check by my Dionysian-oriented colleagues. Most likely a more accurate explanation is that I lacked the administrative skills to persuade them to implement the necessary policies. Of course this persistent contradiction shadows, to a more or less extent, any institutional policy ever made anywhere, so it is no surprise that the Hutchins faculty, like everyone else, continue to wrestle with this issue today as new challenges arise.

When I first joined Hutchins, the workload was heavy. We were teaching eighteen units per semester; six units above the units allowed in the union contract. While supportive of the union, the Hutchins faculty believed, above all, in the ideal undergraduate education championed by Dr. Hutchins. On some Saturdays, we even combined two or three courses to have joint activities like *Bafá Bafá* (an interactive exchange between two distinct cultures) and *Star Power* (a consciousness-raising game of subtle oppression and resistance). In retrospect, the new faculty members consider these Saturday activities sheer lunacy (but some of us remember them as being much fun!). As Dr. Hutchins notes about his own times, it seems that this situation is an example of history repeating itself (what strikes me as akin to a "historical fractal"):

> People who would have been regarded as good sixty years ago would now be regarded as merely dull, perhaps even stupid, because they did not understand that the virtues are outmoded. (Hutchins, 8)

Of course the conditions at SSU back then were supportive of a faculty that was deeply committed to teaching *above everything else*. After decades of decreased public and therefore State support, leading to increasing privatization of public education and the adoption of a corporate model to run the University, much has changed.

Under these different circumstances Universities and academic programs must justify their existence primarily in terms of the budget bottom line (especially in Liberal Studies as I discuss further below) and, consequently, the University's central goal becomes the achievement of prestige and the production of the kind of scholarship that brings funds to the University. For the faculty there is increasing pressure to publish, to apply for grants and to become known nationally and internationally. It almost seems that the ideal faculty member is the one who brings enough prestige and grants to offset her or his salary.

Another consequence of the changed situation is that today the faculty's main preoccupation is with workload. One must not only publish and keep up with changing and increasingly onerous administrative demands for data gathering on every component of teaching, but also changing instructional technology that one is expected to use. Oh, yes, and actually teaching undergraduates. Add to this the high cost of living in the SSU service area, and the line between commitment to a cause (facilitating knowledge for students) and exploitation of labor is becoming blurred. Understandably, some faculty increasingly feel that unless they get additional units or increased salary, they are not going to take on any additional projects no matter how lofty they may be. (Perhaps this illustrates how "virtues" disappear.)

We all feel super busy. We live under information overload and therefore we no longer have time to read an article one of us wants to

ail. Ironically, the old-fashioned way – to circulate a
n faculty member to faculty member via our mailboxes
_ ue more effective, but then again we "had more time."
faculty retreats every semester have disappeared or become
sporadic. We no longer have time for long, reflective discussions
during our faculty meetings. Our cadre meetings are increasingly
focused on administrative matters rather than on the text our
students are reading. The lower division 12-unit courses are now split
into Monday/Wednesday seminars with one professor and Friday
symposium with another professor. Some lower division courses
have a capacity of 200 students and they are open to all SSU
students.

One of the principles of the Hutchins pedagogy is that learning, like
many other human values is a *reflective* and dialogical process. This
is the *personal* dimension of learning and it is being lost in the
corporate model that emphasizes *institutional practices*. And this is
why it is nearly impossible to have a sense of the common good,
which according to Dr. Hutchins, is a prerequisite for an intellectual
community and for a democratic society as well. We are too busy
trying to meet all the increasingly untenable demands on our time
and attention. We simply don't have time for reflection. This is
definitely a different world than the one I knew back in 1990.

We used to take the value of Liberal Arts and of the Hutchins School
for granted. Now, the new faculty feels compelled to explain to the
University administration (as well as potential students and their
parents) *what* we do in Hutchins, *how* we do it, and *how* it brings
some kind of *material value*. And so we must take on the challenge
of justifying our existence: how do we define the dialogical process of
learning or what we call *seminaring*? And equally important we need
to define "value": is a Hutchins education practical in terms of
student demand, the kind of a job one can get, a career with a future?

Is it Socratic Seminar, Dialogical Process, or is it Really Magic?

"Only the invisible is real."

~ Anonymous

When he joined the Hutchins faculty, my colleague and dear friend Dr. M'Panya once deplored the fact that no one had ever written anything to explain the seminar process, which is touted as "the heart of our pedagogy." In my usual impulsive way I responded: "That's because it's magic." We have continued to entertain this notion in subsequent conversations for which I am grateful because they help to deepen my own understanding of what we do.

There seems to be an intangible process in Hutchins seminar that is as mysterious as the elementary particles in quantum physics: you know they are there but you can't determine exactly where they will be next. From another perspective, given what we know about our subjective perception of our world, about how our brain is complicit with our mind in the creation and maintenance of specific beliefs (sometimes in violation of all empirical evidence to the contrary), the magic and the miracle of the Universe is that we can communicate at all. This is evident at this time of political gridlock, fake news, and increased polarization across the globe. Today more than ever it does seem that *cada cabeza es un mundo* (each head does indeed seem a separate world).

Professor Mountain used to talk about the academic "game" some students play. It consists of figuring out ways to pass a course without seriously committing themselves to the dialogical process grounded on reading, reflection and written response. And eventually professors Eric McGuckin and Heidi LaMoreaux (now River) did write about our "seminaring," making reference to the messiness of the process. It is also my experience that sometimes seminars are academic, resembling a graduate level seminar with students surprising the professor with profound insights; other times seminars are conversations about everything except the assigned texts; and sometimes they feel more like group therapy or ranting sessions. This happens anytime you create a space where students (or anyone) can articulate and hopefully reflect on their own thoughts.

In a seminar one attempts to create the conditions where students can explore the deep Hutchins' questions such as: What should I do, what should we do, why should we do these things? What are the purposes of human life and of organized society? How does my specific career goal or orientation relate to the various disciplines? Do we have an idea of the common good of the community in which we are to function as college-educated students? Or are we just perfecting a particular trade?

Though professor Margaret Anderson can develop an entire curriculum through her Dialogue Center about how to conduct seminars; the paradox is that "seminaring" is an art, not a science. So instead of handing out a set of rules for new faculty to follow blindly, we tell new faculty something like: "Don't lecture to them. Let them flounder. Let them come up with illogical conclusions. Don't spoon-feed them 'the answer,' have them wrestle with the text for it." The crucial point here is that there is a difference between 1) memorizing a set of common fallacies and testing students to see how well they memorized them, and 2) having students learn to detect fallacies in their everyday life as well as in text and other media of communication. We strive to be more than just a *learning* community. We want to be an *intellectual* community. We require intellectual qualities other than memory.

Upon further reflection, the difficulty in pinning down a definition for intellectual production is perhaps because radical inquiry is not a conscious choice but a response to the exigency of life itself; because change occurs faster than we can contain it with words, concepts, theories, philosophies, and most definitely, academic disciplines. Add to this that deep learning and memory arise from emotion, not from reasoning alone. There must be some sort of catharsis, a transformation. Thus the constant need to search for the elusive Truth. And perhaps this is at the heart of a paradox; we must *truly* learn despite the learning institutions, as Dr. Hutchins himself points out (Hutchins, 4). And also why in Liberal Studies we try to develop what Dr. Adler cleverly calls "uncommon sense" or a "crap detector" when it comes to dealing with the experts at any level, including representatives of institutions (doctors, lawyers, mechanics, etc.). Truth lives in the intersection of the subjective and the objective, the paradigm and the exception to it. In the more concrete, mathematical terms of Gödel's Incompleteness Theorem, no formal system can apprehend the whole of reality. Imagination triumphs above any formal system; and when imagination rules the challenge becomes how to maintain a balance between fiction and reality.

At any rate, one key to human communication is simply to allow for the space and time to *converse* face-to-face. Despite the advances of our digital age communication, people from around the world–from government to business, to artists and philosophers–hold serious discussions by gathering around conference tables or sitting in circles. Just like humans have done throughout history. Perhaps the expectation is that these conversations increase the probabilities of coming across that one piece of the puzzle that has been missing in our own personal effort to piece together the meaning of life, of knowledge, of our existence or even in a mundane contract agreement. After these reflections Dr. M'Panya looks like he may be agreeing with me: It is magic. But our discussions continue.

Michel Foucault (1978, 1980) would add that these personal connections are necessary due to the nature of discourse and power relations; they are always in flux, never stable, never predictable. This is why seminaring is also a *dialectical* communion because it often leads to uncomfortable experiencing of the Other. It is also why the seminar is considered the soul of Hutchins. We know seminar conversations are not always pleasant. They can challenge our most cherished beliefs. As seminar members, we are sometimes startled when our like-minded friend in the group will sometimes say something totally unexpected: "You believe what????"

With similar incredulity, the University, parents and students may not be satisfied with the above explanation of what we do. They might look at me with eyes wide-open and say: "You mean you train students to be magicians?????"

At which point I would encourage them to notice the vast and essential difference between a seminar, a dialogical communication, and a lecture or workshop. In the latter information is predetermined, measured, timed, with specific goals, and flows in only one direction: from the authority in the field to the recipients of the information. Hutchins students in the Teaching Tracks II and III do engage in this kind of learning in some of their courses in order to meet the educational standards set by the State of California. Those in Track I may do this kind of learning depending on the major they have designed and what their goal is. The point is that if it has to be memorized, it is training for a trade, not an intellectual activity. This is calculative thinking as opposed meditative thinking. I will come back to this later.

The seminar or dialogical process is a reflective, meditative kind of thinking that helps students practice the skills of analyzing and assessing power relations, both as they occur in everyday life and also as they solidify in policies and institutions, with the resulting impact they have on human bodies and societies all over the world. This is a "holistic" skill that will serve students well into any future activity, career, or profession. In short, it will teach them how to maneuver in a changing world. More than just acquiring knowledge, it hopefully leads to wisdom. These are two very different types of education with two different purposes that require further elaboration.

What *is* the Purpose of Higher Education?

Dr. Hutchins believes that students who engage with the great ideas from the past, without authority figures to intervene, are more likely to become educated as global citizens and to provide the leadership their country and the world needs. In this regard he raises several key questions: Are we just a learning community or an intellectual community? Do we demand intellectual qualities other than memory? Do we have an idea of what the common good of the community in which we are to function as college-educated students? Or are we just perfecting a particular trade? How does my specific career goal or orientation relate to the various disciplines? Thus he circles back to the perennial question: What are we trying to do? (Hutchins, 4-5)

In a similar vein my Hutchins colleague Les K. Adler addresses the elusive question of the mission of the University in "Uncommon Sense: Liberal Education, Learning Communities and the Transformative Quest." He sees two roles for higher education. One is to establish a relationship with the current paradigm of knowledge as it is continually renewed, and to understand the "wide variety and elasticity of the human experience" in order to make reasonable judgments. This, along with critical thinking skills, serves as a "crap detector" to avoid falling for the "passions of the moment" The second role for higher education is to attain wisdom, defined as a high degree of self-knowledge and the ability to grasp complex issues and act judiciously in the application of the individual or group ideals.

Echoing Dr. Hutchins, Adler believes that the ultimate goal of the Hutchins School is not to train specialists or to train teachers but to educate students to become conscious of their important role as citizens of a democracy.

> Indeed, the entire premise of democratic government rests on the assumption that self-governing individuals can grasp the complex dimensions of the vital issues of their times in order to make essential judgments as citizens. (Adler, 1-2)

It was easy for me to relate to the Hutchins pedagogy through the lens of the critical pedagogy in Paulo Freire's *Pedagogy of the Oppressed*. And here too the dialectic between the Furies and Apollo makes its appearance. Freire's argument is also that education should be *dialogical*. It should be an equal exchange between the worldview of the teacher and the worldview of each of the students. The goal of this exchange is first for students to articulate and analyze the relations of power affecting their daily lives in terms of economic and health issues. And secondly to address any social injustices that might be inherent in these relations. This he terms *"conscientization"* which means knowledge as conscious awareness of our individual political economic reality leading to *praxis* or the effort to change that reality; in short, this is *education for liberation* with the intent to change the world.

The opposite of this is traditional education, which Freire calls "the banking-concept of education" and considers an *education for domination*. The metaphor refers to the student being considered an empty vessel in which teachers "deposit" their knowledge in the head of the student. And through this process the school system as a whole replicates an undemocratic, unjust, and unequal society.

In Adler's and Dr. Hutchins' writings one finds echoes of Freire's banking-concept of education (in reference to traditional education), and of the notion of *"conscientization"* (in reference to a liberation education). In our curricular (cadre) discussions, however, while the founding faculty members seemed to agree with my comparison, they were ambivalent about its ideological implications. And here we must take a reflective pause because we have come face to face with a challenging paradox at the heart of the question we are addressing regarding the purpose of higher education and along with it the purpose of learning and the purpose of knowledge. I will approach this paradox from the perspective of the Hutchins School and expand on it in the following section.

As an active citizen and community organizer I felt that Freire's pedagogy was much more incisive than the Hutchins pedagogy. And I imagined the potential of the Hutchins School becoming a school for activists that would go out there and change society and the world for the better. After all, I thought, are we professor not keepers of the flame of liberal studies and democracy? But then, my scholar self would confront the same paradox I confronted when teaching Chicano Studies: what then is the difference between a social movement and an academic discipline? In keeping with the academic quest for objectivity, I felt compelled to agree with my colleagues that as a Hutchins School we must commit to an interdisciplinary education for lifelong learning, not a specific ideology; otherwise our teaching ceases to be objective. After all, the idea of a *liberal* education is to be free from any imposed ideologies, allowing students to make their own choices. And even though Freire's critical pedagogy is not doctrinaire, it does call for learning to be based on the most immediate issues affecting the students' well being and the encouragement to address those issues through some kind of social action (praxis). Yet (and here the paradox shines): from an "objective" perspective, this pedagogy is open to charges of being too socialist at best, and rabble-rousing at worst.

Of course this raises another set of questions in terms of defining "objectivity" and why it is that having students analyze their political economic reality and then working toward changing it, is not "objective." Support Apollo's polis or let the Furies out? To be sure, I never felt censored by my colleagues when it came to my ideas or questions. There was and continues to be a tacit agreement that the essential point was to engage in these discussions and, as a Hutchins faculty, to support diverse views. Above all, we collectively value the students' right to make up their own minds.

Going back to the questions raised by Dr. Hutchins in the opening of this section, we can provide some answers. Hutchins is both, a learning community *and* an intellectual community. We demand intellectual qualities other than memory. No, we do not have a concrete idea of the common good of the community in which college-educated students are to function. We are not just perfecting a particular trade. We do explore how specific career goals relate to the various disciplines. As for the question "What are we trying to do?" We in Hutchins are indeed trying to educate global citizens that will provide the leadership their country and the world needs.

Neither the Hutchins School nor SSU exist in a vacuum so we also need to ask: "What is *society* trying to do?" or better yet, "*Who* decides what society is trying to do?" With each passing day, asking this question acquires a sense of urgency. Let us revisit the purpose of a higher education from a wider perspective.

Liberal Studies, Power, and the Political Economy of Knowledge

and i know
that you shall ever
fear
to extend the knowledge
that shall free us...

~ *World,* by Ricardo Sánchez

It is common to hear that "knowledge is power." And thus the answer to the question "What is society trying to do?" usually is "education." And yet, it seems that the inverse is just as valid or at least more prevalent: power is knowledge. Knowledge in the form of free thought has a long and torturous history because it has been considered a threat to the existing power structures (Bury, 2010). Journalists are presently being threatened (even in the United States) and increasing numbers are killed in many countries. Socrates himself was condemned to death for his subversive teachings. In other words, there has always been an unwritten Political Economy of Knowledge that governs what can and cannot be said. No conspiracy theory here; it is simply a corresponding dimension to the dynamic of power relations.

Liberalism itself was once also considered a marginal, radical form of knowledge and a threat to the Church and the Monarchy. Yet, for several centuries the Humanities/Liberal Studies have maintained a respectable place in the University. In part this is because they can be traced to the birth of the University and also because they have served as custodians of humanistic values that are erroneously considered to come only from Western civilization. Most importantly perhaps, humanistic philosophy has served the rise of capitalism (Harari, *Homo Deus*).

Despite the attempts to control knowledge that threatens the status quo, there are many examples of bodies of knowledge, fields of study, that are born out of the imperative for social change due to human suffering (The Furies). Of course, these are marginalized because

98

they do not conform to the established socially accepted knowledge, or to the University curricula and/or to claims of objectivity, universalism, or scientific, analysis (Apollo). Examples from my own research would include the *nationalization of knowledge* as *filosofía de lo mexicano* (Philosophy of Mexicanness), which emerged in non-Western countries in the first half of the twentieth century as a discourse of liberation from the universal claims of European philosophy. Historically this is followed in the United States by the *ethnicization of knowledge* during the late 1960's and 70's with the rise of Chicano, Black, and Native American Studies as discourses of liberation from the Eurocentric academic disciplines. These were accompanied by a *genderization of knowledge* with the rise of Women and Gender Studies. All of these academic disciplines that promote social change and the dignity of human to this day experience complicated relationships with the established disciplines and the University itself regarding the question of "objectivity."

From this perspective of a political economy of knowledge and the struggle for human dignity, it is pertinent to ask: what is the standing of Liberal Studies today?

With its *interdisciplinary* pedagogy, the Hutchins School is the subject of criticism by the established disciplines, which focus on the transmission of content that can be measured and tested. The criticism is that students are not learning anything in-depth and that we have no way of knowing what exactly have they learned because we don't test our students (we do give written evaluations in the lower division and students have a choice of taking a class for a grade or credit/no credit). And not surprising (given the power of objectivism) some of this criticism is even voiced by some Hutchins faculty members themselves; a recent proposal to change the curriculum suggests that, "for the benefit of our students," we limit our teaching to our area of expertise and rotate Hutchins faculty among the various seminars. As noted before, there is an ongoing debate between the "effectiveness" of the disciplines and the "holistic search for meaning" of interdisciplinary studies. And at the heart of this debate is the crucial and serious misunderstanding of the opposition between calculative and meditative thinking, information and knowledge, measurement and meaning, or content and process. Soft and hard sciences emphasize the first item of in these pairs while Humanities/Liberal Studies emphasize the second one.

Perhaps the problem is that Liberal Studies is rooted in students' gaining an intellectual holistic *understanding* of society, while today's society increasingly demands that students prepare for a specific job or career. Dr. Hutchins maintains that training is good for a job but it does not require students to *understand* anything. And consequently we need to teach what lasts a lifetime, not lifelong learning but learning for lifelong reflection. Mr. Clifton Fadiman's sharp response echoes *Brave New World* by Aldous Huxley, and the more recent film *The Matrix*. Fadiman argues that schools and colleges cannot support an intellectual community, because their primary role is to serve as "detention centers" for young people, so as not to impede the "functioning of the social machine" (Hutchins, 7-11). And that's why, he adds, training for jobs that may not exist in the future makes sense: because in the "techno state" it is it not necessary to *understand* anything (in the intellectual sense).

To clarify the increasing emphasis on disciplines, it helps to remember Michel Foucault's (1980) studies of the relationship between power and knowledge, and their effect on the rise and fall of academic disciplines. According to his analysis, knowledge deploys increasing levels of power to the same extent that it validates its claims to be "scientific" and "objective." From this line of thought it follows that science brings analysis, rigorous measurement and accuracy to any academic discipline. From here it is a short distance towards the only kind of value supported by power today: efficiency in terms of the production of economic value and the market.

The perennial debate between inter-disciplinary and discipline-based knowledge has taken a new turn now that the production of knowledge is specifically tied to market forces. This complicates matters even more because now science itself is being devalued and contradicted when it interferes with the market or private or political interests. *Here is another instance where power produces its own kind of knowledge.* And this question acquires a vital urgency when it comes to the question of what society wants. For example, in 2015

Wisconsin's governor Scott Walker secretly tried to change the mission of the university system which is embedded in the state code by removing phrases such as "search for truth" and "improve the human condition" and replacing them with "meets the state's workforce needs." His efforts to do that failed; nevertheless, last year the University of Wisconsin-Stevens Point proposed to eliminate 13 Liberal Studies majors, expand 8 career majors and add 8 additional career majors. Administrators point out that in Wisconsin, as in the rest of the United States, Liberal Studies Programs have declining enrollment. They note that, though the majors are eliminated, upper division courses will offer the opportunity for deep engagement in the liberal arts (Bach, Strauss, and Summers).

Obviously, in the emerging biological and digital technological society, the production of knowledge (the learning process) is increasingly being tied directly to market forces. *It is as if Liberal Studies is again becoming a threat to some kind of status quo, not the religious or political establishment but apparently the digital-driven economic establishment.* Or perhaps it is becoming a relic from the past with no place in the 21st century. One is compelled to ask if the act of reflection itself has become a threat to the techno-state? At any rate, one of the consequences is that, by eliminating Liberal Studies we are depriving students from the space, time and means to ask the kind of "deep" questions which historically have served as a foundation and preservation of a liberal democratic society. But what else can the University do if students (and society) don't value these courses? Who is going to pay for them?

This predicament has hit close to home. At the January 18, 2019 meeting of the School of Arts and Humanities, Dean Hollis Robbins and SSU Provost Lisa Vollendorf shared with the faculty their concerns with declining enrollment in Liberal Studies at SSU and throughout the country, and the need to cut some classes. They both presented a positive outlook and described the measures that are being taken to address the problem by increasing resources and strategies for recruitment. One of the proposed creative measures to counter the under enrollment in the Humanities is a new partnership between the Wine Business Department and Arts and Humanities in which business students would work with students of poetry and dance to design commercials to sell wine. While this fits the logic of the new status quo I was stunned to hear it and I was even more surprised by the lack of reaction from my colleagues in A&H. There seemed to be an air of resignation; faculty members seemed fearful to ask questions directly to the Provost so they asked the Dean. In retrospect, I appreciate the administrators' compassion and their sympathetic efforts to finesse a difficult situation. They reminded me, however, of doctors who reluctantly tell the terminal patient that there are treatments that might possibly help.

The Hutchins School used to be referred to as "a feather in the cap of the CSU system," because this alternative curriculum, with its dialogical if not Socratic small seminars, upholds the ideal of a Liberal Studies education. Given the current situation, there is clearly no room to appeal to the Administration to honor the agreements made in the past between the Hutchins School and the SSU administration regarding our unique status as an alternative curricular program. Honor is a virtue and virtue has no line item in the budget; it is not affordable.

From a historical perspective, however, this is not a new development. One could argue that the arts have always been at the service of the powerful. More to the point, the role of the University has changed over the last millennia and we don't know what is going to happen next.

What are the alternatives? Perhaps we can do both (offer Liberal Studies courses for students who want them, but have no majors) as they claim to be doing in Wisconsin. Or perhaps we are moving back to a time when only small minorities of people in the world were truly educated and everyone else was "trained" as an apprentice in a trade.

Tracing the root of the problem, however, would lead to some of the driving factors behind the financial lack of support for public education and its increased privatization. At SSU one of these factors is the cost of servicing SSU's debt for the Green Music Center. SSU administrators are saddled with decisions made by the previous SSU administration or simply following orders that come down the ladder of power from the Chancellor's Office, the CSU Board of Trustees, and the State of California. Nationally and worldwide another factor is the increasing income and wealth inequality, which in turn fuels political polarization among social classes, racism, nationalism, and fascism. And to some extent this factor points to the ruling class that historically has the most power to decide "what society wants." From this perspective, the question should not be, "What does society want" but "What does society need?" And we certainly do not need more of the kind of polarization that rampant capitalism has unleashed on our species. These events, however, seem to confirm Harari's intimations in *Homo Deus* and *Twenty-One Lessons for the 21st Century* of a decline in Humanism and a consequent waning of Liberal Democracy. The future has arrived. The concept of "We the people" is in danger of disintegrating and being replaced by Artificial Intelligence and Dataism. In the new world paradigm governed by biological and digital technology, no consciousness is required for efficiency.

Upon further reflection, it occurs to me that perhaps this dark view is just a reflection of my own state of mind as I reach retirement and the plain fact that I am old (or in my "third age" as we say in Mexico). I am projecting my short future onto the new generations. Young people are full of dreams and plans for the future. *La lucha continúa,* the struggle continues, as it has for eons of time as reflected in all the mythologies of the world. Like Sisyphus, we roll the rock up the mountain just watch it roll down again. This time, however, the stakes are raised, fasten your seatbelts.

The Wrestling Match of the Century

> *"What we've got here is a failure to communicate."*
>
> ~ Paul Newman in *Cool Hand Luke*

In his 1977 prescient essay "The Intellectual Community," Dr. Robert Maynard Hutchins argues that a University community must be open to dialogue and discussion of diverse, contradictory, critical issues and that such an intellectual community is essential for the role of at the University. His friend and colleague Fadiman responds that, on the contrary, these values no longer matter in an increasingly technological society because they simply do not add to the goal of *efficiency*, which is the goal of the "techno-state." Dr. Hutchins counters: "Perhaps I overrate the power of reason, the resilience of the spirit, and ... the fact that all men by nature desire to know...and it is not clear to me... that the techno-state... is indomitable." On the contrary, Dr. Hutchins believes that it can be tamed in the service of humanity (Hutchins, 11). Who will win this match is one of the most vital existential questions facing our species thus far in this century.

Reading, writing and thinking about this question and listening to the students' seminar discussions during my last year of teaching in the Hutchins School, I woke up with these words in my head:

Twilight Thoughts
(morning of January 25, 2019)

Ought, Virtue
Higher power
God, Law

God is Dead
Law is Dead
Algorithms rule

No consciousness required for efficiency

Efficient production
Capital
Ego
Win at all costs
Me, me, me
Selfie, selfie, selfie

Just tell me what to do
Teach me how to do my teaching job

Don't ask me to ask "Why?"

I hate history, politics and economics
I don't understand philosophy

Why do I have to Search for Self?
I already know who I am
I have no shadow

I already know the truth
It's in the Bible
Or in Wikipedia

I don't need to reflect
Or meditate
Or pay attention
if I can't relate to it

Logic and reason?
That's your opinion
I have my own opinion

What you call critical thinking
I call politics in the classroom

Just tell me what I need to do so I can get a job
Let's stop asking "Why?"
Just Google it...Or better yet, ask Siri or Alexa

I hasten to clarify that this is not necessarily a reflection on all my students. Nevertheless, I can't help but wonder, as Dr. Hutchins continuously does throughout his essay: What happened to the virtues? This question sounds quaint in today's world, yet it is still relevant. For example, Dr. Hutchins states,

> Watergate shows that politics has become the pursuit of power.
> The whole operation of society shows that we expect to get
> along without good people. (Hutchins 8)

Indeed, by this early spring 2019 the pursuit of power has now gone
beyond Watergate with the current politics of winning "at all costs."
This is evident with the election of Donald Trump as President of the
United States; the subsequent investigation of his possible collusion
with Russia to win the election and obstruction of justice, the
building of a wall to keep Mexicans out of the United States contrary
to Congressional wishes. And this is part of a worldwide increase in
xenophobic nationalism, racism, and the consequent rise in hate
crimes. "Friendly" fascism has become the norm while global
problems like climate change and social and ethical issues raised by
biological and digital technology are not fully addressed.

It is no wonder the *Twilight Zone* TV program has remained a
popular program and has proved to be a hit with my students –and
now a brand-new series has opened with comedian Jordan Peel as
the new Rod Serling. I also find it symbolic that Peel is also creating a
new genre of horror films that include a social content.

Fadiman's explanation of what happened to the virtues is that Dr.
Hutchins' world, governed by the concept of "What Ought to Be
Done," no longer exists. It was eroded along with the notion of a
higher authority or force (God, conscience, Natural Law, the inner
light) and that one needed to obey in order to be "...'better' more
'human'..." (Hutchins, 9) Just as it is no longer necessary to
understand anything, Fadiman goes on to say that we no longer need
to make such distinctions between good and bad. We no longer
punish war criminals, or corporations – or politicians one might add
(Hutchins, 11). As opposed to the common stock of ideas based on
human virtues in Dr. Hutchins' world, Fadiman sees a technological
world that "... assimilates war (and crime) to show business, and so
gives it a positive value. Custom... habituates us to death" (Hutchins,
10). Fadiman's examples of "custom" are plane disasters and
hijackings, which had become so common in the 1970's as to no
longer be "shocking." Today one can easily replace those "customs"
with the normalization of mass shootings, the denial of health care to

the poor, the sadistic insistence on the separation of children from refugee and immigrant parents, a war that never ends, and the casual threats of nuclear attack. Everyday life is now framed within a reality show.

We have come/regressed a long way, Dr. Hutchins. Feel free to turn over in your grave.

These transmutations of value do not come as a big surprise. A post-moral world based on a calculus of power has been reflected in literature from all over the world. In Western literature, for example, Nicolo Machiavelli writes in *The Prince* (1532) that virtue applies to the people but not the rulers. Similarly, Friedrich Nietzsche in *Genealogy of Morality* (1887) perceives that the "master mentality" rules over the "slave mentality" on the basis of a "natural rights." And Ayn Rand's *Atlas Shrugged* (1957) – a big hit in Silicon Valley and Wall Street – longs for a world where compassion is a weakness and greed is a virtue. Nevertheless, reading Dr. Hutchins' essay, it is eerie to think that so much of what is going on in the first decades of the twentieth-first century has been anticipated for so long and so recent at the same time, and we appear impotent to do anything about it. It brings to my mind Gabriel Garcia Marquez' short story, *Chronicle of a Death Foretold,* in which a people in a small town know a murder is going to occur but no one, including the protagonists, wants it to happen. And yet it does.

Reflection on the contours of the challenges ahead for the Hutchins Community and the world, should not lead us into negativity or a panic mode, however. There is much we all *can* do and *should* do. And the brightest hope of all is that young people are already actively addressing the issues they have inherited from previous generations by challenging the old concepts of what and how things ought to be based on their experience in this new world.

Dr. Hutchins notes that he was able to create an intellectual community at the University of Chicago in part due to the dire economic circumstances during the Depression, prewar, WWII and postwar periods. In that sense, we in Hutchins may be in a similar situation when it comes to the financial constraints at SSU and higher education in general, and that provides some hope for survival.

Will the Hutchins School survive for another fifty years? Mr. Fadiman provides a silver lining, suggesting that under a techno-state an intellectual community can exist as a "small disorganized, would-be intellectual community" (10). And to some extent, that describes the Hutchins School today. To be sure, the "disorganized" part is due to a long list of internal but mostly external factors that arise from the shifting nature society: the changing requirements for publication, increasing class size, adherence to the changing State education standards for teachers, changes to the lower-division seminar structure, students' apparent resistance to reading and learning for learning's sake, declining attention span due to social media, students working too many hours to meet their financial or family needs, increasing number of students suffering from anxiety, political-religious polarization in the classroom (e.g. regarding science and the differences among fact, opinion, belief, and truth).

And while the CSU institutional fabric is strengthened through the uniformed collection of data and the hierarchical centralization of decision-making, the human fabric is fraying at various levels. There is less shared decision-making, and personal communication is constrained by our assigned roles as students, faculty, staff and administrators. Data-driven administrative logic and the limitations on face-to-face interactions, lead to the feeling that human sentiments are not valued. And this in turn leads to demoralization among faculty and staff and administrators. Within the Hutchins School itself, the Director is no longer compensated year-round; there are threats to cut the academic advisor at the same time that rules and regulations become increasingly complex. Serious discussions to address these issues take time, and in this environment there is little time for careful reflection. Faculty retreats are sporadic rather than every semester. Faculty meetings are conducted during the one-hour lunchtime. Everyone in Hutchins does the best they can, but under these circumstances accountability and coordination become luxuries and this adds to the feeling of disorganization. The common denominator seems to be that change is happening at such dizzily pace that it overwhelms human capabilities. There is simply no time for reflection in order to separate the important from the unimportant.

Yet, despite all these difficulties (and what family does not have disagreements?) the Hutchins faculty maintains a strong sense of camaraderie. To some extent this is because the basic foundation and structure of the Hutchins School as an intellectual community remains very strong. And this is reflected in its many successes. The School proudly holds the top record for student retention in the entire California State University System; its graduates who go into teaching are coveted by school districts. In effect, Hutchins alumni from the teaching or non-teaching tracks, report a high level of satisfaction with their education. This is evident in a survey conducted by the School of Arts and Humanities during Dean William Babula's tenure at SSU and also in every LIBS 402 Senior Synthesis, a capstone course where students evaluate the Hutchins program as part of their Portfolio. Students who go on to law school particularly provide unsolicited praise for our teaching of critical thinking.

This suggests that the Hutchins School is poised to confront the new challenges. In the near and far future, with the specific pressures to address the faculty-student ratio, there may be more onerous workload requirements of the faculty. Yet focusing on the value of the seminar dialogical discussions, it may be possible to preserve "the soul" of the Hutchins School. At the faculty level this includes the lower-division cadre curriculum planning "seminars": clear policies for their functioning as a cohesive four-semester series need to be specified and enforced; consistent retreats each of which consciously addresses a long-term master plan; and faculty meetings long enough to address the agenda (to keep these meetings brief, some preliminary work could be done via email). Though it does require initial time investment, a handbook of policies covering the basic functions of the Hutchins School (like formats for student evaluations) should be assembled for the new and existing faculty; to make it a helpful instrument, however, it needs to be seriously embraced and upheld by the Director and the faculty. The Catch-22 here is that these recommendations increase the workload. As Dr. Hutchins insists, however, *reflection* is one of the key ingredients for intellectual thinking and we need to make time for it.

At the curricular level, this practice of *reflection* can be affirmed via the Portfolio in both the lower and upper division. The Portfolio needs to be preserved and soon turned into an electronic portfolio. Some students and some faculty may not like it, but *reflecting* on previous work in order to get a sense of those areas that show growth and those areas that need attention, is an invaluable exercise. The Portfolio can actually serve as the spine that supports the curriculum for the entire four years. It needs to be thoroughly introduced in the first semester along with a clear explanation of the rationale for the Hutchins pedagogy as a program that first and foremost prepares students to be global citizens and only secondly for a particular career. In a similar vein, the faculty needs to address the difference between being overly directive by providing a format for student responses that consists of specific questions and a format that serves as a scaffold for critical thinking. Another delicate balance that needs to be addressed is that between homogeneity and consistency when it comes to evaluation forms in lower division, workload, etc.

Given the writing on the wall regarding decreasing enrollment, the Hutchins faculty may want to brainstorm what possible (even if draconian and/or unthinkable) scenarios might address future budget cuts and still preserve the seminar. And to begin to address these scenarios before they occur to administrators. For example: Hutchins lower division courses have a 14/15 to 1 student faculty ratio and unique critical inquiry preparation. What other University does that? Does this mean that Hutchins should be an honors program? The elite are apparently sending their children to Waldorf Schools because they understand the value of alternative education. Should we recruit from this elite group of potential students and expand our non-teaching Track I? What would be the implications of such policy for current efforts to increase the diversity of the student body?

In terms of increasing class size, some faculty members, myself included, who have large upper division classes are adept at having several breakout sessions where students seminar on their own for part of the time. This process works for some faculty but not for others, and admittedly, the quality of each seminar discussion in the breakout groups varies. In past years a handful of us, due to a sudden absence of a faculty member, have taught two 12-unit lower division seminars back to back. It is a matter of time before the SSU administration proposes that faculty teach two lower division seminars using this back-to-back format for the same amount of assigned units. Or the faculty may decide to teach the two seminars at the same time using the lecture/break-out group format. Whether the breakout groups are in a large room or in different rooms, *the key to the success of this format is to create a culture where students and faculty feel comfortable with "autonomous" seminars* (where the students indeed assume responsibility for the seminar discussion without depending on the authority of the professor). It would also require the cultivation of administrative skills to keep track of the logistics that include the selection and training of students from the same class who could serve as facilitators for each seminar. (Ironically, this would *fully* realize the ideal of the professor as the guide on the side, not the sage on the stage.)

Epilogue: The Will to Consciousness

We seem to be living through a paradigm shift and a formidable struggle between humanity and an antagonist that is perhaps even more challenging than the "techno-state" described by Fadiman. This century will test Dr. Hutchins' premise that "...the power of reason, the resilience of the spirit, and ... the fact that all men by nature desire to know," can tame the techno-state to serve humanity.

At the end of his book *Homo Deus*, Harari describes the key elements in this spectacular match.

> Yet if we take the really grand view of life, all other problems and developments are overshadowed by three interlinked processes:

1. Science is converging on an all-encompassing dogma, which says that organisms are algorithms, and life is data processing.

2. Intelligence is decoupling from consciousness.

3. Non-conscious but highly intelligent algorithms may soon know us better than we know ourselves.

These three processes raise three key questions, which I hope will stick in your mind long after you have finished this book:

1. Are organisms really just algorithms, and is life really just data processing?

2. What more valuable—intelligence or consciousness?

3. What will happen to society, politics and daily life when non-conscious but highly intelligent algorithms know us better than we know ourselves? (402)

It is significant that even Harari who presents us with distressing future possibilities finds, if not salvation, at least consolation in reflection. "Meditation," the last chapter in his book *21 Lessons for the 21st Century,* ends with a recommendation to practice self-observation as a means of focusing on who we really are. This means that ultimately, it does not matter which mythological lens appears in our Hutchins kaleidoscope. Whatever the archetype or the cultural metaphor, as members of the *Homo sapiens* species we confront the same set of questions we've always had: What should *I* do, what should *we* do, why should *we* do these things? What are the purposes of human life and of organized society? The Hutchins School has invited students to wrestle with these questions during the last fifty years. And this is a proud legacy. I am grateful and feel blessed to have been a part of this legacy. We celebrate today and we look forward to continue to encourage reflection on this struggle for meaning in this new century. And echoing Nietzsche (1974) we wonder, "What ... games shall we have to invent?"

References

Adler, Les. 2001. "Uncommon Sense: Liberal Education, Learning Communities, and the Transformative Quest." In Barbara Leigh, Smith and J. McCann (eds.). *Reinventing Ourselves: Interdisciplinary Education, Collaborative Learning and Experimentation in Higher Education.* Jossey-Bass.

Bach, Natasha. 2018. "Why One University Wants to Drop its English, Philosophy and History Majors." Fortune.com. March 12.

Bury, John Bagnell. 2010 [1913]. *A History of Freedom of Thought.* HardPress Publishing.

Coates, Ta-Nehisi. 2015. *Between The World and Me.* Spiegel and Grau.

Foucault, Michel. 1978. *The History of Sexuality, Volume I.* Pantheon. 1980. *Power/Knowledge: Selected Interviews and Other Writings, 1972-1977.* Pantheon.

Harari, Yuval Noah. 2017. *Homo Deus: A Brief History of Tomorrow.* Harper. 2018. *21 Lessons for the 21st Century.* Spiegel and Grau.

Hutchins, Robert M. 1977. "The Intellectual Community." *The Center Magazine.* Jan/Feb.

King, Martin Luther. 1963. "Letter from a Birmingham Jail."

Márquez, Gabriel Garcia. *Chronicle of a Death Foretold.* Reprint edition. New York: Vintage, 2003.

Nietzsche, Frederick. 1974. *The Gay Science: With a Prelude in Rhymes and an Appendix of Songs.* Vintage.

Strauss, Valerie. 2018. "A University of Wisconsin Campus pushes plan to drop 13 majors — including English, history and philosophy." *Washington Post.* March 21.

Summers, Greg. 2018. "The Liberal Arts and the Meaning of a University." *Inside Higher Ed.* April 2.

Unamuno, Miguel de. 2014 [1912]. *The Tragic Sense of Life.* CreateSpace Independent Publishing Platform.

A Reminiscence

Nelson R. Kellogg

Nelson R. "Buzz" Kellogg taught in the Hutchins School from 1991 through 2014, where he developed and taught a dozen novel upper division seminars, including "Machine as Metaphor," "Space, Time and Culture," "Anatomy of a Virtual Community," "The Roots of Empathy," and "Storytelling and the Search for Meaning," among others. His Bachelor's degree is in physics; he has taught math and physics at various levels, and worked as a researcher in electro-optics.

He attended both Princeton and Johns Hopkins universities, receiving his Ph.D. in the history of science and technology from the latter. He was a pre-doctoral fellow with the Institute of Electrical and Electronics Engineers and a resident fellow at the Smithsonian Institution. He has published in the history of science and technology, as well as in educational philosophy. His primary passion, however, is teaching, and the Hutchins School turned out to be the perfect fit for many years.

When I moved to Northern California in the summer of 1991, it was for the sole purpose of taking a position on the faculty of the Hutchins School at Sonoma State University. Coming from several attachments on the East Coast, including graduate school and several teaching positions, I had no family, friends of family, or other acquaintances in this region, and, being financially zeroed-out, this new step in my life just had to work out. It did, and beautifully.

The opportunities were as inviting and stimulating as the geography of this frontier. Within a generous framework of curricular requirements, I was invited to invent novel configurations and contents for courses that excited my curiosities with the eager anticipation that my students would relish these adventures with me.

I was not disappointed. The evidence of new insights being embraced came directly, right from the start. I sat down at a seminar table, along with 12 to 15 students instead of pontificating from a distant lectern and telling myself that I had just delivered an immortal address to several hundred young people. The Hutchins seminar is a rare and, in these times of pecuniary profit-motives, endangered species. In the best of these seminars, the intellectual interactions and inspirations among the student participants are vibrant, vital, and vivid.

Working with other faculty of widely varied academic histories and different life-experience lines of sight was also critical. Even casual conversations among colleagues could begin and lead anywhere, often catalyzed by something that had just occurred in a seminar. I have, for most of my adult life, identified as a teacher at my core. After teaching at Hutchins for twenty-three years and looking back, I find it quite plausible that I wouldn't have thrived in any of the more traditionally defined educational settings.

Of course, some events or situations left me disappointed. One of the more painful kinds happened when a student shone brightly, with insistent curiosity, analytic skill, and beauty of presentation, but who did not know it and could not be persuaded to believe it. I recall a few such students whom I felt impelled to take aside and try to impress upon them a recognition of their rare, recondite intellect, and to let them know I would be willing, as their teacher, to vouch for them whenever they pursued opportunities in the future. Sadly, a few who seemed not to fully believe this about themselves, for whatever personal or historical reason. Perhaps a positive reading of this is a reinforcement of the idea that, however humble the life-path, brilliant and gifted individuals are marbled throughout society. In itself, this knowledge is reason enough to find joy in all types of associations we chance upon in life. My teaching life has been generously blessed with many associations with remarkable people.

A few occurrences in my first several years register as important for my Hutchins sojourn. These were times where I was ambivalent about remaining in this position, not because of a paucity of strong feelings of attraction, but because there were many pulls, but in different directions. I felt deep yearnings to return to the East Coast. The sources of this dynamic included the death of my father, the fact that most of my family (siblings and their families) lived in northern Virginia, my long academic involvement in the Washington, D.C. area, and the presence of strong friendships cultivated over many years and, frankly, the absence of those factors in my new environment.

What held sway in keeping me at Hutchins and in the North Bay region were the connections and attachments offered to me in abundance by both students and faculty. Among the faculty were a half dozen colleagues who extended their friendship and support beyond the ordinary. Les Adler was the Hutchins Provost (as the chair was then designated) when I was hired. My individual interview with him, as part of the hiring process, immediately impressed me that here was a possible colleague to whom I could relate, not just academically but personally. This intuition proved itself again and again during those early years. We shared interests, novel ideas, and a slant toward the comedic, at once rare and treasured. As a result of many late afternoon conversations, Les and I also composed and delivered for state and regional educational groups many outreach programs inspired by the Hutchins pedagogy. I have told Les many times that he was the primary reason for my taking my position at the Hutchins School of Liberal Studies. Les and I remain close friends to this day.

Others who made conscious efforts to create a home for me at Hutchins included Ardath Lee, Tony Mountain, Lou Miller, Lu Mattson, and Roshni Rushtomji-Kerns. These individuals engaged me in deep and supportive conversations, and they always fully supported each new course I devised and taught. They invited me into their homes as both colleague and friend, often at the very juncture when I most needed these heart-felt associations.

Then there were the students from my introductory years. I had come prepared to teach courses within my areas of expertise, especially in the histories of science and technology with an emphasis on the episodes when trends in these arenas both reflected and propelled shifts in cultures and society. I was also eager (but unprepared) to contribute in the evolving design and teaching of the four-semester sequence that comprised the Hutchins lower division curriculum. In fact, it was largely through my initiation into the vast subject material of the lower division that I soon began imagining course designs utterly new to me. These included two courses that were heavily dependent upon students actively and willingly creating and completing their own projects.

The first of these was "Biography of a Community." For this class, students had to choose a community – most often an established town – and immerse themselves in it. However, those projects could transcend the traditional definition of a town on a map. One student chose a Native American tribe of this region. Another chose the homeless community of Santa Rosa. Regardless of the choice, the theme of this class was to expose and describe the many ways in which a community affects those who belong to it. One's community is, in many ways, like an alternate family of origin, with complex and emerging personalities, truth stories, and environmental cues that subtly but powerfully engage in producing who we become. During the semester, along with our assigned reading discussions, each student offered updates on their experiences and discoveries about their community of choice, so the seminar provided each member with comparisons and commentary. The students might be looking at historical records of their subjects, and doing interviews within the community, as well as doing even deeper dives by spending some days and nights in location. The final presentations, which included every variety of exposition, including theatrically composed impressions and enactments, went beyond my (or the class members') expectations. Indeed, these creative pieces were revelatory.

A follow-on to "Biography of a Community" was the course titled "Anatomy of a Virtual Community." This came about in the very early stages of the publicly available internet and the World-Wide Web (the "www" that is the prefix for nearly all of our online communications today). Personally, I wished to know more about how this modality, completely new to society at large, would reconstruct what we had come to know as community and redefine interpersonal relations, for better or worse. My incipient feeling was that this technology could actually rejuvenate very powerfully the best of traditional neighborhoods and neighborliness given certain preconditions. One was that the primary function would be to make it possible for people to become conversational (face-to-face) friends if only they could emerge from the modern work-a-day demands of career-only acquaintances, commuting and only returning home after hours, within a toxic mixture of frightening newscasts and "fear of the other." The other precondition was to allow oneself to be known in this new cyberspace. In other words, no anonymity.

Within our exploration of the new virtual community, we modeled different takes on discussion space architectures using our own seminar group as the test subject. Toward this end, one of the students and I developed a virtual physical space called Morphburg. As this was very early in the technology, and the campus server was an ancient one, everything we did needed to be text-based. In our investigations, we held regular in-person weekly seminars on background readings, as well as seminars (both synchronously and asynchronously) in the Morphburg meeting room. We tried having these seminar discussions using a virtual "talking stick" (where you could contribute to the discussion after a previous speaker had handed you the "stick"), and using an "annonymizing" function, whereby we would know that the speaker was from our in-person seminar, but not who that individual was. We were all struck by the nature of different conversational spaces, and the ways they affected what was said and how.

Out of this background, the first cohort of this class formed an "activist group," which we called "Project Group One," or Project GO. There were only a small handful of towns in the whole country at that juncture experimenting with primitive versions of a town or community bulletin board system (BBS). Our class decided we might actually help towns develop their own website, with different alcoves for different uses (local events, interest clubs, discussion spaces for ideas, whether philosophical, practical or simply entertaining). Still, we wanted to encourage the idea that any uses could be a catalyst for locals to actually meet face-to-face, as we felt that encouraging in-person connections was the ultimate community virtue. And we discouraged anonymity. Believe it or not, we had not even considered a community website might evolve into a long-distance commercial exchange, this being years before Amazon and its clones. If we had imagined that possibility, we would have considered it a poor utilization of the technology, since it would only exacerbate the tendency in contemporary culture to isolate oneself behind closed doors.

Within short order, our group initiative (Group One) received a California State Grant, and we went on to help two local towns, Petaluma and Sebastopol, to configure and set up their own community websites. We did trainings and tutorials for community groups and received public recognition through newspaper coverage. This was a memorable time for me, and especially for the student members of Group One, but in hindsight it seems that our work is "locked in amber." And yet, as with the efforts of any group of students and educators, it is unreasonable to "require" the work to become something permanent. The work is the work, and any inspirations or imaginings that arise in the process need not be anything of any tenure that continues after the learning experiments conclude. As educators in good faith, blessings do come our way if we let them, but the primary objective is to realize them when they occur, not bemoan their passage.

During one of my "Biography of a Community" classes, I was worried that if each student failed to realize that their own chosen project was an indispensable part of the experience of the entire class, the class would not work. Every week I began our seminar by trying to impress them with the need to work on their projects every week or the whole course would run off the tracks in disarray. Finally, about a month in, one of the students looked across the seminar table at me and stated, simply, "Yeah, don't worry, okay, we GET it." Looking back, I can happily say that, yes, they certainly did get it. That was their gift to me.

Apollo and Dionysius in the Era of Standards and Risk Management

Eric McGuckin

Before coming to Hutchins in 1998, Eric McGuckin conducted two years of ethnographic research in India with Tibetan refugees. He earned his PhD in Anthropology in 1997 from the City University of New York (Graduate Center). At first a skeptic of seminar process, he became an adherent of student-centered, dialogic pedagogy witnessing its power to transform and empower. He particularly enjoys teaching LIBS 201 Exploring the Unknown in the Lower Division, and among other courses, Death and Dying, and the Anthropology of Humor in the Upper Division. McGuckin served as Director of the Hutchins School for two terms, 2005-2011.

Despite external and internal challenges to its unique pedagogy, the Hutchins School of Liberal Studies at Sonoma State University has maintained a commitment to interdisciplinary inquiry and the seminar format since its inception in 1969. It has been shaped by a continuous dialectic between what the School's founder, Warren Olson (1992), characterized as Dionysian and Apollonian tendencies – between a freewheeling, experimental spirit and more rigorous structures and "accountability." In the past two decades, the Hutchins School has repeatedly been forced to incorporate state-mandated prescriptions in teacher education that threaten its practice of student-centered, thematic exploration by the expectation that students master impossibly detailed and specific content unconnected with a concern to the construction of meaning. Another challenge currently facing the school is the reduction of seminar time in the Lower Division General Education program – the original "heart" of the School – in order to align instructors' actual workload with their credited (paid) work. In addition, there has been reduction in the number of General Education units offered, in response to an Executive Order from the Chancellor's office of the California State University (CSU) aimed at streamlining requirements to facilitate earlier graduation. In the last decade, another significant change in practice has been the introduction of grades in the Lower Division. Along with these changes that have made the program more similar to others at Sonoma State, there has been a continuing infantilization of the student body through risk management practices that narrow the range of activities the school can include. Put together, these shifts threaten to institutionally "normalize" the Hutchins School to an extent that some alumni and long time instructors protest that they no longer recognize "the Hutchins Way."

The Hutchins School has always sought to put into practice the vision of a truly general education for citizenship enunciated by its namesake, Robert Maynard Hutchins, who asserted that the objective of a liberal education is not to teach all the facts and skills students will ever need to know, but to encourage them to develop habits of learning such that they continue to educate themselves over their lifetimes (Hutchins, 1953). In our effort to foster "lifelong learners" and the development of "learning communities," the Hutchins School long offered an alternative general education curriculum consisting of an intensive four-semester sequence. Each of these block courses is interdisciplinary, and combined fulfill the entire lower division general education requirements in the CSU with the exception of mathematics. The curriculum is constructed collaboratively by instructors holding doctorates in a variety of disciplines (which have included History, Engineering, Literature, Philosophy, Geology, Anthropology, Visual Arts, Theater, Film, History of Science, Psychology, and Environmental Sciences). Content is organized thematically, supporting integrative inquiry and openness to multiple perspectives on issues of social concern, as opposed to the transmission of specific disciplinary expertise or the pursuit of a monolithic "Truth."

At the time of its founding, in the "interesting times" of the late 1960's, Sonoma State University in Northern California was a hotbed of counterculture ideals and lifestyles. Olson remembers it as a time of open pot smoking on campus, skinny-dipping, and sweat lodges (which earned it the nickname "Granola U"). The Hutchins School reflected this era of experimentation and freedom, and was originally structured as a semi-autonomous "cluster school." It aimed to overcome "1) Passivity, 2) Fragmentation, and 3) Alienation" through a practice that was "Student-centered, concerned with process, and committed to allowing the affective realm a central place" (Olson, 1992: 1). All courses were conducted as small seminars, and graded Credit/No Credit. The curriculum resembled a "Great Books" program, supplemented by contemporary literature and consideration of the burning issues of the day. Olson has called the first year a "Tragicomedy," as "Apollonian and Dionysian" tensions exploded into open conflict between members of the faculty. Several of the founders recognized that minimal structures – including an agreed upon booklist – were essential to a program that took texts as the focal points of each session. The Dionysians, however, considered any requirements at all an authoritarian imposition, and refused to collaborate with "punitive motivators." After a tumultuous first year, the Dionysians were exiled, and the program hired a new cadre of young instructors that reached consensus on what were, in fact, extremely loose structures. The central philosophy of the School, then as now, is grounded in "dialogic" (more than Socratic) learning. It trusts students to take ownership of the seminar, demands they construct their own meanings from each text, and encourages them to find their "voice" through writing. The *process* of collaborative learning has always been emphasized, rather than any particular *content*. The program once eschewed testing in any form, and still fosters close relationships between students and instructors who previously deployed largely narrative evaluations and face-to-face meetings, a practice that is partially slipping away in response to new time and labor constraints.

A wave of retirements and the hiring of new scholars now under increased pressure for vigorous research and publication agendas has also changed the tone and content of the curriculum, as well as the willingness to put in the long hours demanded by collaborative course planning. There has been a noticeable de-emphasis on the

Greeks, an infusion of post-structural and post-colonial influences, and a much increased use of media and instructional technologies (in 2018, most seminar classrooms were outfitted with large flat screen televisions connected to the internet). The conduct of the seminar, in which all viewpoints are interrogated and no single truth is taken as authoritative, has meant that in practice the School has been implicitly "postmodern" from the beginning. What has changed, to some degree, is the theory and terminology that explicates this practice ("multivocality" and "incredulity to metanarratives"). Most new instructors push the program in a more Apollonian direction (at least at first). Generally fresh out of graduate school, with a deep commitment to their hard won expertise and often adept at lecturing, new professors sometime mourn the loss of disciplinary content. While new academic arenas such as postcolonial and critical race studies are interdisciplinary in research methodology and publication, they are often quite "traditional" in their pedagogy, emphasizing the transmission of content from teacher to student, an approach sometimes dismissed in Hutchins, following Freire (1970) as the "banking concept of education." The notion of interdisciplinarity that has always been implicit in the Hutchins pedagogy is not one of grafting one disciplinary approach onto another, that is, with identifying, accumulating and connecting discrete disciplinary knowledge. Rather it focuses on questions with multiple possible answers that may require more than one discipline to address. Our students tend not to think of "disciplines" at all, rather of *problems*. The organization of the seminar around discussion of issues, rather than the transmission of knowledge, sometimes means that students may not mention what the instructor feels are the key points of any text. New instructors thus tend to be "too directive" in seminars, perhaps launching into mini-lectures or deploying various methods to assess competency in subject matter. For example, I was once quite impressed with how students in a seminar were making connections between Darwinian ideas and social ideologies, but was appalled to discover that not a single student could adequately define natural selection. I launched into a long-winded explanation, which one student – a creationist, it so happened – challenged as the imposition of a single truth on the group.

Over time most new instructors come to see, as I did despite initial doubts, that the program *works*. A turning point for me was the day two graduates of the program, seeing me with a course reader in a local café, approached me to enthus about their Hutchins experience. They told me how honored they would always feel that they had had the opportunity to sit for long hours surrounded by books and discuss ideas with a PhD who treated them as equals. Students do indeed learn what they desire to learn (which may not accord with the instructors' ideas!), but more significantly, *retain* what they learn, having "made it their own" through synthesis with knowledge obtained in other courses and with their own experience. Students become skilled critical thinkers, infamous on campus as creative and outspoken questioners of authority. Our alumni, among the most generous in the California State University system, often express how inspiring it was to be taken seriously as co- learners, rather than passive recipients of professors' knowledge. Hutchins aims to develop socially conscious, broadly educated *citizens*, though in the process we may admittedly lose depth in any particular discipline. The mix of innovative thinking, outspoken independence, and lack of discipline-based expertise led one of my colleagues in another department to tell me that Hutchins students are both her "best and worst students."

Placing trust in students *works*, though only when students fully invest in the process and challenge themselves. Because the seminar format works best with *narrative* materials, there has been a constant struggle to adequately educate students in the natural sciences, which many of our students have a tendency to avoid. Other "Apollonian" changes included an attempt to increase explicitness about the theory and practice of interdisciplinary inquiry, constant attempts to come to (near) uniformity in what are fairly idiosyncratic assessment practices, and the use of Portfolios. In my opinion, many of these changes are motivated more by faculty than student demand, and represent responses to trends in pedagogical theory – such as the "outcomes assessment" movement of the 2000's – as well as the requirements for repeated program reviews. While there is clearly a need in contemporary students for more explicit guidance and criteria for excellence in integrative learning, our students generally enroll in the program not because of any theories, but because we are seen as "the teacher program." We still hold out hope that more than a few come for our practices – for the seminars, for the opportunity for independent study and program design, for the close collaborative relationships with peers and instructors. The Portfolios, intended as a "tool of student empowerment" are loaded with self-evaluation tables, integrative matrices, structured writing assignments and question sequences. Some of our students complain that these structures are "make work" with little real meaning for them, and I worry that we may overload our students and ourselves with "assessments" and matrices that may look good in program reviews, but are top-down, overly busy, and homogenous, threatening to bury what one Apollonian himself called "the Zen" of the program. A push by some for the program to move to electronic portfolios, in my opinion, does little to address these problems. In fact, I fear that while making compilation more convenient (and saving paper) students will not value, save, nor deeply process texts read on screens (as research has repeatedly shown).

Each time a structure is introduced faculty members soon make it their own in response to their personal inclinations and in dialogue with students (every seminar has different needs and dynamics). Then, as a new hire objects, or a veteran is confronted with a chaotic seminar, another Apollonian innovation is proposed. This dialectic is a lively part of the faculty's ongoing collaborative "seminar," conducted for the most part in good humor and collegiality. The more serious challenges to the Dionysian spirit have come from external institutional forces.

Over time these forces and changes in demographics have led to an increasing "rationalization" of the program. The once autonomous program was folded into the university's School of Arts and Humanities, and although it has been able to hold onto its own full time faculty, providing continuity and commitment to the essentials of the pedagogy, the program relies ever more heavily on part-time lecturers (as is the case across university systems nationwide). By the late 1970's, a new generation of younger, more career-oriented students led to a drop in demand for non-specialized degrees in Liberal Studies. In response, the Hutchins School developed a graded upper division program including a "teacher track" for pre-credential students, who now make up the vast majority of the student body. State requirements for this track, in combination with budgetary constraints, demanded significant curricular changes, a certain loss of experimentation, and the need to offer a number of large lecture/discussion courses. In response to demands in the 2010's that the program increase its student-faculty ratio, as well as offer General Education courses open to non-majors, the Hutchins School now offers one large lecture (or lecture/film) course every semster with enrollments of up to 185 students. Instructors have been forced to reduce written requirements, and many deploy multiple-choice, electronically graded exams, something once absolutely anathema.

Further "Apollonian" shifts are a result of changes in average age, aptitude, and literacy of the student body; most of our students are now fresh out of High School, attending college because they're "supposed" to, steeped in social media rather than literature, and ever more career focused. Fewer students enroll in the program out of a sense of exploration and excitement for learning for learning's sake. The Lower Division seminar program remained ungraded into the mid-2000's, and seeing little consequence for not completing assigned reading, many students simply did not do them carefully, resulting in seminars filled with personal anecdote and tossed out opinion rather than close textual analysis and critique. In an attempt to promote "accountability," most professors now demand typed response papers with questions directly relating to the texts at each seminar session, a practice once frowned upon as "policing." Some instructors engage in what one called "disguised lectures," finding that contemporary students often simply do not have the contextual knowledge to make sense of many texts.

The Lower Division is now graded after the first semester, a change I pushed for when I was the program director. I saw that other programs and institutions were becoming ever more suspicious of credit/no credit courses, and Hutchins students were increasingly facing significant difficulties in entering other majors, applying to law and graduate schools, and studying abroad. I was also spending more time every year writing letters explaining the program, and pleading that Credit marks not be translated as C's in student GPA's. As predicted by some, this has made the program less distinguishable from what one of the founding generation of instructors criticized as the traditional "game of school."

For decades, the faculty of the Hutchins School supported the low student-faculty ratio enjoyed in seminars by engaging in a large degree of unpaid overload instruction. In the Lower Division program, students earned 12 units for approximately 12 hours of classroom time (9 credit hours in small seminar sections, and 3 in multi-section "symposia"). Instructors, however, were only credited with 6 teaching units, and taught another 6 units in the Upper Division, for a total real teaching load of 18 units, an outlier at the university level. As the demands for research and publication ratcheted up, and new generation of instructors, some with small children, were hired, this became increasingly untenable. Some faculty and a new administration also insisted that the teaching load be aligned with the California Faculty Association's union contract. In addition, in 2017 an Executive Order from the Chancellor's office reformed the California State University's General Education structure. The result of these changes has meant a reduction of units in the Lower Division from 48 to 36, with both students and faculty credited for 6 rather than 9 units in seminar, and one instructor taking responsibility for the formerly collaborative 3 unit weekly symposia. Thus, there are fewer hours in seminar, less faculty collaboration and participation in symposia, and less time for shared curriculum planning (which formerly, due to the large number of seminar hours, could be carved out once a month during classtime). One consequence is a radical reduction in the percentage of shared texts across sections and fewer opportunities for faculty discussion of curriculum (as opposed to practical business). The content in some seminar sections sometimes only tenuously connects to the symposia. A further constraint is that the university's risk managers, in addition to demanding an almost laughable amount of liability release paperwork from students and faculty, have forbidden students under the age of twenty-one to drive their cars on field trips. The School must now hire expensive buses to travel even to sites quite close to campus (such as the Sonoma Mountain Zen Center), severely reducing the number of field experiences we can provide.

Is this then, finally, what many over the years have feared: "the end of Hutchins"? Certainly, the changes of the past fifteen years have greatly transformed the program. But I don't believe we should despair the loss of a mythical "golden age." The former teaching overload on faculty was not only out of compliance contractually, but exhausting and unrealistic given the increased requirements for publication. The former demand for nearly lockstep uniformity of content in the Lower Division seminar sections frequently led to endless meetings and a good degree of conflict. Instructors are now freer to construct syllabi that truly excite them and play to their strengths. In the current climate, grades in the Lower Division have, in my opinion, led to more serious engagement by students in their work, though admittedly this reflects extrinsic motivation more than the intrinsic rewards we hope to nuture. We are certainly challenged to "work smarter, not harder," but we should recognize that a 4 semester sequence requiring 6 hours of seminar a week in the Lower Division, along with a minimum of 4-5 required seminar courses in the Upper Division, provides considerable opportunity to practice our pedagogy, and remains an outlier not only at Sonoma State University, but across the nation.

We are challenged, as always, to communicate the value of a broad, interdisciplinary liberal arts education to students, parents, and administrators increasingly focused on specialization and the job market. We must become far more explicit, from outreach to graduation, about what we mean by integrative pedagogy, while not allowing imposed theories and top-down structures to interfere with the student-centered processes we promote. We are called upon to reach out and defend our Dionysian Ivory Tower outside its walls, *to be political* as well as practical. We will be required to "tighten up," with less time for free exploration, but will strive to remain loyal to the experimental, even rebellious spirit the School has embodied since its founding. We need to be Apollonian Dionysians. We still recognize, as did our founder Warren Olson (citing Nietzsche), that one must have a bit of chaos in order to give birth to a dancing star.

References

Freire, Paolo. 2000 [1970]. *Pedagogy of the Oppressed*. Continuum.

Hutchins, Robert 1953. *The Conflict in Education in a Democratic Society*. Harper and Row.

Olson, Warren. 1992. "The Origin and Birth of the Hutchins School of Liberal Studies." Unpublished manuscript.

The Hutchins School: A Crucible for Creativity

Riversteadt LaMoreaux, PhD

Riversteadt (River) LaMoreaux, known then as Heidi Kieffer LaMoreaux, taught in Hutchins from 1999 to 2016, where she used her expertise in physical geography to create outdoor field experiences. River has a PhD in Geography from The University of Georgia with emphases in paleoecology, speleology and archaeology. While teaching in Hutchins River added graphic novels to the curriculum, created an annual art show, and served as Director from 2010-2014. She currently teaches online courses, in-person workshops, completed a couple of years of training in British Shamanism, and is working on several creative projects including snarky earth-science diagrams, a memoir, an Inner Geographies workbook, and a play.

The Hutchins School of Liberal Studies (Hutchins), a dialogic cluster school within Sonoma State University, creates spaces for creative growth for both students and faculty through the use of undergraduate seminar discussions, symposia and field trips, student-centered curriculum, flexibility in both course structure and student assignments, and emphasis on alternative assessment methods rather than formal examinations. Through active participation in the Hutchins community, faculty creativity is enriched by: 1) course planning in collaboration with a cadre of five or six professors from varied disciplines who plan lower division classes; 2) introduction to new interdisciplinary ideas which may result in new avenues of individual scholarly research; and 3) the creation of upper division courses in alignment with faculty interdisciplinary interests and passions. Student creativity is encouraged through: 1) student-centered and student-driven curricula; 2) seminar discussions of "big questions"; 3) open-ended and inquiry-based assignments; 4) symposia and speakers; 5) field experiences; and 6) a sense of community. With its unique curriculum and many opportunities for personal connections between students and faculty, Hutchins encourages active learning, interdisciplinary connections, and integrative thought.

Losing My "Discipline"

When I tell someone I'm a retired professor, they usually ask, "what did you teach?" At the beginning of my career this question was easy to answer as I operated mainly within a set academic discipline – in my case, physical geography. The answer became complicated when I began to teach in the Hutchins School of Liberal Studies at Sonoma State University.

When I entered Hutchins in 1999, I had been looking at pollen grains under a microscope and trudging through peat bogs for several years. Hutchins needed someone to create outdoor lab experiences for their students; I needed a place that not only tolerated my academic schizophrenia but embraced it. I first knew I was entering unusual waters when, instead of presenting scientific research during my job interview, the Hutchins faculty asked me to present the syllabus and content of my "dream course" – in this case "Experiencing Nature."

In preparation for my interview I created a book of nature prints and polaroid transfers during a romp through Robert Louis Stevenson State Park the afternoon before. I wanted to show my potential colleagues that students could visually capture the natural essence of a place in an afternoon. To my surprise, rather than wondering why I created art for a science interview, they were delighted. I felt understood – something polymaths rarely feel in academic settings. My colleagues in Hutchins considered my interests in bookbinding, nature journaling, creative writing, comics, caves, religious studies, and earth art, as assets rather than distractions. Hutchins became a space capable of containing my varied interests and allowed me to transform passions into interdisciplinary courses, field trips, and student projects. I lost some of my academic disciplinary specialization but found new interdisciplinary spaces for creativity. By the time I retired in 2016, the crucible of Hutchins had personally and professionally transformed me.

"Hutchins": What It Is And How It Works

Creativity is not linear and predictable. In fact, creativity is more as David Sill (1996) stated:

> Creativity relies on non-logical and non-linear thought processes, filled with digressions and diversions. Creativity is a messy, complex process, and therefore difficult to confine within a simple, precise, definition. By its very nature, creativity violates the present order in creating a new order. (295)

Hutchins was constructed, in part, to "violate the present order" of 1960s academia.

The Hutchins School, named after Robert Maynard Hutchins (with his permission), was formed in 1969. Five dissatisfied faculty members of the newly created Sonoma State College decided to create a "school within a school" that could overcome 1) passivity, 2) fragmentation, and 3) alienation through creating a pedagogy that, as Professor Eric McGuckin stated in 2003:

> "involves a serious commitment to "dialogic" (more than Socratic) learning... trusts students to take ownership of their seminars, demands that they construct their own meanings from each text, and encourages them to find their "voice" through writing. The process of collaborative learning is emphasized, rather than the mastery of any particular content" (Newell et al. 22-23).

Of the first five faculty members, only three survived the first year due to a battle over academic structure. The three who endured insisted that at least some structure was required – the two who left the program wanted students to have ultimate freedom from any faculty interference. Additional faculty members from various disciplines were subsequently hired to create what is now one of the largest and most robust departments at Sonoma State University (SSU).

The first Hutchins courses were interdisciplinary and structured around "big questions," similar but not identical to "great books" classes. These beginning courses, though modified through time, are still the model for the four-semester lower division program in Hutchins. Each of these four classes is worth twelve credits and combines ideas from many disciplines to explore a central theme. These four lower division courses, "The Human Enigma" (which explores questions of what it means to be human and how humans differ from other species, including Darwin's theory of evolution); "In Search of Self" (which examines concepts of "self," individual personality expression, gender, and human physiology); "Exploring the Unknown" (which scrutinizes how humans explore the unknown both through religious ideas and through science paradigms like quantum physics); and "Challenge and Response in the Modern World" (which studies ecology, problems of globalization, wealth inequity, and social injustice) are planned by five or six faculty members from different academic disciplines, called a "cadre." Each cadre member adds their own expertise, in the form of books, movies, symposia ideas, or field experiences, to the courses they teach.

Each faculty member in the cadre teaches a smaller group of 12 to 15 students in a dialogic seminar format. Every few weeks all the seminar groups combine into a large group to hear guest speakers, watch films, go on field trips, or have large group discussions. Upon completion of the four-semester sequence, students complete all their general education requirements except mathematics. Some students choose to leave Hutchins after lower division to pursue other majors; many remain through upper division or stay connected to Hutchins through completion of a minor. Hutchins also includes a degree-completion program for students who wish to finish their BA through online discussion and weekend seminars, and once included a Masters program, "Action for a Viable Future," which required completion of a civic engagement project rather than a traditional thesis.

The upper-division Hutchins program, which was originally a major left open to student design, became "Track I." Pressure to adapt to changes in academic requirements imposed since 1969 resulted in the addition of a pre-credential "teacher track," or "Track II," and then an accelerated "blended track," or Track III," which allows students to obtain both their bachelor's degree and their teaching credential in four rather than five years. Through all these changes, the basic Hutchins major – "Track I" has remained a constant, though approximately two-thirds of Hutchins students are in the "teacher tracks."

Track I, the ultimate playground for "multipotentialites" as popularized by Emily Wapnick (2017), allows students to design a liberal studies degree according to their interests, and gives them the freedom to take courses from other disciplines in the greater campus community as well as within Hutchins. Track I students are also required to take independent study classes, complete an internship, and if possible, "study away." All of the Hutchins tracks end with the "senior synthesis," a capstone course, during which students compile a portfolio of papers and projects, complete a final project, examine their writing and speaking skills, and write an "intellectual journey" paper. These projects are showcased in a science-fair-style symposium at the end of each semester.

Student and faculty interaction are maximized in Hutchins. Exams and large classes are rare and only found in a few upper division courses. Most upper division classes have 12-15 students and are seminar-based. Faculty members are known by their first names and are seen less as authorities than as informed seminar facilitators.

There are no grades in the first semester of lower division; students may opt for grades for the final three lower division courses or continue to take classes credit/no credit. Students are given general, rather than specific instructions regarding assignment requirements, and often modify the assignments to fit their individual interests. Every participant in the seminar is seen as both student and teacher, whether student or faculty. David Sill (1996), in reference to integrative studies programs, states that:

> Environmental factors can either encourage or discourage creativity, and an environment that encourages creativity can enable creativity in both the individual and the group. The implication is that through the shaping of class activities and assignments, the instructor can encourage integrative thought. (306)

Hutchins is an environment that creates spaces for both faculty and students to approach learning more creatively. Each participant in the learning environment is asked to "bring something to the table." Those offerings, when combined into the crucible of a creative class environment, allow ideas to mix, opinions to reform, and collaboration to occur.

Spaces For Faculty Creativity

Cadres: Interdisciplinary Melting Pots

Gunnar Tornqvist (1983) said, "Creativity flourishes when different specialties and competencies are squeezed together on a small surface. What is needed is a meeting-place for more or less random contacts and new combinations of pieces of information and fragments of ideas" (103). Putting five or six scholars from disciplines ranging from physics to poetry together into a small room to co-create a course is definitely "squeezing" different ways of thinking onto a very "small surface". Cadres meet on two levels; once a week to discuss the current class they are co-teaching, and once a month to plan the lower division class they will teach during the following semester. These cadre meetings give faculty members the chance, several times a month, to interact and to learn from each other.

I was silent during most of my early cadre-planning meetings. (Remember that my world had consisted of microscopes, pollen grains, and peat bogs for several years). My colleagues threw around book titles and names of philosophers like acrobats throw each other in Cirque de Soleil. I was afraid to get in the way, and to admit that I had last heard of Descartes and Plato as a freshman in college. The only thing I added to that first course was a field experience at a regional park which taught students to measure stream capacity, test soil properties, and identify a few plants – activities in alignment with my disciplinary specialty and my job description.

I was also silent during most of the faculty meetings that first year – afraid of "doing it wrong" or looking as stupid as I felt. My experience was not unusual; most first year Hutchins faculty experience a similar major transition into this new culture, including mourning the loss of their disciplinary content and resisting the urge to control seminar discussions (Newell, et al, 24). Over the course of that first year, I went privately from faculty member to faculty member, asking each instructor how to "do Hutchins." The answers varied as much as the personalities of my colleagues. Finally, at the end of the first year, I realized that there was no one way to "do Hutchins." I resolved to find my own way to creatively contribute elements from my disciplinary background, personal interests, and academic obsessions.

After that point, and up until my retirement in 2016, cadre meetings became one of my favorite creative spaces. During weekly cadre discussions and monthly planning meetings I learned ideas from a wide range of disciplines and details from colleagues' fascinating backgrounds. One cadre member might mention his experiences growing up in pre-colonial Zaire, another his newest backyard laboratory invention, another her latest trip to concentration camps in Europe. During monthly planning meetings, each cadre member would lobby, sometimes fiercely, for course content they felt would enrich the course; one colleague might hope that we include short stories by Mexican writers, another a book about quantum physics, another poetry by Adrienne Rich, another a Bollywood movie. I always learned something valuable from the unique disciplinary perspectives of my colleagues. I miss the synergy of these interactions.

Tornqvist, who participated in an experimental seminar of scientists and humanists from a wide variety of disciplines also found his multidisciplinary interactions promoted creativity. He said, "a significant synergy effect calls for multiplicity and variation. Uniformity and homogeneity do not seem to form a suitable climate for creative processes" (1983, 105). Cadre members in Hutchins still create a richer experience for students than any one professor could create alone. Additionally, faculty learning in lower division only *begins* with the cadre process; throughout the semester, professors, along with students, experience the texts, movies, and field experiences which comprise the course. Even if a professor teaches the same two lower division courses every year, the content is constantly morphing; usually 50% or more of the books, articles, field trips or symposia topics change each time a class is collaboratively constructed.

Cadre Collaboration: Raw Material for Creativity

The greatest gift that the cadre process gave to me was the feeling that my creative ideas are valued and supported. I agree with David Seamon (1983) that "beyond movement and dialogue, there is a need that the person involved in creative work feels part of some larger whole to which his insights can contribute" (62). When I felt supported in my creative excursions, I was more likely to think outside of my discipline. In fact, all the information from cadre meetings, intersections with new reading materials in lower division, and multiple perspectives from seminar discussions sparked creativity within professors as well as students. As a faculty member I encountered ideas and perspectives that would have been impossible for me to think without this disciplinary cross-pollination. As Margaret Boden (2003) states, "the deepest cases of creativity involve someone's thinking something which, with respect to the conceptual spaces in their minds, they couldn't have thought before. The supposedly impossible idea can come about only if the creator changes the preexisting style in some way" (6). Through contact with the ideas and perspectives of my cadre colleagues, I was able to boldly think thoughts I could not have thought before.

Sill explains: "integrative thought consists of taking disconnected material or ideas and synthesizing them into something new, a task that is certainly a form of creativity" (293). Most of my art and creative writing pieces while I taught in Hutchins were responses to ideas from lower division course material. Some examples include: a "reference slide" of cultural attitudes toward women, which stemmed from learning about issues of gender and social justice in "In Search of Self"; an oversized board game "spinner" that showed different countries and how the U.S. policies negatively impact those countries, inspired by teaching "Challenge and Response in the Modern World"; a 3-D collage of cocoons (world problems) and butterflies (possible solutions), which came from ideas in both "Challenge and Response in the Modern World" and "Exploring the Unknown"; a world tree sculpture from ideas in mythology and religion from "Exploring the Unknown"; creation of a comic about maps and world views, from the upper division class "Graphic Novels"; and a 3-D collage of photos and artifacts (gathered with permission) from Adams Springs, the site of a field trip in one of my upper division courses, "Terrain"; and a sediment core model of my life history created in "Inner Geographies." Curriculum that is always in flux keeps learning fresh for faculty, and through formation of new curriculum and instructor development, for students as well.

Upper Division Course Creation: You Mean I Can Teach What I Want to Teach?

In academia, much of the curriculum is set or difficult to change. While I taught at SSU, I also moonlighted teaching a world regional geography class at a local junior college, one of my few direct ties to my academic discipline. While teaching in a more traditional format at the junior college I often felt restricted by the "have to's" imposed upon me by the requisite structure – requirements like tests, strict guidelines regarding what material must be covered for the class to be transferable to other schools, and the encouragement to use mainly lecture-based pedagogy. Luckily in Hutchins space for creative pedagogy, rather than institutional mandates, is built into the system.

In Hutchins, every upper-division student is required to take one class in each of our four interdisciplinary core areas. Core A classes explore issues of history and society, Core B classes connect science to society, Core C classes include art and literature, and Core D classes delve into mysteries of psychology and religion. This system provides ultimate flexibility for Hutchins faculty to pursue their individual interests as they create classes which contain elements from many different academic disciplines. Upper division classes are required to contain multidisciplinary content. The core class content guidelines, which are purposefully general, allow each faculty member to craft classes that fit within the core areas and at the same time parallel the passions of the instructor. As one of my colleagues Tony Mountain said to his students, "If you can find a class that explores an instructor's obsession, take that course."

It is also possible for Hutchins instructors to teach upper division courses which lie outside of their academic disciplines. During my first few years in Hutchins, I taught all Core B classes which aligned directly with my background in physical geography – classes like "Experiencing Nature," "Caves," and "Terrain." Over time, I took classes in artistic techniques and natural history at Point Reyes National Seashore and received a grant to learn Polaroid Transfer techniques. I used this new expertise to create a Core C class called "Earth Art" which taught students how to use artistic techniques to explore natural phenomena and record their observations in nature journals. Emboldened by my successful move into Core C, I developed another Core C class, "Graphic Novels," reflecting a longtime passion. Use of graphic novels from this class spilled out into lower division courses as well. A later foray, into Core D, called "Inner Geographies," combined scientific metaphors, maps and creative writing to explore personal history and sense of place. Just before retiring, I created a Core B class which employed critical thinking skills to the study of cryptozoological creatures in "Cryptids: Fact & Fiction."

Most of my colleagues teach in at least two core areas, though they may have originally been hired to teach classes in only one. Rather than teaching the same classes every year, Hutchins professors are granted the rare opportunity to create new courses that reflect their changing interests and academic growth as interdisciplinary scholars. Creating new courses also gave me an "excuse" to pursue academic interests outside of my discipline that I would likely not have had time or energy to otherwise explore.

Spaces For Student Creativity

Through email outreach, social media, and information gathering as part of a program review of the Hutchins school conducted in 2013, I asked current and past Hutchins students how Hutchins influenced their personal creativity. Their replies led me to identify several ways that Hutchins promotes student creativity.

Student-Centered and Student-Driven Curricula: "This is Your Class, Not Mine."

Hutchins professors make every effort to move responsibility for learning from the teacher to the student. Hutchins professors facilitate discussions rather than tell students how or what to think. Sarah Miller et al. (2008) pointed out that in active learning situations, "although the teacher is present and engaged in the activities, active learning exercises place the learning responsibility into the hands of the student and require that the student come to class prepared to learn. This attitudinal shift alone will enhance learning because the student is ready and willing to participate" (1330). Hutchins students are usually prepared for class and interested in learning because they, along with their classmates, direct the flow of the seminar discussion. They become "co-learners, rather than passive recipients of knowledge" (Newell et al. 24).

In some of my upper division classes like "Graphic Novels" and "Terrain," I came to class the first day with a bare-bones syllabus that only includes required information (like contact information and office hours), a few books to read during the first few weeks, and blank spaces for weekly topics. I handed out a list of possible topics or readings, and the let students use the first day of class to create the course. They argued back and forth about what topics to include, what order to put the topics in, and who should facilitate the discussion of each individual topic. Students also had a voice regarding percentages to be assigned to each of the graded portions of the class as well – deciding how much each assignment will be worth. Based on comments from student evaluations of these courses, students had a strong sense of involvement in the course because they helped to design and facilitate the class; they cared about the course because it is as much their course as it was mine.

The Seminar: Broader Questions, Deeper Learning

The seminar is the bedrock of Hutchins pedagogy. Most lower and upper division classes are seminars, except for a few large or workshop-based courses. The emphasis in most seminars is not with finding the right answer, but rather with asking the right questions. Jacob Getzels and Mihaly Csikszentmihalyi (1964) state that "the most important part of the creative process may not be the creative product... but may well be the framing, discovery, and envisioning of the creative question" (125).

Hutchins seminars tend to focus around large moral and intellectual questions rather than specific disciplinary material – in fact, most questions in Hutchins require perspectives and information from multiple disciplines to be understood (Newell, et al., 24). Hutchins interdisciplinary courses require students to combine ideas from disparate disciplines, which can create creative tension, which can lead to discovery. Sill states, "in general, creative tension results from the mind's need to construct order turning in on itself. When two or more ordering systems (i.e., matrices of thought) contradict or conflict, then the mind feels tension until the conflict is resolved through the creation of a new order. Such resolution is an integrating thought process" (303). Since the Hutchins seminar combines the thoughts and opinions of all seminar participants, the instructor, and the author of the text, there is ample room for integrative thought as various ideas are presented and discussed.

Students see the seminar as an effective way to promote both learning and creativity. Based on student answers to my question "How does Hutchins create spaces for personal creativity?" the seminar plays a big role in student learning. One student stated:

My Hutchins experience has taught me that ideas and thinking are much more interconnected than they may appear to be. By seminaring on a broad variety of topics and learning to connect information, I have gained a deeper understanding of myself and a better ability to explore why I think the ways that I do. I have gained information and even facts over the past five semesters, but more importantly, I have gained a better way of thinking deeper and more critically. I have learned how to research information on topics that I care about and forge connections between myself and information. I can listen to others' ideas even if I don't agree, and I can separate myself from my personal opinions in order to explore a topic.

Other Hutchins students concur. One stated that "if you get the right group of people together you are able to learn and explore in ways you otherwise wouldn't"; another, that "the Hutchins Program encourages students to speak their minds and discuss important issues, which sparks creativity and learning."

Not all seminars, however, work all the time. Some students will come to class unprepared. Sometimes personalities conflict. Some more introverted students don't speak up as often as extroverted students. Robert Maynard Hutchins, anticipating problems like this, said in an interview with Keith Berwick (ca. 1970) that "real dialogue is a very difficult thing and requires certain moral qualities. You cannot participate in the dialogue if you are a show-off; you cannot participate in the dialogue unless you really want to learn... but by what other method could you really obtain a clear and rounded view?" The main purpose of the faculty member in a Hutchins seminar is to help students work out these difficulties as a group. Often when a seminar was not working, I would leave and have the students retrieve me when they decided on a solution. My absence allowed the students to honestly and openly express their dissatisfactions with their peers without fear of it affecting their grade. This method, however, is not advisable if faculty absence might leave vulnerable students at risk for increased marginalization.

Despite possible flaws, "... the program works. Students do indeed learn what they desire to learn. More significantly, they *retain* what they learn, having made it their own through synthesis with knowledge obtained in other courses and with their own experience. Through the seminar experience, students learn from the text, from the instructor, and most importantly, from each other." (McGuckin in Newell et al. 2003, p 24)

Open-Ended Assignments: "No, I'm not going to tell you exactly what to do."

In Hutchins, faculty members make every effort not to "spoon feed" students. As Sill pointed out:

> E.M. Forster once stated, "Spoon feeding in the long run teaches us nothing but the shape of the spoon." By engaging the student in the complexities of the material, interdisciplinary study attempts to go beyond spoon feeding so that the student learns not only the shape of the spoon, but the shape and nature of thought as well. (291)

For students already familiar with the shape of academic spoons, this sudden departure from lecture-based classes, rubrics and elaborate essay prompts can be disorienting – at least at first.

Students often resist not being told exactly what to do and how to do it. Assignments do come with guidelines, and yet are constructed to leave room for student interpretation. Inevitably in "The Human Enigma," the introductory class for freshman, and "Introduction to Liberal Studies," the introductory class for transfer students, a student will plead for, even demand, that I tell them "what to write about" in their first essay. They ask me to "give them the prompt," or to "give examples of papers from previous years." Hutchins professors rarely, if ever, oblige, and yet miraculously, by the end of the first semester in Hutchins, students usually don't ask for specific direction in assignments any more. As one student stated:

Assignments were rarely given as essays, but more often as personal challenges, such as "put yourself in a situation you've never been in before and come back prepared to share your experience," "as your final, I want you to learn a new craft of your choice and bring in your results to share," "create your own graphic novel," "create a waste management system for future colonies on mars" and so on..."

Spaces for creativity are opened wider when students have to discover and uncover their own topics and their own interpretations of assignments.

Some examples of student assignments, besides response papers and essays, include landscape photo essays, body sculptures, student centered voting symposia, laboratory-style write-ups of field experiences, short film projects, autobiographies, nature collages which include nature prints, Polaroid transfer prints, and block prints, nature journals, short comics, dances, musical compositions, carpentry, quilts, mobiles, graduate school plans, resumes, elementary school field trip plans, astronomical observation logs, food diaries, personal atlases, and diagrams or models of theoretical earthwork monuments.

Students, after surviving the initial shock of having to "feed themselves", regularly seek out studies and experiences that support their developing interests and passions. Students also create independent study projects, search out internship opportunities, participate in study abroad programs, and create both a yearly a literary magazine and community art show.

Symposia and Speakers: Multiple Voices, Multiple Perspectives

One of the hallmarks of lower division courses is the "symposium" – occasions when all of the small seminar classes and cadre members meet together for large group activities. Some upper division classes also invite guest speakers to interact with their students. Students often comment that their interactions with speakers and information presented in symposia are life changing. Since entering Hutchins, I have witnessed student poetry slams, watched student-created films, participated in Sufi dancing and Chi Gung exercises, heard young women from different countries describe their experiences with globalization, heard the life story of a male to female transgender woman, heard students ask questions of a LGBTQ panel of their peers, watched movies on topics ranging from dystopic futures to media manipulation, been instructed in autobiographical writing techniques from the daughter of a beat poet, heard details regarding how an author created their most recent book of fiction, heard a lecture about cosmology from a physics professor, listened to a rabbi explain Judaism, and witnessed students share their feelings about 9/11 and Operation Iraqi Freedom. These opportunities to experience voices from within and beyond the Hutchins community have sparked student independent projects, art projects, essays, and other creative enterprises for both students and faculty members.

Field Experiences: Trips Away from the Center

Much of the curriculum in Hutchins happens in the familiar territory, the academic center of Hutchins – SSU. The physical center of Hutchins is in Rachel Carson Hall, a collection of office-classrooms arranged in large connected squares around small open areas filled with benches, trees, plants and wildlife. Most Hutchins classes try to leave this common space at least once a semester in the form of a field experience. Lower division courses include multiple excursions away from campus each semester; these trips are designed to give students interdisciplinary and direct experiences that tie to curriculum. Many upper division classes also include field trips. Randy Burke Hensely (2004) reminds us that "engaging all the student's physical senses in a learning situation provides support for engendering curiosity, and using problem-solving approaches to learning also helps foster inquiry" (32). Field experiences are an effective way to engage the students' physical senses.

Field experiences are usually directly tied to the big questions and texts that the students are examining in seminar. Students take a ferry to San Francisco to visit the Museum of Modern Art to connect the experience of viewing art to texts about art history, use of visual imagery in media, and propaganda techniques. Texts about Chinese American experiences in the West prompt a visit to Chinatown, complete with dim sum lunch. Discussions of the underground in mythology and ancient religious sites lead students into the unfamiliar environment of caves. A trip to the Alternative Press Expo or to Wondercon allows students using graphic novels in class to directly experience comic subculture. Students learning about the role of garbage in society take trips to a local garbage dump. Excursions to Alcatraz or San Quentin are tied to issues of social justice. Studies of world forests and the study of biomes lead students to the California Academy of Sciences rainforest and coastal environment exhibits. Ecology studies at a local beach teach students about plant identification, soil sampling and other elements of salt marsh and dune habitats. Texts about water pollution lead students to collect and test water from local habitats, including campus water supplies. Questions of landscape history and archaeology lead students to Adams Springs, where they compare the foundations of crumbling buildings to photographs of those buildings at the height of the "springs" industry in early 1900s California. Students travel to Bloody Island, the site of a local massacre of Pomo people at the hands of the U.S. army, hear stories and songs from descendants of the massacre survivors, and then tie these accounts to historical versions of the massacre; they also compare present environments near Bloody Island, through landscape analysis, plant and animal identification, and use of maps to the historical landscape described in early anthropological literature.

Field experiences encourage, and even require students to actively participate in their own learning. Active learning "provides opportunities for students to talk and listen, read, write, and reflect as they approach course content through problem-solving exercises, informal small groups, simulations, case studies, role playing, and other activities – all of which require students to apply what they are learning" (Meyers and Jones, xi). These experiences outside of the familiar environment of SSU encourage students to actively learn and then to apply their new knowledge as they create art, or poetry, or complete field experience reports. In the final Hutchins class,

"Senior Synthesis," students frequently mention field experiences as turning points in attitudes, as fodder for creative projects, and as highlights of the Hutchins experience.

An Extra Bonus: A Creative Learning Community

Hutchins is more than a major; it is a learning community. As Barbara Smith and Jean MacGregor (1992) state:

> Learning communities directly confront multiple problems plaguing under-graduate education: the fragmentation of general education classes, isolation of students... lack of meaningful connection-building between classes; the need for greater intellectual interaction between students and faculty; and lack of sustained opportunities for faculty development. (7)

A sense of community is heightened through repeated interactions between faculty, between students, and between faculty and students that arise in seminar classes. Crises like the sudden death of a faculty member, deaths of students, and 9/11 made this sense of community obvious and tangible as we met together to share our grief, laugh and cry the memories of the ones we lost, and discuss our shock and growing uncertainty.

Hutchins pedagogy fosters creativity as well as a sense of community. Jennifer Leach (2001) argues that "creativity – be it in music, science, business, poetry, technology, education, art, industry, the philosophy of ideas or politics – can be viewed as an essentially social process: a process dependent on, and arising out of, the participation in particular kinds of communities, rather than any innate or unusual gift" (179). The social processes within Hutchins encourage students and faculty to find their own innate and unusual gifts; and though those gifts may not be world changing, they can be shared within an accepting environment and change the lives of individual members of the Hutchins community.

Hutchins also provides a nurturing space for new creative ideas. As Margaret Boden (2003) stated:

Creativity, whether in children or adults, involves exploration and evaluation. The new idea must be compared to some pre-existing mental structure and be judged to be interesting by some relevant criteria. A person who can evaluate their own novel ideas will accept them or (sometimes) correct them, but will often be unable to explain in just what way they are interesting. (63)

One of the benefits of the sense of community in Hutchins is that students feel supported enough to give voice to their new ideas, and also find a community of people willing to tell them how and why their ideas are interesting.

Hutchins also provides a sense of community through shared activities like an annual art show and reception, and publication of an annual literary magazine. Other group activities outside of classes include an annual trip to Bloody Island for a sunrise ceremony, and student-led activities through the Liberal Studies Student Association.

Losing A Discipline: Finding An Education

In the end, perhaps the greatest benefit for me, personally, is that I finally feel "liberally educated;" educated far beyond pollen grains and peat bogs. I can now throw around titles and names of philosophers with my colleagues, even if those books and ideas lie far outside of my personal Ph.D. training. Though disciplinary knowledge gives much to academia and to the world, there is also much to be said for cultivating a broad-based interdisciplinary view of the world, especially while completing an undergraduate degree. I now believe that it is possible for an individual person to become a life long learner in multiple fields of knowledge. As Heinlein said in *Time Enough for Love* (1973):

A human being should be able to change a diaper, plan an invasion, butcher a hog, conn a ship, design a building, write a sonnet, balance accounts, build a wall, set a bone, comfort the dying, take orders, give orders, cooperate, act alone, solve equations, analyze a new problem, pitch manure, program a computer, cook a tasty meal, fight efficiently, die gallantly. Specialization is for insects. (238)

The more time I spend as a part of the Hutchins community, the more willing I am to give up a bit of my discipline to embrace new forms of creativity and community.

References:

Berwick, Keith. ca. 1970. Interview of Robert Maynard Hutchins. Center for the Study of Democratic Institutions Collection, Box 611: 1 n.d.

Boden, Margaret A. 2003. *The Creative Mind: Myths and mechanisms.* Basic Books.

Florida, Richard L.. 2002. The Rise of the Creative Class: Why cities without gas and rock bands are losing the economic development race. *Washington Monthly online.*

Getzels, Jacob W., and Mihaly Chsikszentmihalyi. 1964. *Creative Thinking in Art Students: An exploratory study.* University of Chicago Press.

Heinlein, Robert. 1973. *Time Enough for Love.* Putnam.

Hensley, Randy Burke. 2004. Curiosity and Creativity as Attributes of Information Literacy. *Reference and User Services Quarterly 44(1):* 31-36.

Leach, Jennifer. 2001. A Hundred Possibilities: Creativity, community and ICT. In: Anna Craft, Bob Jeffrey, and Mike Leibling (eds.). *Creativity in Education.* Continuum. pp. 175-194.

Meyers, Chet, and Thomas B. Jones.1993. *Promoting Active Learning: Strategies for the College Classroom.* Jossey-Bass.

Miller, Sarah, Christine Pfund, Christine Maidl Pribbenow, and Jo Handelsman. 2008. Scientific Teaching in Practice. *Science 322(28):* 1329-1330.

Newell, William H. 1994. Designing Interdisciplinary Courses. In: Klein, J. T. and Doty, W. (eds.). *Interdisciplinary Studies Today: New directions for teaching and learning 58:* 35-51. Jossey Bass.

Newell, William H., James Hall, Steven Hutkins, Daniel Larner, Eric McGuckin, and Karen Oates. 2003. Apollo Meets Dionysius: Interdisciplinarity in Long-standing Interdisciplinary Programs. *Issues in Integrative Studies 21*: 9-42

Olson, Warren E. 1992. Unpublished manuscript.

Sample, Steven B. 1995. The Great Straddlers. *Liberal Education 81*: 54-58.

Seamon, David. 1983. Creativity, Center and Horizon. In: Anne Buttimer (ed.). *Creativity in Context, Lund Studies in Geography, Series B. Human Geography, 50:* 54-90.

Sill, David J. 1996. Integrative Thinking: Synthesis, and Creativity in Interdisciplinary Studies. *The Journal of General Education 50(4):* 288-311.

Smith, Barbara L. and Jean T. MacGregor. 1992. What is Collaborative Learning? In: Anne Goodsell (ed). *Collaborative Learning: A sourcebook for higher education.* National Center on Postsecondary Teaching, Learning and Assessment at Pennsylvania State University.

Stein, Morris I. 1975. *Stimulating Creativity Volume 2: Group Procedures.* Academic Press.

Storr, Anthony. 1988. *Solitude: A Return to the Self.* Ballantine.

Tornqvist, Gunnar. 1983. Creativity and the Renewal of Regional Life. In: Anne Buttimer (ed.) *Creativity in Context, Lund Studies in Geography, Series B. Human Geography 50*: 91-118.

Wapnick, Emily. 2017. *How to Be Everything: A guide for those who (still) don't know what they want to be when they grow up.* HarperCollins.

The Art and Science of Transformation in the Hutchins Seminar

Wendy L. Ostroff

Wendy Ostroff is an applied developmental and cognitive psychologist who first joined the Hutchins faculty in 2000 (and again in 2015). She is the author of the books *Understanding How Young Children Learn: Bringing the Science of Child Development to the Classroom*, and *Cultivating Curiosity in K-12 Classrooms: How to Promote and Sustain Deep Learning*. Wendy relishes the radical interdisciplinarity and freedom that Hutchins allows, and has invented and taught seminars on existential philosophy, the concept of time, nostalgia, technology, feminism, neuroscience, children's literature, Dostoevsky's *The Brothers Karamazov*, and desire, to mention a few.

By some confluence of persistence, destiny and dumb luck, I wound up a professor in the Hutchins School of Liberal Studies at age 26. A first-generation student on a mission to finish at all costs, I had high-achieved my way through a B.A., M.S., and Ph.D. in psychology at large research universities, and all without so much as a hint of a liberal education. I had never participated in a Socratic seminar, never mind facilitated one. When I accepted the job, and began discussing the plays of Aeschylus, the art of Kollwitz, the philosophy of Foucault, and the poetry of Rich, my entire reality cracked open. Another way to say this is, I know first-hand that Hutchins seminars are transformative, because they completely transformed me.

But what, you may ask, is so special about a Hutchins seminar? This is something I have puzzled over for two decades. There is most certainly an alchemy to the way in which a series of discussions can irrevocably change who we are and how we think. And these discussions stand in stark contrast to the "contests of analysis and brilliance" I experienced in graduate-school seminars. There is both an art and a science to the Hutchins seminar –some of this magic can be carefully planned, but much of it has to emerge authentically and in real time. Seminaring is about un-doing as much as doing. And it doesn't come easily.

One reason it does not come easily is that our brains operate by maximizing efficiency. Human brains find workarounds to the problem of taking in so many details, thanks to tens of thousands of years of evolutionary history. In essence, our brains smooth out our realities, making perception effortless for us by removing complexity. The visual system provides a good example. In any given scene that we look at, we can only see the middle of the landscape in color. Since only the centers of our retinas have the closely packed neurons that are sensitive to color (called 'cones'), it is actually *physically impossible* to perceive color in the periphery. But, although the edges of our world are *technically* blurred and colorless, we experience full color and detail! Un-seeing what our brains have done to make our world seamless might seem counter-productive. After all, who wouldn't want to perceive everything in color?

Painters must undo automatic perception when trying to capture a scene. First they need to undo seeing the scene as three-dimensional, and translate the shapes and angles onto a flat canvas. Then they must un-see the colors as continuous, and re-see them as broken into many shadows and hues. Whereas a purple tablecloth in afternoon shadow will read as a single color to our eyes, the artist needs to recognize that the shadows don't actually look purple at all, but deep brown and blue and green, reflecting from the fruit upon it. This undoing and redoing, focusing and unfocusing, contextualizing and decontextualizing must *also* be the work of the critical reader, writer and seminar participant. It is the art and practice of non-automatic thinking, and it is hard work. Just as the prisoners who escape Plato's cave feel unspeakable fear and pain at first; ultimately, encountering another realm outside of the cave is worthwhile. It takes a similar kind of labor and discomfort to unhook the automatic responses of our brains and minds, and to begin understanding differently.

Learning in the Hutchins seminar can't be about getting things "right." With all this switching perspectives, how could one version ever be "right"? Learning instead must become about attempts at meaning together. Success, then, is not about being "smart," because intelligence (it becomes immediately apparent) is merely the outward expression of different sets of initial conditions; a comparison to some arbitrary outside metric. Further, as the teacher-learner roles in the Hutchins seminar become blurred (à la Paolo Freire), seminaring becomes about pushing ourselves, and noticing and witnessing ourselves getting pushed. But once the trusting and intellectual risk-taking community has been built - once we have gotten in the habit of challenging the automatic responses of our minds and brains - there is not a sweeter, easier flowing feeling in the world.

At the end of a semester spent seminaring in Hutchins, I often ask my students to review the texts and passages that have changed them as people - that they will never be the same after having read, contemplated and discussed. This stands as an attempt (by the cognitive scientist in me) to pinpoint and document *the* thought or insight that opened or moved the learner beyond automaticity. On this occasion of the 50th anniversary of the Hutchins School of Liberal Studies, I find myself reflecting on texts which have transformed my thinking, teaching, and learning as a facilitator of seminars. The passages that come to mind share the same message: that in order to transform we must struggle to not take the smoothest route.

"Curiously enough, one cannot read a book; one can only reread it. A good reader, a major reader, and active and creative reader is a rereader"

~ Vladimir Nabokov

Anyone who has ever spent a semester in Hutchins knows that the best seminar groups earn their understanding via really delving into the text at hand. And if we do put in that work as careful and critical readers, the concomitant pleasures emerge: shared bliss in the creative act, shared possession of epiphanies. "Ok," I can imagine my students saying, "I am willing to put in the effort and deeply read. But why do I have to reread?" Rereading has to do with zooming out and seeing things whole. Just like we only can know the arc of a life story after that story has ended, we only can know the arc of a text after we have seen it completely and gained some perspective. We need to take the time to experience it whole. In subsequent readings of a text, we don't just review what we have already viewed, we construct the story *entirely anew* (Smith, 2009, p. 50). This is how remembering works in the brain, too. Our experiences do not passively sit in files or neural circuits, waiting to be called up and recounted. Every time we tell a story, we are re-conjuring that story, reimagining it and recreating it - literally - in a newly enhanced and strengthened string of neuronal connections. Remembering, like learning, is always a verb – our histories always impact our thinking, even in the immediate situation.

Each time I read and discuss a text within the seminar, I *do* have an entirely different experience of it. First, my own work in preparing for seminar is completely dependent on what I am bringing to the reading experience, what is currently going on in my mind and in my life. I take notes in the margins and in the blank pages at the beginning and end of the book (really in any spot I can squeeze in a thought or musing or connection). We are in conversation together, the book and I, and this conversation bursts open into a conversation with others. One of the most powerful examples I have witnessed of this textual plurality is reading and seminaring on Camus' *The Stranger* (perhaps the one book that could be said to reside in the Hutchins canon). I have had seminars in which we approach the anti-hero, Meursault, from the angle of anger (that is, fallen right into Camus' trap of wanting him to please us with his responses); I have seminared on the text from Marie's point of view, a kind of power differential, wondering about the limits of unconditional acceptance; I have read this story as a mother, giving love without expectation of it being returned. My students have looked at him as a neuro-atypical man, without responsibility; as a Buddhist, boldly in the present; as a puppy, merely reacting to what is in his face. It is the going back around to reread and rethink about this text that has enabled such rich and complex thinking.

In Hutchins, we revisit books and ideas time and time again during a semester of seminaring, always with an eye to finding new ways to see things, including ourselves and our thoughts, from varying angles. As the starter for transformative dialogue, texts become our companions on a journey. They may enable us to begin down a path less trodden; they may spark a moment of revelation; give resources to make sense of something; share a feeling, or question the way we are going. But most importantly our companion books give us the sense that we have a lot of visiting to do; and that we are not alone (Ahmed, 2017).

"... to best exploit that singular gift of study, to question what I see, then to question what I see after that, because the questions matter as much, perhaps more than, the answers"

~ Ta-Nehisi Coates

In a way, all knowledge results from questioning. This is especially true in the Hutchins seminar. Asking begins the conversation, and therefore is the fundamental medium by which we transform. Although educators always extol the virtues of creativity and insight in learners, even in the university classroom, questions have tended to come from the teacher. But even at their most inspiring, teachers' questions guide students' thinking along some predetermined path. They are designed to elicit correct answers, or at least answers within a certain mode of thinking. And, of course, whoever asks the questions holds the power. French philosopher Michel Foucault (1982) was acutely aware of this problem in formal education; he noted that those in power can severely limit the bounds of knowledge.

The genuine questioning of a Hutchins seminar forges new paths and challenges assumptions, including the basic frameworks of reality. Such students can then approach any content and find a new way to consider or investigate it (including the habits of mind of creativity, innovation, and critique). In Hutchins, the goal is to teach students how to articulate their own sincere and genuine questions—and while they're at it, to question everything around them. This is always a challenge at first. In thirteen years of formal education, many students have never been asked before what they are genuinely interested in. When they are assigned to post, or share their genuine questions, or when an essay is due and there is no prompt, students sometimes feel as though it's a trap. They want to be told what to write about; want to know how to please me 'the teacher' and get their A. But here again, the cognitive science research supports what we have known for decades in Hutchins. When it comes to questioning that fuels learning, sincere wonder is always best. In one research study, scientists recorded and catalogued students' questioning behaviors as they completed a difficult problem-solving task. The questions that the students came up with *on their own* were much more likely to lead to further inquiry than the questions the researchers or others asked them. They noted, "The critical factor was that what the [students] said and did came from themselves, as a personal question.... Even if someone else originally asked a question, it only became a genuine question for the students when they asked it themselves" (Cifone, 2013, p. 52). Margaret Mead reportedly noticed the same in her students –what they remembered over time was never what she had remarked or asked throughout the class, but rather what they themselves had asked or said.

My students' own questions reveal to me not just what they understood from the particular text or experience, but also many facets of their developing learning process: things they want to find out about, their partially developed ideas, their attempts to find out what works, and—ultimately—their personal discourse with themselves. They expose their biases—and mine—and help me see what's being taken for granted and what might be possible.

"Opinions appear like rescue ships on the horizon,
a promise of terra firma, the known"

~ Susan Griffin

If our own strong opinions can limit the scope of our knowledge, we must learn to challenge such emotionally ensconced feelings and thoughts. In the realm of cognitive science, it is well documented that emotion makes us attached and inflexible. Indeed, once we have an opinion, we want to hold it, and will look for data to reinforce and confirm those existing beliefs. Known as the confirmation bias, humans will go to great lengths to interpret new information in a manner that keeps their prior conclusions intact.

Like other brain shortcuts, the confirmation bias can be explained by the immense mental energy required to evaluate complicated evidence. To stave off overwhelm our brains search for, favor, interpret, and recall information in a way that confirms their preexisting beliefs. Also, the confirmation bias minimizes cognitive dissonance, that uncomfortable feeling of stress that we humans experience when data contradicts our beliefs. Strong, emotionally motivated opinions activate centers of the brain which are separate from and anathema to the critical thinking prefrontal cortex (e.g., Westen et al., 2006).

Cognitive dissonance has ramifications in the cultural realm as well. Our efficiency-based society tells us that those without strong and immediate opinions are not only considered unintellectual, they are considered flaccid thinkers. Changing your mind, being unsure, waiting for information to crystalize and mature is tantamount to being morally suspect. But instantaneous emotional opinions may provide a false sense of strength. In the Sufi and Buddhist traditions, inquiry must begin with an open-ended attitude: the experience of not-knowing. If we take the position that we know already, then no inquiry is possible. The moment we fully recognize that we don't know, inquiry may proceed. Not knowing, even if uncomfortable, is the starting point to learning (Almaas, 2002).

Suspending opinions and the comfort of knowing is also central to the best seminars. If we already know what we believe, think, know, the conversation may as well be scripted. To understand our contexts and biases means to wait and give them a chance to surface. It is risky for the teacher to not have a prepared lecture or even a set of questions for the students to respond to, it is also risky to let things unfold - to not control how we think and feel; to have no idea what is going to happen. But it is also more fruitful. Knowledge that emerges collaboratively in a free space can take learners to much deeper understanding. Our minds can build insights together, with thoughts not being owned by any one member of the group, but co-created in a dynamic stream of meaning-making. Sometimes during a Hutchins seminar, it feels as if all of the individual minds become blurred, with insights flying out of us - in a fast paced flurry of ideas! I try to write down my own thoughts, the shared insights as they are happening, and it is extremely hard to catalogue. It is an experience cannot be scripted, must be authentic and energized and active.

On the neurological level, this occurs in our mirror neurons - highly specialized brain cells that fire when we share actions with others. If someone touches my arm, neurons in the somatosensory cortex of the brain fire. But a subset of these neurons (mirror neurons) also fire when I watch someone else being touched. If you anesthetize or remove my arm, and then I watch you being touched, I will literally feel it in my numbed hand. In essence, mirror neurons allow us to adopt another's point of view and gain from their experience. They have been credited with many of the rapid cognitive advances of our species, especially the speed with which children can watch and learn complex skills in just one step (Ramachandran, 2009). For conversational collaborators in the Hutchins seminar, mirror neurons dissolve the barrier between participants, allowing minds to openly share and collaborate - becoming what poet John Keats described as "a thoroughfare for all thoughts."

"... I am a child of the age, a child of nonbelief, and doubt till now and even (I know it) until my coffin closes. What terrible torments this thirst to believe has cost me and still costs me, becoming stronger in my soul, the more there is in me of contrary reasonings. And yet sometimes God sends me moments in which I am utterly at peace"

~ Fyodor Dostoevsky

When Russian novelist and activist Fyodor Dostoevsky was sentenced to execution for his political views, he received many letters from family and friends, praying for his soul. He made the strangest statement in a letter to the wife of a fellow political exile who had given him a copy of the gospels. He basically said he can't believe in God no matter how much he wants to, but in the next breath, mentioned how God sends him moments of utter peace. This statement stands out to me as an emblem of contentment with uncertainty and not knowing; not just to wait and suspend opinions, but to sit with discrepancies and even complete contradictions! It is perhaps the trickiest thing we can ask of ourselves in seminar. We might not believe and then in our non-belief something might bubble up that completely contradicts what we just thought or said. If we can simply be ok with mucking around with ideas and possibilities; if we don't decide yet (or ever) what we know or believe or understand, we can reach a place of genuine inquiry. Our smoothing brains fight us tooth and nail on this one. In one study of ambiguous information, brain scans revealed activation in the amygdala and orbitofrontal cortex, two areas of the brain that are heavily involved in fear reactions. Anxiety and fear rise, while the ventral striatum (which helps respond to rewards) simply stops functioning (e.g., Hsu et al., 2005). But deep intellectual growth requires challenging fixed emotional and action patterns.

Over the past 50 years, the Hutchins School of Liberal Studies has been a space of unconventional and authentic learning. It is the place where I have been so fortunate to become a thinker and learner, while at the same time being a teacher and facilitator. On the world stage, it is an immense privilege that we get to spend our days in seminar –considering books and questions and ideas. Yes, at times the seminar is laborious, but at times it is filled with a free flowing and almost inexplicable magic. What I believe makes it so are the practices of revisiting, questioning everything (especially ourselves) and taking our genuine questions seriously; noticing, embracing, and remaining open to complexity; being wary of strong opinions. To participate in a seminar, to facilitate a seminar (and, it turns out, to live a meaningful life) is to fight against the shortcuts, efficiency and smoothness our minds and brains and social hierarchies want, and to hold out for the more complicated openness required to let ourselves be transformed.

References

Ahmed, Sara. 2017. *Living a Feminist Life*. Duke University Press.

Almaas, A. H. 2002. *Spacecruiser Inquiry: True guidance for the inner journey*. Shambala Publications.

Camus, Albert. 1942. *The Stranger*. Vintage.

Cifone, Maria Vittoria. 2013. Questioning and Learning: How do we recognize children's questions? *Curriculum and Teaching Dialogue, 15:* 1&2, 41–55.

Coates, Ta-Nehisi. 2015. *Between the World and Me*. Random House.

Dostoevsky, Fyodor. 2002. *The Brothers Karamazov*. R. Pevear & L. Volokonsky (trans.). Farrar, Straus & Giroux.

Foucault, Michel. 1982. The Subject and Power. Afterword to H. L. Dreyfus & P. Rabinow, *Michel Foucault: Beyond structuralism and hermeneutics*. Harvester.

Freire, Paolo. 1970. *Pedagogy of the Oppressed*. Seabury.

Griffin, Susan. 1993. *A Chorus of Stones: The private life of war*. Anchor.

Hsu, M., Bhatt, M., Adolpis, R., Tranel, D., & Camerer, C. 2005. Neural Systems Responding to Degrees of Uncertainty in Human Decision-Making. *Science, 310:* 5754, 1680-1683.

Nabokov, Vladimir. 2002. *Lectures on Literature*. Mariner Books.

Piaget, Jean. 1973. *Main Trends in Psychology*. Allen and Unwin.

Ramachandran, Vilayanur. 2009. *The neurons that shaped civilization* [Video file: Ted.com].

Smith, Zadie. 2009. *Changing My Mind: Occasional Essays*. Penguin.

Westen, D., Blagov, P.S., Harenski, K., Kilts, C., & Hamann, S. 2006. Neural bases of motivated reasoning: An fMRI study of emotional constraints on partisan political judgment in the 2004 U.S. presidential election. *Journal of Cognitive Neuroscience, 18*

CREATIVITY, THE ARCHIVE, AND ACTION

Janet Hess

"What is it that you like to do?
If you have twenty different responses,
surely nineteen of those responses could be somehow turned to
promoting the movement for social justice globally.
Do what you like, just save a little bit of your time for activism
and for social justice globally.
And that will keep this movement alive."

~Paul Farmer

Janet Berry Hess received her J.D. from the University of Iowa and her Ph.D. from Harvard University, and has taught at U.C. Santa Cruz, Northwestern University and the University of Cape Town, South Africa. She integrated art and creativity into the teaching of history and art history since joining the Hutchins faculty in 2002. Hess has published and lectured widely in the area of African post-liberation art and architecture and Native American culture, and is Project Director for the National Endowment for the Humanities Digital Advancement grant, "Mapping Indigenous American Cultures and Living Histories."

Arlette Farge states in *The Allure of the Archives* (2013) that "[a]n archive presupposes an archivist, a hand that collects and classifies." Scholars and students alike often imagine that received knowledge—in the form of texts and prestigious speakers—is indisputable. One of the shining virtues of the Hutchins School of Liberal Studies is that, in many cases, claims to objectivity have been challenged by "the claims of groups who have typically been disenfranchised by dominant regimes of truth." Those who are the margin of dominant discourse—the poor, people who are vulnerable due to their "race," those discriminated against due to gender bias, ableism, ageism, appearance, or non-academic belief systems—have challenged the academic standards and scholarly archives that marginalize them. This is one of the hallmarks of Hutchins: that students and scholars alike push against what the philosopher Hans-Georg Gadamer (1975) describes as "the limits and possibilities of the archive as a site of knowledge production, an arbiter of truth, and a mechanism for shaping the narratives of history."

The committed nature of Hutchins instructors (each of whom have their own disciplinary backgrounds) can lead, at times, to redundancy or bias (although, as Gadamer suggests, bias is inevitable and even positive). The complex combination of liberal arts study and teacher preparation, the heavy reading (and teaching) loads, and the struggle to achieve and champion diversity (in many forms) invariably leads to challenges. Yet students consistently praise Hutchins for its seminar-based instruction and the close faculty-student interactions that are generally only found in graduate school; the interdisciplinary nature of the material, and the creative nature of Hutchins learning; the respect and dignity afforded to students by most; the fact that close reading, rather than testing, is valorized; and the building of a community in which most students feel safe, acquiring confidence and learning to speak respectfully and mindfully. The passion, care, and variety of instruction is also frequently praised, and the "extensive dialogue on readings that question authority" (from a Senior Synthesis survey 2018). Indeed, it is typical of the Hutchins School that we acknowledge our challenges—breaking through the "archival," or academic, narrative of perfection —because in doing so, we build one of the strongest programs in the country for taking students who have been served at various levels by an underfunded California state system, and teaching those students how to excel according to their own goals. Hutchins is the only seminar-based program of its kind that forms the basis for further training for future teachers. As many have said, the Hutchins School provides an Ivy League education at a public school price. I often tell students, "the only difference between learning here and at Harvard is how much you want it." And creative, compassionate, gifted students frequently rise to the occasion to inspire and astonish us.

An often-posed question – asked of a range of humanities majors – is, "what can graduates do with this degree?" Such a question perpetuates the recent pushback against humanities programs throughout the country in general. One of the hallmarks of the American higher education process is precisely its emphasis on the humanities. An AAC&U address in 2014 emphasized that it is precisely for its humanities strengths that many students from other countries attend schools in the U.S., because they know creativity and innovation is key to advancements in all fields. Creativity and collaboration has in many studies been revealed as essential to the success of corporate endeavors (see Landry, 2017). Many of our students graduate and continue to obtain teaching credentials and jobs in teaching, a noteworthy achievement in itself, but we also mentor students who continue to law school and the practice of law; entrepreneurial enterprises; and, after obtaining their Masters, jobs in social work, special education, and creative fields such as acting and performance art.

One of the most transformational aspects of Hutchins is that one learns as much from one's peers and colleagues as from the texts themselves. This mode of learning in community also serves to shatter the obsession with the academic archive, or canon. Teaching in close proximity to students and becoming familiar to some degree with their lives and concerns, faculty gain respect for students' gifts, insights, modes of intelligence and courage. In the face of the pressure and even trauma which increasingly accompanies student life at every college, the close relationship among faculty and students at Hutchins allows teachers to witness the strength, resilience, and capacity for reinvention students demonstrate. This, as well as the contributions made by many Hutchins faculty to the community and the willingness of many to share their achievements and insights in team-taught courses, is a unique feature of the program.

The Hutchins School has led me to a new appreciation for my own limitations alongside the gifts of my colleagues, a humility that I believe is healthy and appropriate in light of the political landscape we now face. Experiential, cultural, communal, and spiritual understandings can be a deep source of knowledge, and Hutchins often allows for these too. Interdisciplinarity and a willingness to share expertise with colleagues—and to air differences of perspective—provide many faculty and students with an intersectional awareness, respect and optimism that are rare and essential today. The spirit of inquiry that pervades the program, a skepticism about the absolute truth of the archive, an awareness of the motivation on the part of institutions and people in power to present false narratives, and a sense of empowerment about innovation and resistance, are all consequences of a process that pushes students to dig deeply and—at moments—valorize the educational process over the individual grade. I am proud of students in the moments when they break free of the focus on grading, proud when they grow beyond whatever previous level of understanding or perception they previously acquired, proud when they accept criticism humbly and employ it to produce greater work, proud when they venture into creative and therefore more risky territory to find their identity—to become their truest selves. I'm proud of students with physical or psychological challenges who struggle to achieve their best. Hutchins facilitates close conversation among students of greatly varying political and religious beliefs, and I am always proud when the students themselves—due to the seminar format and the community of Hutchins—create a safe environment for respectful navigation of these differences. Of those students whose achievements—and leading a healthy and meaningful life, particularly one chosen by the individual against outside pressure, is in itself an achievement in the current economic and political state—I learn about after graduation, I am immensely proud.

As a faculty member, I have found the Hutchins School transformative and positive in life and career. Having obtained a J.D. from the University of Iowa College of Law, an M.A. in non-western art history from Columbia University (African, African American, Oceanic, and Native American Art History were once combined!), and a Ph.D. from

Harvard (in the Art History of Africa and the Diaspora), I arrived at the Hutchins School of Liberal Studies well indoctrinated into the intense competitiveness and publish or perish mentality (along with my own set of challenging life experiences). With this background, I was initially confused by the collegiality and genuine warmth freely offered by Anthony Mountain, Richard Zimmer, Debora Hammond, Eric McGuckin, Wendy Ostroff, and Mutombo M'Panya, and later, Stephanie Dyer and Ianthe Brautigan, among others. I was overwhelmed with the notion of interdisciplinarity in teaching (what I imagined as interdisciplinarity was vastly larger at Hutchins, stretching from science to grammar), the teaching load, and what at first seemed a lack of focus on research (later belied by the great research accomplishments demonstrated by other colleagues). I wondered if the institution could accommodate my interests or if I could fulfill its expectations. Still, I was charmed and engaged by the students from the first moment.

What occurred slowly and gradually over the years was a shedding of the competitiveness, individual focus, and single-track research focus that graduate school had given me, and the acquisition of a new knowledge of the joy of collaboration and creativity. Hutchins taught me the innovative modes of research and community service Hutchins fosters, the value of having one's perceptions tested and one's deeply held values and interests affirmed—even interests abandoned long ago. Hutchins is astonishing in its professional patience with faculty and student alike who have the authentic desire to create and grow beyond limiting experiences that they bring to the program, and in some faculty's humility about their achievements both academically and within the community at large (Wendy Ostroff and Francisco Vazquez come to mind in these realms, respectively). In sum, the Hutchins experience has been humbling and enlightening. These two qualities, it seems to me, are precisely what faculty should model to their students.

An unexpected benefit of the Hutchins School of Liberal Studies has been its accommodation and encouragement of experiential knowledge and beliefs. This experiential knowledge in my case relates to my legal career; relatively useless at other institutions, I have found it a vital bridge at Hutchins in teaching such subjects as "African American Culture" and "Native American Art." What seemed tangential before emerged as an essential component of instruction related to marginalized voices. Thus, teaching from original Supreme Court decisions such as *Dred Scott v. Sanford*, *Plessy v. Ferguson*, and *Brown v. Board of Education* (in "African American Culture") and cases such as *Johnson v. M'Intosh* and *U.S. v. Kagama* (in "Native American Art") became a way of embedding historical observations in mechanisms and institutions of power. In sharing the words of Justice William Brennan—whose dissent in the United States Supreme Court of *McKlesky v. Kemp* allowing a racially biased death penalty system to proceed was so artful and shattering that it shaped the course of my life—I was able to link my work and life experience to my teaching in a way that is highly impactful. As Brennan stated,

> Those whom we would banish from society or from the human community itself often speak in too faint a voice to be heard above society's demand for punishment. It is the particular role of courts to hear these voices, for the Constitution declares that the majoritarian chorus may not alone dictate the conditions of social life... It is tempting to pretend that minorities on death row share a fate in no way connected to our own, that our treatment of them sounds no echoes beyond the chambers in which they die. Such an illusion is ultimately corrosive, for the reverberations of injustice are not so easily confined... and the way in which we choose those who will die reveals the depth of moral commitment among the living.

This case, so deeply personal to me (I was a research assistant for David Baldus, the attorney behind the study at question in *McKlesky*), and my opportunity to teach about Japanese American internment during World War II (my son's father was born in an internment camp) enriched and expanded my investment in teaching, because it brought personal investment into my scholarship (as it does so often for students) and articulates the core of my own value system. I had the opportunity to share those values in texts about historical figures inspirational to me, such as Paul Farmer and

Martin Luther King (*Mountains Beyond Mountains: The Quest of Dr. Paul Farmer, A Man Who Would Cure the World,* by Tracy Kidder; *Bearing the Cross: Martin Luther King Jr. and the Southern Christian Leadership Conference,* by David Garrow; and the film *King: From Montgomery to Memphis*) –and the Hutchins format allowed me to teach texts in full, rather than in abbreviated form. The expansive and interdisciplinary nature of Hutchins also allowed me to investigate the intersection of gender with all of these issues: my gender studies-oriented class, innocuously entitled "Barbies," enriched and strengthened through collaboration with Don Romesburg, the brilliant creator of the Queer Studies minor who shared our modest but lovely Rachel Carson Hall, was enriching for many on a personal level that traditional class sizes (and standard classrooms) could not permit.

Studies have shown that creativity enhances *all* aspects of learning by employing and rewiring regions of the brain, and has a wide range of health benefits, which in turn benefit personal growth (see Gute, 2015 and Nunez, 2016). In one of my favorite courses, "Unblocking Creativity," students have demonstrated over many years that releasing obstacles to their own dreams can facilitate lives of joy and deep fulfillment. Few colleges, and no art history departments, would have facilitated the teaching of such an unusual and cross-disciplinary course. Indeed, Hutchins allowed me to integrate art making with art history at a level pursued at only a few specialized institutions of learning in this country. In many cases, students astonish me with their progress in overcoming obstacles to realizing their life goals, their "creative dreams," and their progress in becoming comfortable with the notion that they *are* creative, and can visualize and move forward through small movements toward what they can contribute to the world. Visiting university and local art galleries has been an integral aspect to most of my classes, and Hutchins has allowed unfettered freedom to faculty in this regard.

The Hutchins School also shifted the focus of my scholarship. This shift led me to become involved in the development of the HUB (formerly the Multicultural Center), and Humanidad (the non-profit educational and counseling agency located in Santa Rosa). Students in my classes and other faculty's classes have engaged in community service for such organizations as Verity (the domestic violence shelter), The Living Room (an organization that helps house homeless women and their children), and Habitat for Humanity (the Carter Foundation's home-building initiative for low income individuals), as well as efforts toward sustainability and safeguarding the environment. The focus on social justice action embedded within Hutchins culture, its embrace of multicultural interdisciplinarity, and its acceptance of creativity led me to shift my focus to Indigenous Studies, and to embrace my dream of creating a digital map of Indigenous America to raise awareness of the presence of its cultures, for which I received a National Endowment for the Humanities Digital Advancement grant. This grant was deeply personal to me, springing as it did not only from friendships with elders, but as well from my family's two centuries-long history in Oklahoma among the Osage and Pawnee peoples in Oklahoma. This personal shift reflects another virtue of Hutchins: its strong appreciation for the fact that "the personal is political." It is doubtful whether the confines of discipline, and the "self-first, student-last" focus of many research institutions, would have led me to the fulfillment of this family legacy and dream.

In shattering the seeming perfection of the archive—that glossed-over, Eurocentric, canonical model of knowledge that dominates many disciplines and institutions of learning—we at Hutchins make mistakes. The crushing, unpaid teaching load faculty willingly took on until recent years had a price; yet without that load, collegiality has diminished. Hutchins faculty have to work hard and should work harder to support diversity and create space for conservative as well as liberal perspectives and the validity of a wide range of religious (Christian, African, diasporic, and Native American) views. Hutchins should advocate more strongly for an increased counselor-to-student ratio in campus counseling, for improved facilities, for the enforcement of Title IX, and for the integration of teacher-track goals with seminar subjects.

From my own disciplinary viewpoint, Hutchins would do well to integrate more creativity and more digital resources into its curriculum. We need to work harder to push back against the notion that social media and Google searches constitute "research" (these platforms can become their own dead-eyed "archive"). We can work harder to hold our students to a high level of academic achievement (in part by assigning less reading, which usually goes unfinished), as well as hold students to a standard of civic engagement and responsibility (the students I polled in 2018 received all of their news from Facebook, and we can do better in encouraging them to delve deeper). We need to continue to support students of low income, single parents, students of color, and those who otherwise have family or personal situations disrupting their academic careers. Above all, we need to underscore for future teachers in particular that social justice, community involvement, and concern for those "whom we would banish from society or from the human community itself... [who] often speak in too faint a voice to be heard" (Brennan, in *McKlesky*) is an urgent and pressing need. Now more than at any other time, Hutchins faculty and administrators need to fight to keep the program alive. Due to cutbacks in humanities courses, the program itself is in danger. For students and faculty who may not remember the faculty mentioned in this book: it is the creativity, innovation and spirit of inquiry this school encourages in its small seminars that can fight the allure of received, pre-processed, or propagandistic information, as well as the individualism and competitiveness that characterize our culture today.

Should the Hutchins program be eliminated in the future, I hope you will fight to revive some version of its spirit in your life. Fight to think for yourselves, fight to make a path for your life that is chosen by you, fight to hold on to your values and morals in the face of authority. No matter what others have told you, you have the right to create and choose your own path, one that gives you joy and meaning, compassion for others, and a sense of openness to the world. Indeed, a sense of compassion for others and a concern for the wider world is the best solution for students who feel hopeless, heartbroken, or unable to find a place in the world. You are worthy and you matter. Suffering may be inevitable, but on a broad social level you have the capacity, even the responsibility, to assist in social change—and in doing so, you may find yourself a part of a community that lessens the burden of self. Such a community can save us in the most dire of circumstances. The current social and political climate, and above all the challenges of climate change, call for our awareness, creativity and engagement, and resistance to the dangerously uncreative narrative of the archive. As Stephane Hessel, a member of the French Resistance in World War II, stated in *Time For Outrage: Indignez-vous!*,

> There are unbearable things all around us. You have to look for them; search carefully. Open your eyes and you will see... This is what I tell young people: If you spend a little time searching, you will find your reasons to engage. The worst attitude is indifference... You must engage—your humanity depends on it.

References

Farge, Arlette. 2013. *The Allure of the Archives*. Yale University Press.

Gadamer, Hans-Georg. 2011 [1975]. *Truth and Method*. Continuum International Publishing Group.

Garrow, David. 1999. *Bearing the Cross: Martin Luther King Jr. and the Southern Christian Leadership Conference*. HarperCollins.

Gute, Deanne and Gary. 2015. *How Creativity Works in the Brain*. Santa Fe Institute Working Group. National Endowment for the Arts.

Hessel, Stéphane. 2011. *Time for Outrage: Indignez-Vous!*. Hachette.

Kidder, Tracy. 2003. *Mountains Beyond Mountains: The Quest of Dr. Paul Farmer, a Man Who Would Cure the World*. Random House.

Landry, Lauren. 2017. "The Importance of Creativity in Business." Northeastern University Graduate Programs. Northeastern.edu. November 9.

Nunez, Kirsten. 2016. "5 Proven Ways Creativity is Good for Your Health." *Verily*, January 14.

A Dialogue on Hutchins with Margaret Anderson

Benjamin Frymer

Benjamin Frymer joined the Hutchins faculty in 2005, having previously taught at Columbia University's Teachers College, UCLA, and Trinity College. He earned his PhD in Sociology from UCLA and conducted post-doctoral research in Education at Columbia's Teachers College. He has helped organize and facilitate numerous on campus dialogues with the Hutchins Dialogue Center and was co-organizer, with Margaret Anderson, of the Modern Media Dialogue Series at Sonoma State University. He writes in the areas of education, self and society, media, and cultural studies focusing on the study of film education, contemporary alienation, violence, and ideology.

Margaret Anderson graduated from Hutchins in 1994, and returned in 1996 as a lecturer in the program, where she has taught for the past 23 years. Margaret received her Masters in Liberal Arts at St. John's College in Santa Fe, which uses the seminar format in all of its classes. Margaret has spent most of her adult life either participating in or facilitating small group seminars. In addition to her work as a lecturer, Margaret is the director of the Hutchins Dialogue Center at Sonoma State, designing and coordinating programs using dialogue to explore and reflect upon difficult topics and issues such as race, class, gender, sexuality, equity, etc. Margaret has facilitated discussions in a variety of settings, including prisons, schools, and businesses, and she has engaged in numerous community and inter-generational dialogues.

Ben: Do you want to talk about why you chose to go to Hutchins as a student, and what your experience was as a student versus now as an instructor? What was it back then that attracted you to Hutchins?

Margaret: The question should be what attracted my father to Hutchins, because I wasn't attracted to formal education, period. Anyway, my father was a teacher and thought a lot about education; he inspired me to attend Hutchins. He felt that the cultural and political changes that were happening around the country would liberalize education and this could positively affect the whole country. He was part of what he and others viewed as a revolution in education, emphasizing active student participation in class with seminar based discussions. Radicals at the time thought that empowering students with critical thinking tools would create independent thinkers genuinely engaged with the world in a way that would shake up the status quo and lead to a more equitable and democratic country. I remember clearly how he juxtaposed his radicalism with the radicalism of my Uncle Rob, who spent time in prison rather than fight in the Vietnam War and who distrusted the system so much that he saw working within it as nothing more than giving in. So I am a product of the experimental education that was so exciting at that time. Like my father, I found formal, lecture-based education and the dead zones of schooling hard to conform to.

Somehow, I prioritized learning that felt honest and alive and I developed a big taste for reading, watching movies, and interacting with and observing people. My father ran a group home for juvenile offenders where a constant exchange of ideas, outrageous humor, and insights coexisted with deeply uncomfortable truths that exposed life in ways that fully captured my attention. This was the place I developed my taste for dialogue. This was one of the best classrooms in my upbringing. To this day, I love that raw, "real talk" experience, even though it often included a high dose of pain and suffering. I couldn't get enough of it.

I miss that belief that we were heading toward something better as a country or species. Many people around me were just starting to talk about the cultural revolution that was taking place and there was a palpable excitement about changing the world through liberal studies and assessments. It was all about reading, discussion and collaboration, and very linked to the 1960s and 70s encounter group model based on relationships, and rigorously addressing sexism, racism, class issues and all those things. My dad thought it was critical to get a good education and Hutchins was one of the few colleges in existence at the time that really fit these ideals. He really thought the country was heading in a fundamentally different direction. Maybe it did. I expected much more than what I see today.

Ben: Me too...so did you eventually go to Hutchins for any career reason?

Margaret: At the time my dad convinced me, "You're so good with kids. Why don't you become a teacher? Get a liberal studies degree though and then maybe consider teaching." And, then came Hutchins, the love of my life. I had no idea learning and academia could be so alive and exciting. It is where all the light bulbs came on. Sitting in a circle with incredible books. Watching films, exploring topics and quenching a thirst I had deep inside.

Ben: You started on the teacher track [which included requirements for admission to credential programs]?

Margaret: Yes, initially, but I stopped as soon as I understood I could be in Track I and do much more exploring beyond a discipline. I had a desire to learn more, more, more, and I also loved film so I took a film minor. I did not believe that I would be a good student because my previous schooling lacked the rigor that I thought everyone else had applied to their studies. I was simultaneously working in group homes with teenage girls off and on as a counselor, and that still seemed like a career path of sorts. I miss that work and am probably most suited to work with "at-risk" kids. They capture my undivided attention and heart, corny as it sounds.

Ben: What was your experience with lower division?

Margaret: I was 25. I was a re-entry student. They considered that re-entry.

To me it was nirvana. It really was. I had Jeannine in LIBS 101. I had to develop mental muscles to meet the these new reading, writing and thinking challenges – and it took a new desire matched with discipline to make it. Jeannine used some semi-conventional "high standards," but incorporated them within an unconventional Hutchins approach. I could tell she thought I was probably like a diamond in the rough or something – not just me in particular, but all students were like that to her. I agree with this attitude. She was going to be patient but she definitely did not allow superficial reading or thinking; she expected more. Jeannine wasn't a cheerleader, but she was exactly what I needed at the time. She had an intellectual honesty and brought rigor to a subject.

However, the one thing I remember from Jeannine that was so pivotal in my life in 101 is what she said at the midterm evaluation, "You know what? You are a natural facilitator. I notice you draw out other people's thinking, and you respond very well and you interact very well."

Ben: So students were able to take the rigorous workload?

Margaret: Yeah, students seemed to be more excited when I was a freshman to tell you the truth, but I'm not sure if that is clouded by my own perceptions at the time. We'll see when we all get together at the Hutchins Anniversary gathering this September and have a chance to reflect with students from different decades. Freshmen can be on fire intellectually and of course that's when it's a real treat for teachers too.

Ben: Yes freshmen absolutely can be intellectuals.

Margaret: When it's just a few students raring to go, something good happens. If there aren't enough students like that, then I think some students resent those working hard in a way. But, with most Hutchins faculty there's a trust that rigor and discipline could emerge at any time and to keep the faith even when the quality does not look so promising.

Ben: I have found that the first semester freshman are typically the best students. Very open and willing.

Margaret: Willing but not always able to sustain it at times and they regress a bit. It seems harder for them to buy in second semester when some decide to experiment with seeing how little they can do, in terms of skimming through texts, writing the obvious and general in response papers, and beginning to challenge the Hutchins honor system; anyway, I see a pattern. But, back to that first semester openness – that kindergarten of the adult world openness! – to me, it's an amazing state of wonder. They're excited and they finally have bigger words, concepts, and understanding. They are eager for more context and want to go beyond test taking results. Of course some students struggle with shyness, introversion or lack of social confidence in the first semester and awaken toward the end of the second semester. There are so many ways to arrive at motivation in our program.

Ben: They don't quite know what we're doing at first.

Margaret: I agree.

Ben: When students read Allegory of the Cave you can see the thinking, but still there's not necessarily a direction to it because we don't contextualize it or "teach it". It's exploratory, wide open to them.

Margaret: It is wide open.

Ben: We connect it to the film, *The Matrix*, maybe.

Margaret: It's interesting when a group truly gains the discipline and attitude, and that whole Dweck "not there yet" thinking is allowed, and students support and help each other. There's a trust students will intellectually catch, I think. Of course, in Hutchins it's not about the content. It's about wrestling with ideas and seeing connections with texts from different centuries, cultures and perspectives, at least trying. This is when real critical thinking begins and articulation and depth take hold.

That transformation is key and I don't think I've ever worked a semester where I haven't seen a majority of students – if not all – change substantially, which I don't think is true in a traditional lecture-based school, where students can become passive.

Ben: When you were a student, were the students who were taking the reading and the seminars seriously a little bit marginal because they were not playing, as one of our colleagues would say, not playing the game of school?

Margaret: Mm-hmm (affirmative).

Ben: There were enough of those students that it became a dynamic where the learning was taken seriously?

Margaret: Yeah, although I think if you spend time in Hutchins as a student and a teacher you will always see times where people are not doing real reading. Everybody knows it's happening, but again, there's that honor system aspect which is so essential and often needs to be challenged. I think there's a lot more to it we all don't fully grasp as faculty and students.

Ben: Like not doing the reading? And as a student?

Margaret: My experience as a student is I don't remember any authoritarian behavior. I just don't remember any of that. I don't remember people scrutinizing each step and telling us, "You need to do this much at this time." I don't even remember font size. I don't remember any of that and I'm not saying those things aren't important, but I just don't remember those things being first priorities. I do remember, though, reading "Attacking Faulty Reasoning" in 101, so we looked at critical thinking and reasoning and fallacies. I do remember getting MLA and looking through grammar and structure but, again, if those were the highest priorities of Hutchins I would have laughed, because I would never have been very good at them, at first. I would have known all the answers to different fallacies and would have forgotten them two weeks later. That's just the way my mind is and the same with grammar and structure. I forget them over and over. Even as a teacher I look them up over, and over and over again.

Ben: They change.

Margaret: Yes, and I don't remember one teacher in Hutchins who didn't have incredible patience in terms of allowing and looking for different kinds of intelligences.

Ben: What exactly was the goal or what did the students think the goal of the seminar was? If it wasn't "you need to understand this idea, that idea in the book," but rather "tell me what it's about"...

Margaret: Yeah, I think we took to it – like a fish to water, I think the attraction to dialogue is hard wired in humans. I don't know if it was these incredible texts or being exposed to important questions, topics and themes? Really, in seminar it often felt like a birthday or being on a holiday, all these incredible books were being given to us. As a teacher I have heard so many students in LIBS 402 Senior Synthesis say how amazed they were that their peers and teachers really wanted to hear what they thought – in response papers, and assessments and evaluations; graduating seniors constantly addressed this point. They would conjure up something you said from two months ago to ask your opinion, to ask if you've changed your mind, really caring and interested in each other's ideas and thoughts. If you think about this, it's just amazing. It's also kind of sad that they are adults who have never experienced this in formal education.

Ben: Even with their own family or friends.

Margaret: Yeah, even at St. John's where we're reading great books, literally Great Books, and even though there was a damn good faculty and extraordinary student learning, there was still a lot of that – stick to understanding the text. Your own personal connections are not relevant. I like a good mix of strong focus on text and our own connections and meaning making.

Ben: Mastery of material was the goal at St. John's?

Margaret: Not exactly mastery, but the goal was to understand the texts. We also developed a huge respect for our peers and tutors which is what all faculty called themselves at St. John's. We did have to call each other by our last names to keep it formal, so there was definitely a different approach that was important in my development. In fact, the focus on a very close reading of texts and that kind of labor was an incredible skill to have, and the teachers and students at St. John's were just as passionate and alive as those at Hutchins, but there was also a type of elitism I detected, even though it was a weird one, because they believed any common person could join the liberal education club. But it was definitely, I think, a little bit of a club. I'd like to have a conversation about St. John's and its philosophy another time, and its connections with Mortimer Adler, Robert Hutchins, Stringfellow Barr, Scott Buchanan and all those incredible philosopher-educators, but I think that will get me even further off track – maybe that's the track I should be on?! Anyway, I just feel like anyone could join our Hutchins club. It is this openness that makes us unique, I think.

Ben: And what would it mean to have answers for, or mastery of any of these texts anyway?

Margaret: What answers? You know? There's no doubt about the better questions and answers, but academia's over reliance on expertise often goes way too far. It's very anti-Socrates. Hutchins tries to wean us off that way of viewing knowledge – we are so much more about following that pedagogical method Socrates was up to. Admitting what we don't know and searching for truth, or at least more understanding.

Ben: Back to your time as a student.

Margaret: In LIBS 102 I had an unusual split course – an 8/4 unit distribution, as faculty were experimenting that semester. So I had something called "The American Experience" for four units and eight units with Susan Barnes in my seminar section "Exploring Self." How cool to have a Jungian Analyst as my teacher. Susan's art from her dreams hung on the walls – the best environment for me to be exploring the self; Hamlet, Wizard of EarthSea by Ursula Le Guin...

Ben: That was four units built into 102?

Margaret: A separate teacher taught that, so we had separate sections of people teaching American Experience. I think Les Adler and Lou Miller? I remember learning much more about Catholicism and Protestantism and about how that played out in the United States and around the world. I remember reading Horatio Alger's *Ragged Dick*. I remember reading *Benjamin Franklin's Autobiography*. I remember concepts like the City on the Hill and all those things; I really did think we were able to explore the books and not look just for answers and yet have a much clearer context.

Ben: But it wasn't a classics curriculum.

Margaret: No, but there were more classics than we are using today. I think that's because they were at a crossroads where I think they were still holding on to more of the Adler, Meiklejohn, Hutchins tradition. They were from different generations perhaps, so they were still going with the idea that the canon was important. And, some of those classics are still being used. Thankfully, we improve and become more inclusive and progressive with each new faculty's perspectives, knowledge and choice of texts. Thank you Mercy, Ianthe, and Justine! I think Warren Olsen was looking at Alexander Meiklejohn for a great deal of his curriculum model to start with; again this will be fun to explore in September at our 50th Anniversary Celebration.

Ben: It was basically a common, lower division curriculum and upper division was organized how? Core areas...

Margaret: I don't know. What I always remember is the first two years. Whenever I looked at any of these different programs, whether it's Meiklejohn, or Hutchins, or Adler, any of those, even St. John's, I don't fully know the difference in their approaches and emphasis. It seems like they were influencing and shaping one another. St. John's, Shimer, Evergreen – we should have a history of all these different liberal arts colleges, I don't know how they distinguish between lower division and upper division. I imagine it would be more focused on content and teachers having a stronger role in leading discussions more deliberately?

Ben: In Hutchins we have upper division specialization – Cores A, B, C, and D, which are connected to general education, but under the new CalState system there may be increasing pressure to assess content learning in these areas and not, say, an interdisciplinary learning trajectory or something like metacognition.

Margaret: Yeah, because I think, again, the other thing about Hutchins is our theme-based and question-based curriculum.

Ben: Do you remember your own views about your role as a student and as a future teacher changing, in terms of Jeannine telling you that you're a natural facilitator, or as you became interested in dialogue?

Margaret: Yeah.

Ben: You wrote your senior project on dialogue.

Margaret: Which was just the most average research paper. It was a typical example of how not traditionally academic Hutchins was. It wasn't bad. I learned a lot exploring the topic but it was mediocre at best in conventional academic terms. Most of us Hutchins students didn't sound like traditional academics nor would we necessarily fare well competitively.

Again, traditional standards and measurements were not driving us. I certainly looked at different texts and sources from around the world in my research; I conducted interviews, and I met Dennis Gray who ended up teaching me in his Socratic Seminars training. He was a student of Mortimer Adler and a collaborator with Paideia Proposal Educational Model. Also, I went to his workshops and got certified, so all those things came out of my senior research paper and project. Needless to say this became my career and passion. Yay meaningful senior synthesis!

Ben: But you also became interested in different philosophies of dialogue.

Margaret: Yeah, I was. I am.

Ben: People like Martin Buber.

Margaret: Martin Buber, absolutely, and again all the outcomes of liberal education like the Paideia Program I mentioned.

Also, I found out about Junior Great Books, Tribes – all these programs doing really interesting seminar-based, interdisciplinary curriculum in elementary, middle and high schools.

Ben: Then it turned into Touchstones.

Margaret: Actually, the path for dialogue work and eventually being the director for the Touchstones California Program was first developed with two of my Hutchins peers, Kathy Hatcher England and Victoria Allen. We were interested in seminar process and kept saying, "Hey, there's still some problems in class where people aren't aware of extroversion, introversion or rigor, discipline or asking questions," and we're learning all this stuff from Dennis Gray. After training more with Dennis Gray, Victoria and Kathy and I got excited and started North Bay Socratic Seminars.

Ben: And what happened with that?

Margaret: Then I found out about Touchstones and started to work for them a little while I was teaching at Hutchins. Eventually I became the California Director of Touchstones. And I went to prisons to observe and be a guest of their conversation. It was Touchstones that used the saying, "Texts are Touchstones to get to our lives and each other."

Ben: Why were they using Touchstones? The texts are not for presenting ideas, but for understanding each other? But they selected particular texts to...

Margaret: To provoke.

Ben: When you came back to Hutchins to teach did you immediately start a dialogue center or did that come years later?

Margaret: That came literally as my father was dying. At the time I had many lunches, conversations and connections with

John Esterly, a Hutchins alumni, who's such a gentle, kind and unique thinker.

Ben: So, you say John Esterly was a Hutchins...

Margaret: He was a grad. He was a transfer student. A perfect example of that beautiful mix of sharp intellect with high doses of kindness and empathy – a great person to be around. Very giving.

Ben: When you went back to teach at Hutchins did you find that it was in a way too limiting? I was just thinking, you didn't go into the dialogue center work because you felt like your teaching wasn't enough or wasn't...

Margaret: I really thought it was a solution to campus problems and in other places where dialogue and quality intellectual activities were scarce. How interesting it is to have dialogue with international students and to do it with Osher Lifelong Learners? I rarely felt on campus what I experienced daily in the Hutchins world, and I was a little surprised Hutchins pedagogy hadn't spread more on our own campus. Of course, people like Les Adler, Buzz Kellogg and Francisco Vazquez have contributed greatly through the Hutchins Institute for Interdisciplinary Learning and, later, the Hutchins Institute for Public Policy. Through Les I got to go to Evergreen College and work with Jean McGregor at the Washington Center.

Ben: Moving to the present, there seems to be more of a... I don't know. There seems to be definitely, right now, tension between Hutchins and the university, and some incompatibility maybe between Hutchins and the CSU general education reform. Tensions to the extent maybe that people in Hutchins are wondering whether Hutchins can survive as an alternative, liberal education program, or any kind of alternative program. If, like you're saying about structure, if the requirements...

Margaret: Are the emphasis?

Ben: and assessment changes to a large extent, and even the
            number of students that the university is requiring us to
            have in a seminar, and the elimination of seminars in
            upper division Cores, can Hutchins maintain itself with
            any real integrity or is it just going to become another GE
            program?

Margaret: Yeah, I would say on a good day it looks like some of the
            qualities and characteristics of Hutchins are alive through
            dialogue. There is still genuine interaction with faculty,
            but not nearly enough quantity time. But I see so many
            fractures within our department because of what you
            mention – the University's disregard for what we do and
            how we do it – in terms of retention alone we've got such
            a high level in our department. Students stay and get
            support to make it through successfully.

            That's the danger as we know. When you're not even
            paying lecturers to actually do all the planning and
            professional development, the very important meeting
            time that's part of the lower division. I feel like it has
            really changed since 1996 when I first taught, and we've
            heard about all the transformations since Hutchins'
            inception. We know there are economic reasons. We
            know there are attitude changes.... There are also people
            coming with a different sense of what the job is. Back to
            what you're saying about the tensions between the
            university (and the CSU system as a whole) and the
            culture of Hutchins – it's that they want proof in this very
            narrow way. To me, you can't "celebrate diversity" this
            way. I think that was one of the arguments years ago –
            that you can't celebrate diversity if one size fits all in
            academia – the supposed center for higher learning.

Ben: We are in a way teaching to the test, the CSET [required
            for admission to credential programs] has been directing
            our curriculum.

Margaret: This semester I've seen that kind of fierce intelligence of examining culture with students big time especially in LIBS 302. After one semester they aren't asleep any longer; they're awake. There's that whole woke thing. They seem to be much more woke.

Ben: In a time where everybody... needs to wake up.

Margaret: Wake up, wake up, it reminds me of the *Control Room*. Remember when the producer says, "Hey, everybody wake up, wake up." He's talking about media and news stations.

Ben: Yeah, *Control Room* was one of the keys to our curriculum I think, ongoing.

Margaret: Right but even right now in our conversation there's some kind of authenticity or honesty being attempted; it's not like it's there every second, but it really is important I think with human beings. I keep thinking that all this false flattery and this power tripping of who's most important and who gets to talk and who's who – all that is killing us. It's killing our culture and academia often really feeds into that. Hutchins at its best doesn't feed into it.

Ben: Some of these problems with maintaining Hutchins pedagogy are real time pressures, real economic pressure or lack of money.

Margaret: God yeah, we see that dismantling happening over the last fifteen to twenty years I'd say.

Ben: Yeah, the old neoliberal shift, the university changing priorities. The idea that faculty are coming into the classroom as an expert is the institutional model.

Margaret: Exactly.

Ben: An institutional model that we've had for who knows how many decades or centuries now. And it's the one where we're expected to, like you said, impart some kind of special insight or information on the text that only we can have. And the students are expected to see us as these specially-trained, unusually knowledgeable and wise people.

Margaret: And I've got to tell you, being raised by my father, I never had that illusion. You know what I mean? Because he was Mr. Question Authority. So yeah, I'm with you.

Ben: Yes. It all depends on the reason you are together with other people during that time. Is it to learn a set body of information? Are you trying to learn the different parts of the Constitution and is that the goal of the time you're spending together? Or, do you trust that people can read it and learn it, and then your reason for being there is to actually share different perspectives, ideas and understandings?

Margaret: Exactly! But that's hard to articulate to other people. It can sound very abstract, hard to really imagine people developing the muscles and attitudes to hear each other and carry multiple lines of inquiry simultaneously – if you haven't experienced that, whether you're an expert or a novice, you don't get what the hell we're talking about. It creates a very different kind of a person.

But it really is an amazing... what is it, what is the word? It's not hope, trust, maybe more like an expectation that happens in its own time. You have to really believe in what you're doing. The long haul.

Ben: Right. And I think, you know, in terms of who our students are and seeing them for who they are, they are living and growing up... they have grown up in a society where almost nothing that's said is even meant to be truthful.

Margaret: I know, that's horrible.

Ben: When everything that is publicly stated on the media or by government officials is not even meant to be true, how do you even bring people together for a purpose of getting at different kinds of genuine understanding?

Margaret: No, I totally get it. Because if culture teaches us who we are and there's nothing carved out for that kind of integrity, most of us aren't experiencing or expecting it, then you just don't know how much better we could be. Yeah.

Ben: Even what we were saying about gender and relationships, with all the expectations that go into the relationships that seem to be full of these false conventions that come from wherever, media, or movies, or...

Margaret: With all that, I feel like it's weird how you can intellectually understand the complexity of these things and still be playing the games.

Ben: Mm-hmm (affirmative).Yeah.

So not only are we not in a reading culture, the culture can't, intentionally doesn't want to, identify quality or what's of value in reading. It's another thing that goes back to the situation our students are in. If you grow up in a culture like that, how do you recognize the value in what you're reading or what you're watching?

Margaret: I know, it's horrible. They/WE don't know.

Ben: Can you watch a great film or can you read *The Stranger*? Can you read *Crime and Punishment* and see... even see what's different about it?

Margaret: *Ways of Seeing*, John Berger?

Ben: Right; ways of seeing. Art.

Margaret: And it seems so clear once you start in...you get lost or drown. And it is accumulative, I think. And we didn't talk much about how to stay healthy as students and as teachers, we can get sick. And I think a lot of students do get sick with this big wake up call – Richard Rodriguez talks about being a border person in *Hunger of Memory*, and how after being formally educated he could really never go back to his family and be accepted and fit in the same way-because his culture had changed, his academic culture kind of distanced him from his own family. I remember my brothers and I becoming totally alienated from my Mom's parents for similar reasons based on class not race issues.

I remember one student in particular crying and leaving class after watching Control Room, because her brother was a vet. And somehow, in her four years, she has learned to hold onto all these different value systems. In four years, she can carry so much. A kind of brilliance I'd say, and yet, she has tensions with her family. I think they're probably good risks, but all these things can be a big can of worms, too, for students and faculty alike.

Ben: Exactly.

Margaret: Or, look at how much we don't know and let that be okay.

Dialogue to me is never really about teaching. It really isn't. It really is getting people to get into a certain state of mind. I think it's a kind of altered state. People know it when they're altered too. When they're sitting around the table and time goes out the window, and that doesn't happen every seminar, but people know that they're doing something unusual and meaningful.

Ben: Altered as individuals but also an alteration of the group, the group dynamic.

The Hutchins Hybrid/Online Degree Completion Program

Ardath Lee

Jack Wikse

Beth Warner

THE SOCIAL DIMENSION OF LEARNING

Ardath Lee

Ardath Lee joined the Hutchins faculty in 1989, after having served in the administration as Dean of Academic Programs and before that as a lecturer in the English Department. She writes that joining Hutchins felt like coming home because she had an interdisciplinary background, with a Ph.D. in English as well as Masters degrees in Humanities and Art History. Since retiring in 1999, Ardath's interests have included studying and teaching Qigong and working on climate issues through the Center for Climate Protection.

When she came up with the idea for the Degree Completion Program, the Hutchins faculty was entirely supportive and helped develop and critique the program in many ways, and many of them taught in the program from time to time. Modeled after the Hutchins integrated general education program, it consists of four ten-unit seminars: LIBS 380: Identity and Society; LIBS 382: Work and the Global Future; LIBS 381: Technology and the Environment; and LIBS 470: Senior Project. Students meet once a month on Saturdays, with weekly on-line assignments in between.

When I was first thinking about adapting the Hutchins program to a distance learning format, my first concern was figuring out how to insure that the social dimension of learning was prominent. For the most part, we are accustomed to learning in groups, and this includes such seemingly unimportant things as nodding to the person next to you, chatting at the break, rolling your eyes with someone else when the instructor makes some incomprehensible remark.

Even more important, given the philosophy of the Hutchins program, is the interchange of ideas around the seminar table. This carries the social dimension of learning to a different level, and makes learning an active process. It involves constantly formulating one's own ideas and then reformulating as other points of view are taken into account.

In a recent book, *The Case Against Education*, Bryan Caplan (2018) argues that most of what is "learned" in college is almost immediately forgotten. Those cases where what is learned is not forgotten involve learning by doing; he gives the example of social science students who retain what they learn about statistics because they have to keep using that knowledge. The seminar approach to learning seeks to develop lasting learning "muscles" by engaging students in actively discussing and debating ideas. When students wrestle with these ideas, they become internalized because the learning has been active rather than passive. It is another approach to "learning by doing."

For these reasons, we decided to keep an on-campus face-to-face dimension in our distance learning program. Students come to campus one Saturday each month for an all-day session. This limits enrollment to those who can attend the Saturday sessions, but we felt that the trade-off was worth it.

The Saturday sessions are comprised of a three-hour morning seminar, followed by an afternoon which might include a lecture and hands-on activities related to the course work. On two Saturdays over the course of a semester, students are required to give a speech to their classmates, without using power point or reading the speech. We want them to learn to think of their feet, to make eye contact with their audience—in short, to be prepared to speak to a city council or town hall meeting. This too is learning by doing.

A further dimension of building intellectual "muscle" involves a weekly on-line seminar in which students post a response to the week's readings, and then are required to respond to at least one other student's posting. As students get to know each other over the course of the semester, this fosters the social dimension of learning and involves the formulation and reformulation of ideas.

We are satisfied that the distance learning approach has been successfully adapted and remains true to the basic mission of the Hutchins program.

Practicing Public Discourse

Jack Wikse

In 2003 Jack Wikse came to the Hutchins School from Shimer College in the Chicago area, where he was Dean of Adult Education, and Chair of Social Sciences. Shimer's "great books" curriculum began when Robert Hutchins developed his early entrant program for the University of Chicago after WWII. As a political theorist (PhD, U.C. Berkeley), Jack is the author of *About Possession: the Self as Private Property* (1977). His other writings have explored dreams as social information, dialogue as meditative thought, and the ethics of globalization. *The Human Dream: Carving a History of Myth* (2019) presents photos and narratives of fifteen of his carvings and his reflections on myth and art and his journey carving stone. He has been the faculty coordinator for the Hutchins Saturday Degree Completion Program since 2010.

When I orient new students into the Hutchins Saturday Hybrid Degree Completion Program for working adults (DCP) I say it's not going to be like junior high school. Higher education dominantly continues to follow a pattern of learning in which a teacher imparts knowledge to students who remain largely a passive audience. Off to history, then to literature, then government. Memorize what is transmitted, and replicate it through examination. How much you can retain of content and method to recreate on demand is what matters. Students are structurally isolated from one another, still often in rows. Academic disciplines are also structurally isolated from one another. Inter-disciplinary approaches and trans-disciplinary questions are absent. Teaching history offers a multi-disciplinary framework of questions, but Americans seem to be one of the least historical peoples ever, and of course, history is about the past, not understood in its root meaning as "inquiry." In the lecture hall, engagement and participation is to anticipate being "called on." In on-line classes which are an increasing proportion of higher education, driven by IT not by faculty, this is not usually at risk for a student at all. This is an atomistic, competitive learning situation which enhances the privatization of consciousness. Students are anonymous to one another. Writing a paper is a privileged communication between student and teacher. Students are not teachers. Teachers are not learners. That's junior high school. We might better call this approach to learning "training."

In the DCP, adult students returning to college to complete their BA Degree in Liberal Studies have mostly experienced this model in prior education, and in their work lives. It is based on largely unexamined dualistic assumptions regarding individualism and dissociation as cultural givens. It mainly ignores the cooperative, collaborative, social dimension of learning, or rejects it as "cheating." There are occasional team exercises, but this also reinforces the characteristic agonistic character of contemporary culture.

Alternatively, a dialogue-based learning model invites students to teach one another, avoiding what Chimamanda Adichie (2009) calls the danger of a single story. Acting as a kind of coach, or conductor, our faculty members feed back and comment on the seminar's developing "co-inquiry" which over time develops shared meaning and understanding. The interchange of ideas between fifteen adults around the seminar table brings the social dimension of learning into focus. As Ardath Lee writes, learning is a social (*socius*, shared) process. Atomistically organized, it replicates the contemporary structures of inequality and hierarchy. Dialogue involves being "drawn out" (*e-ducare*) by others through mutual questioning and reframing ideas that are moving through a group of people learning together what they think and feel. This opens insight, because human problems don't lend themselves to narrow, disciplinary "single story" solutions. Insight is multi-perspectival. The ability to develop creative, shared meaning and understanding of controversial questions by following the logic of a conversation means that both students and teachers "facilitate" the dialogue.

We live in a time in which shared or common goods and values are difficult to conceptualize. The distinction between public and private has become blurred. Awareness of the "public things" (*res-publica*) is disappearing. This is a crisis of the republic. "Public choice" has become the libertarian ideology of the ego and his own. Unexamined subject/object dualism reifies "society" and "the state" as abstractions over against the isolated individual person. Government is ruled by an "aristocracy of manufacturers," as de Tocqueville foresaw developing in the 19th Century. He worried that U.S. government would become a "powerful stranger" to the people. When I teach political theory, I say the United States are balkanizing. What is "political" has become a dirty word, confused with "partisan." "Social media" project the spectacle of racial, class and religious fragmentation, factionalism, fear and violence: a discourse of animosity preoccupied with corruption.

The Hutchins School at Sonoma State University was created to address the problem of passivity, fragmentation and alienation in higher education. Warren Olsen wrote in 1992:

> Students will make considerable strides toward intellectual and emotional liberation in which they will have a much better than average chance to become engaged with various worlds each of us lives in...by studying the relationship of values to action, and of the significance of the individual in history, to improve the quality of their lives by adding the usable past to their experience, including cultural and aesthetic achievements, and to provide them with the tools and motivation for continual self education.

This approach acknowledges that learning is a process of relationship and reciprocity, not a one-sided exchange. Thinking and feeling and knowing are interpersonal and inter-subjective – experienced between and within us. There is no private language. Education as public discourse involves weaving together a reciprocity of standpoints and worldviews, integrating fact and values. It involves respectful dialogue and deliberation. This pedagogy follows the legacy of Robert Hutchins' study of democratic institutions. I dreamed once that adult education on the Hutchins model was "the old humiliation overcome." We tell our students they will need to shift their thinking to be teachers for one another. There will be no exams, lots of workshops, some guest lectures and films. They will read a lot and write and converse with one another weekly. There will be only one textbook (on ecological science) throughout their junior and senior years. They will read original thinkers. They will stay together for two years as a seminar cohort of fifteen students through four 10 unit trans-disciplinary core courses, culminating in a semester long senior project of their own choosing.

In the DCP, our learning community approach seeks to practice the skills of mutual engagement in discussing and debating great ideas – what Hutchins called "The Great Conversation." We say the questions are more important than the answers: What is the nature of human freedom? What makes work meaningful? What does a citizen need to know in order to evaluate the climate change debate? What would a coherent community look like? These are questions without simple answers. Over two years, as students get to know one another's views, the seminar cohorts become a "public" in which controversial topics (self and society, work and the global future, technology and the environment) open a wide general education for active citizenship and life-long learning. I think there is a genuine human need for a space in which to be free to express and inquire safely with others: a need for dialogue.

In the DCP, a writing instructor works with students in their first semester in order to develop competencies in academic writing. Thinking and writing develop each another. The curriculum is based on weekly themes that integrate humanities, social and natural sciences in each seminar. Readings and workshops involve original sources and texts. A self-evaluation matrix is used for grading so that students can develop the ability to recognize their strengths and potential. The final semester is an independent senior project in which students integrate their studies in the light of the curriculum and their career goals.

Seminar participants come to campus one Saturday each month for an all-day session. In the first semester, cohorts introduce themselves to one another by sharing one of three short memoirs.

They regularly share extemporaneous presentations of their work with their classmates. In the second term, they present research into their family's work history to help them locate one another in relation to broader socio-historical events and migration patterns. This helps them to perceive what Gregory Bateson called "the pattern that connects." It fosters understanding that they are part of a public culture, where common factors and aspirations cut across divisions of age, class, race and gender separations. In the third semester, they do collaborative research on a current environmental issue. In the senior seminar, they present the results of a semester-long project integrating creative, analytical, and research skills into a 20 minute presentation. In this way they learn to think on their feet, to communicate well, to develop their own voices – in short, to be prepared to speak to a city council or town hall meeting.

A further dimension of building social awareness involves weekly on-line discussions in which participants post a response to the week's readings, and then respond to at least one other student's posting. As in the face-to-face seminars, this is also an "emergent" aspect of the curriculum. Students pose the questions and interpretations they explore together. They initiate what concerns them. They develop their voices, finding a safe environment to engage one another as adult learners in a collegial setting. When someone approaches one of the seminar rooms, it is often laughter that they hear. I'd say this is the sound of trust. When I tell new members of the introductory seminar that they will be joining a learning community, I emphasize that through this process they will be learning and practicing community. Public discourse takes practice. Within our individual bodies, our proprioceptive sense enables us to coordinate and move as a whole. There is also a "socioceptive" awareness that can be developed in our social bodies through which we can recognize and better organize ourselves as socio-political animals, working to foster greater holism and integrity, and learning together.

References

Adichie, Chimamanda Ngozi. 2009. "The Danger of a Single Story." Ted.com.

Olson, Warren. 1992. "The Origin and Birth of the Hutchins School of Liberal Studies." Hutchins School Publications.

Somewhere Over the Rainbow: Hutchins from the Outside In and the Inside Out

Beth Warner

Beth Warner graduated from Hutchins in 1989 and has taught several elective courses in the Saturday Hybrid program, so she knows the pedagogy from the inside out. She was the first advisor/administrator for the program and is now Senior Academic Programs Coordinator for the School of Extended Education. She received her MA in History from SSU in 2009.

This introduction to the Hutchins pedagogy was written for students entering the Saturday Hybrid Degree Completion Program, a program for working adults launched by Dr. Ardath Lee under the Hutchins umbrella in 1997. The program adapts the Hutchins seminar approach to accommodate the busy schedules of adult re-entry students, and the sentiment expressed is applicable to traditional-age students in the regular program as well.

I want to make this clear from the outset: when you join the Hutchins School, you are not in Kansas anymore, but in a good way. Recall the flat, black-and-white landscape of Dorothy's farm life: solid, predictable, and ringed with narrowly-defined rules of what you can and cannot think. The Miss Gulches of that world will make sure that Dorothy never steps out of line. This is the school life most of us have had. But hold on, here comes the tornado!

The first few weeks in the Degree Completion Program will be totally different than anything you have experienced. This adjustment period can be confusing and unsettling, but exhilarating at the same time. As you move through the program, you will begin to rediscover your own ways of learning. You will have many opportunities both to encounter new ideas and to re-examine your habitual ways of thinking and your belief system. The result is a sort of tune-up that clears your mind of any dust that has accumulated and gets things humming along again.

The student-centered Hutchins approach to education is Technicolor. You will encounter strange beings in the texts and a whole different set of rules. You will find allies in unlikely places: even humbugs may have their worth. But unlike Oz, you are not left to flounder alone through unfriendly apple trees or across fields of poppies. Your companions will help guide you on the way, and Glinda will be with you in the form of your seminar instructor.

Although we feel the content is extremely important and many faculty hours are devoted to crafting the reading list and honing assignments, the program is as much or more about process. The point is not to memorize facts or theories. Rather, the content of the courses is a vehicle to learn frameworks of understanding that can be applied to other situations. The informal Hutchins motto is, "We do not think of education as 'knowing things.' Rather, we believe that it consists of being able to think about the 'things' you know." And it is learning to ask and answer questions. What did you learn? How did it connect with what you already know? What don't you know that you wish you did?

Events and ideas don't occur in a vacuum, and they are not interpreted in a void. Where did they come from? And what is our framework for understanding them? It is vitally important to understand the context in which something happened, and also to understand the interpretive context. This is one reason Hutchins uses primary texts as often as possible: you need to encounter the thinkers and the theories on their own terms, not working from what somebody else said about them.

In fact, one could say that the whole point of the Hutchins program is to assist you in reclaiming your own learning process. A large part of that is getting in touch with your curiosity, which may have been stifled by many factors. As a child, you most likely encountered an education system that considers questions a distraction from the knowledge a teacher is trying to impart.

Further, the fear of ridicule by peers and instructors is a potent suppressor of inquiry. We are all too busy and don't have time to pursue anything other than practical matters. In our day-to-day lives, there is no space to contemplate questions, either our own small wonderings or the larger issues that face humanity. The Hutchins School creates that space to explore these questions in a safe environment in gently-guided seminars.

A Hutchins seminar is based on dialogue, not debate. This means stating one's opinion (and how you got there) while being respectful of others' viewpoints. This is the opposite of the current cultural trend toward shouting matches from entrenched positions: this is what we see on television in what are supposed to be news programs. Commentators with dubious credentials fling empty, inflammatory rhetoric to provoke a reaction, with no particular concern about the nuances of the matter under "discussion." The questions presented by the far-from-moderate moderator are designed to generate a shoot-from-the-hip emotional response. This makes for good theater, but could not be further from the way our seminars are conducted.

Humans are social creatures, and we learn best in a collaborative, nurturing environment. There is no doubt that you will encounter controversies and difficult questions that have no answers. But the seminar is not winner-take-all. It is a place where students assist each other in mutual inquiry, a learning community that supports its members in the difficult task of making sense of the world. The text acts as a jumping-off place, a common point of reference, to explore these controversies, examine their implications, and perhaps propose answers.

Some readings will be more accessible than others. You will have your favorites, and there will be ones you have to fight through. Someone will love what you hate and vice versa. We encourage you to examine your own thinking processes as you encounter the different viewpoints in the readings and in seminar. Why do you react the way you do? When do your buttons get pushed, and when do you shout "yes!"?

We have high expectations of you, but not in a traditional classroom sense. We expect you to prepare for discussions both online and in seminars. We expect you to ask the hard questions, and to be willing to explore them with your cohort. We expect folks to stretch outside their comfort zones, to be open to new ways of looking at the world and to new experiences. Our integrative inquiry model allows us to walk around a subject and view it from multiple perspectives, so there is something in this program for everyone.

Your journey through this program is a transformative process. You will be exposed to new ideas on a scale that you may not have experienced before. On the way, you will find that you are no longer a passive recipient of the knowledge that others deem important: you have become an active learner, able to make your own connections between your experience and what is happening around you, and to learn what you want to know about. You will gather a formidable set of skills: in clear writing, in focused analysis, in presenting your ideas to others both informally and formally. Most of all, you will develop your own ways of sorting through information to come to the kernels of knowledge about self and society that will deepen your experience of life.

We do not expect all this to come quickly or necessarily easily; people take differing amounts of time to master the different skills. Just keep in mind that faculty and advisors and your cohort of fellow students are there to provide support and guidance along the way.

At the end of the journey, we hope that the Scarecrows among you will find their brains; the Cowardly Lions, their courage; and the Tin Men/Women their hearts; and that all of you, like Dorothy, find your way home enriched by your experience. We know you will find that it is no longer black and white.

Reflections

from

Hutchins Alumni

John Esterle

Meredith Caplan

Owen Laws

Lena McQuade

Kevin Cody

Finn Menzies

AnnMarie Miller

Hutchins: A Gallery Walk

John Esterle

John Esterle transferred to Hutchins as a junior in 1976 and graduated in 1979. After that he helped a couple of other friends run a movie theatre in Petaluma before moving to San Francisco in 1981 where he has lived ever since. He received a Masters in Broadcast Communications Arts at San Francisco State still wondering what he was going to do career wise. After a few different nonprofit jobs, most notably leading a pilot educational project called Crime and the New Media, he landed at The Whitman Institute (TWI) in 1988. TWI is an independent foundation that links dialogue, relationship building, and inclusive leadership with efforts to advance social, political, and economic equity. Currently, he serves as its co-executive director as well as being a trustee. He lives in San Francisco with his wife of 39 years, Mary Beth, and they have two grown children, Lauren and Brian, who bring them great joy.

I recently had the good fortune to visit the Modern Art Museum in New York. Entering the museum, I had been thinking of Hutchins, a not uncommon occurrence since I graduated there in 1979. In this instance though I'd been wondering – struggling actually – with what I might contribute to the collection commemorating its 50th Anniversary. I had already asked for an extended deadline more than once and my final one was now not too far off. With those doubts swirling around in my head I headed for the floor featuring late 19th and early 20th century art.

Entering the gallery, a wall of Cezanne's greeted me. I immediately thought of Jeannine Schulerwill and her seminar "Expressionism in the Arts," which introduced me to a number of artists and writers I hadn't encountered before. I ended up doing a class presentation on Cezanne, something I remember being pretty nervous about. I also recall how good I felt when it went well; the group alive with discussion, Jeannine, fully present, right there with us.

I often think of Jeanine when visiting a museum or seeing an exhibit, for she opened a door to thinking about art I hadn't stepped through before. She had a special way of holding her expertise lightly and making you feel like you had something new and fresh to say about work she knew well. Her passion and knowledge, her listening and empathy, her questions and encouragement, all invited you in.

"What do you see?" "What do you think?" "What do you feel?" "And how does that connect to the other things we've been talking about?" Of course, she wasn't alone at Hutchins in bringing that sensibility to her teaching; she just embodied it for me in a way that represented Hutchins at its best.

And suddenly, thinking about Jeanine and Hutchins and the art surrounding me in the MOMA, the metaphor arose of Hutchins as a gallery, a gallery of memories with many rooms. I sat down for a moment to let that picture sink in.

And then I started my own personal gallery walk....

I imagine a room full of portraits of my Hutchins professors, who, like Jeannine, also opened doors to thinking critically and creatively about a host of topics and ideas. And not all of them did so through a seminar.

For instance, I never took a class with Lu Mattson – she taught lower division seminars and I transferred to Hutchins as a junior – but I felt like I did. Whether visiting her during her office hours or seeing her at social gatherings (otherwise known as parties) she was open and engaging; eager to listen and eager to talk about ideas, of which she had many!

And in that way she represented another element of Hutchins at its best: a sense that the entire faculty were accessible and that they and the students were all part of a learning community – a sum of relationships that equaled more than the parts of its individual classes. A community of learners with shared values that dialogue rooted in curiosity and empathy matters, that inquiry is more interesting from a systems perspective than a siloed one, that professors and undergrads can be co-designers in their education.

And then it strikes me how many of the faculty I knew, including Jeannine and Lu, are no longer with us; gratitude mixes with sadness as I move into the seminar room.

Featured prominently here is the best class I ever had, a yearlong experiment called Experiencing History taught by Les Adler. It featured a heady mix of simulated role plays, discussion, fiction and nonfiction reading, and creative journaling (I pretended I was writing as Eugene Debs and Clarence Darrow). It was one of those fortuitous moments when instructors, students, and design came together in a pretty magical way. An old sepia toned class photo of us all dressed in period costumes hangs before me and I linger awhile with a smile on my face.

Exploring the room of classes I took, I'm reminded of their interdisciplinary bent and the different ways I experienced them: seminars, independent study, and being a TA. Thinking about the smorgasbord of subjects I sampled I'm suddenly aware how many people have their cell phones out in the MOMA gallery I'm sitting in. And then I think, "A seminar on technology, mediated experience, and its effects on individuals and society – or something like that – would make for an interesting class. I bet someone at Hutchins is exploring that in a seminar – and if they aren't, that would make for a good independent study." Another smile of recognition crosses my face as I think how much Hutchins contributed to my own spirit of lifelong learning.

And that gets me to thinking of all the students and teachers who have passed through Hutchins over its fifty years and carry their experience with them; and that links to thinking of all the seminars and independent studies that have taken place over decades; and then to all of the efforts to bring the values and processes at the center of Hutchins to wider communities both inside and outside the classroom.

Thinking these thoughts, the walk through my own personal Hutchins gallery of memories expands dramatically to a more collective one. And Hutchins reveals itself as a gallery of countless rooms, constantly changing, evolving, and growing – both from the perspectives and experiences of its new teachers and students and from the shifting memories alumni ascribe meanings to with the passage of time.

So my "I" becomes a "we" and I'm no longer alone in this gallery of the mind. With me is the circle of friends – students and faculty – from my own experience as well as a much wider circle of Hutchins fellow travelers I've never met but feel connected to nonetheless. There's a buzz of energy and ideas, the sound of laughter, and a palpable sense of community. I realize I'm envisioning my ideal 50th anniversary celebration. I signal I want to make a toast and begin:

> Hutchins was not just a positive undergrad experience for me, it was a set of values and perspectives and processes that I internalized; a thread that I ended up weaving through my life in different ways.

> On a philosophical level, it helped nurture and grow a budding interest – which became lifelong – in dialogue, thinking, and meaning making. Career wise, my life's work became leading The Whitman Institute, a philanthropic foundation that links dialogue, relationship building, and inclusive leadership with advancing equity and social justice. And personally, inviting one Hutchins Professor to serve on TWI's board and supporting another as she established the Hutchins Dialogue Center were but two strong ways I stayed connected with the idea and ideal of Hutchins over time.

> At a time when the value and purpose of an undergrad liberal arts education is more in question than ever, the type of program Hutchins was – and is – matters.

> (I raise my glass)

May the experiment that Hutchins remains continue to evolve and grow, and may the vision of education Hutchins' embodies shine brightly in a world full of too much dimness and darkness.

Here's to you, Hutchins!

Hidden Treasures: Deepening the Joy of Learning

Meredith Caplan

Meredith Caplan graduated from the Hutchins Program in 1988. This education continues to have a critical influence on her teaching career. She has used the seminar process in public schools by choosing picture books on topics such as death, war, love, dreams etc., to help first graders discuss these important topics. Now she teaches home-school science classes that are based on the interests of the students in the class. She seminars with students about science topics, including environmental issues, evolution, and dark matter; as well as social issues and literature.

The two most important things to teach in education are the love of learning and the ability to communicate with others and learn from each other, and it is this that my Hutchins education was all about. It is my ideal for teaching others and for the continued teaching of myself. Caleb Gattegono says "Each of us has been by far the best teacher each of us had." It is the teacher's job to create the conditions for the students to teach themselves. Gattegno goes on to say, "Only awareness is educable." That is the hidden treasure— the awareness to see and go deeper into learning. This supportive way of learning started for me in high school and has continued throughout my life. I wish to share my experiences of my love for learning and the art of facilitating seminars/discussions and how I have tried to foster this love in my students. Connecting is a key aspect of teaching and we do this by engaging with others and bringing out their ideas and reflecting back what we see. Letting them steer the class with their ideas and interests. Empowering students with their energy of connection to what they like and what they are interested in learning. Knowing that we are all able to express ourselves in different ways and setting up different ways to do this from sharing with the group, doing projects together, breaking up in groups, working alone, to working with a partner.

My Hutchins professors where true and wise teachers who facilitated the learning and growth of the people in their program. Most of my classes were set up in the fashion that we read something which we then responded to by writing. Next we shared with others in the class by discussing these writings together. We also did our own research in areas of our interest that were on topics that were the theme of the particular class. The readings were fantastic and some where more in the area of literature and the humanities and others in science and philosophy. Every professor responded to the writing we did with insightful and supportive comments. They did not spend time in class lecturing to us. The reading we did was the lecture and they were there after we digested, brainstormed and pondered what we read to help facilitate the best conversations I have experienced.

Hutchins professors modeled what it means to be a facilitator of learning by encouraging conversations, deeper thinking and the sharing of ideas. A seminar is a place where people are loving learning and the professor is holding a place for people to say what they think and to help them develop their ideas. It is a place a person can test the waters of what feels right for them; even if it means saying something they are not sure they even believe, in order to see if they do. There is an open mindedness that allows others to express their inner selves. Making connections with others so that they can connect to their own process of learning and growing is also an aspect of the seminar. On the Hutchins website there is a quote from a student named Taylor Terhune that illustrates the power of the seminar, " I cannot stress how thankful I am to have taken part in Hutchins...I came into Sonoma as a close-minded and shy student, and I left Sonoma as an empowered woman ready to debate, defend and take on the world."

When joining the Hutchins program I read two papers by people at SSU that have long guided me. Owen Laws starts out his paper by saying "A seminar is a contract between people to be prepared—every day— to explore the boundaries of knowledge." What is more exciting than exploring these boundaries and possibly coming upon an idea that may later be proven true? His quote, "There is likely to be nothing more exhilarating in your years at college then the experience of a really good seminar." I say shift that to life—what is more exhilarating than having a great discussion with others. Michael Kahn wrote an essay called "The Seminar" in which he goes into depth about the seminar process. He talks about the four kinds of seminars; the first being "the free for all"; the second "the beauty contest"; the third "the distinguished house tour"; and the fourth being the ideal: "the barn raising". Seminars do have people trying to be smarter and expressing ideas to impress others. Yet the ideal seminar includes every voice in the seminar as important—as Kahn states, "Everyone in a seminar is, as we have seen, everyone else's teacher and everyone else's student."

In high school I experienced my first kind of discourse that was similar to the Hutchins program. It was in my favorite class, in my junior and senior years, and was called Masterpieces, in which we read a large variety of books ranging from *The Little Prince* to *Dante's Inferno*. I loved reading *The Odyssey, Beowulf, Don Quixote,* and *Zorba the Greek* among other books. This class was structured much like a Hutchins class, in which we read, wrote our thoughts, ideas and reflections about what we read, and then in a small group of twelve people we discussed our insights into these books and life. We made connections between the books and our lives, and we noticed the connections between the different books and history, and this helped us develop our own philosophies. My guess is that my teacher, Dr. Robert Farrington, may have read Robert Maynard Hutchins' *Great Books, the Foundation for Education.* He was amazing at facilitating conversations and allowing people with differing ideas to respectfully discuss their insights. This unique class was the only one of its kind at my high school, and by far, my favorite. My best friend, Christine, took this class with me and I remember staying after school with her as we walked around the halls of Byram Hills High School discussing books, politics, philosophy, history and science which I am sure was partially the result of taking Masterpieces. When I applied for college at the age of seventeen I applied to schools in my home state of New York and for some strange reason I applied to Sonoma State University. I decided to go to SUNY at Oneonta, but the foreshadowing did not escape me. Ten years later I was at Sonoma State University in the Hutchins Liberal Arts Program. It was the best education I could imagine.

In high school the importance of writing essays was stressed. Every senior, at my school had to write a thesis paper that was well researched. The art of writing an essay was very much deepened while in the Hutchins program. Professors wrote many and lengthy comments about the content of what we wrote. They still did corrections and pointed out flaws in writing, but it was the content that they focused on. This is something that can ever be improved. I work at teaching this process to students. In the final paragraph of an essay one is supposed to retell the thesis, but from my Hutchins training this is also the time to reflect and tell about how the process of writing that paper has caused one to have an insight into oneself or something about the topic while doing the essay. One of the insights I am having writing this chapter is that I circle through information and people that I study and deepen these ideas and thoughts. I have an even greater appreciation for the seminar process and the engaging of thought and ideas with others.

The hidden treasures in the Hutchins program continue to move me daily as a teacher. How do I bring Hutchins into my teaching? I respect my students and have them discussing in groups their ideas and thoughts after learning information about a topic. I encourage them to think critically and express their thinking. I also find out their interests and help to teach by bringing in these areas of interest. In the science classes the students help choose the topics and their questions help direct the lessons. Good conversations are encouraged and nurtured. Their suggestions are respected and I try to find a way to include these in the classes. Just this year one of the students brought up his desire to study different countries. I was not sure how to bring this into our science class when one my students showed me her powerpoint on Ancient Egypt and I got the idea. I asked if she would want to share this powerpoint with the class and she said yes, and this was how we could bring in the study of different countries.

They are now sharing youtube videos they made on their topics as well as keynotes and other ways of sharing their research. They decided as a group to work in teams, with one person providing information about a country or place, and the other presenting an interesting plant from that area. They have been doing a great job researching, organizing the information and presenting this to the group. The group responds by talking about the presentation and sharing their appreciation for learning. They asked to continue this throughout the rest of the year. These presentations have been well researched and cover a broad area of information.

During the time I was in the Hutchins Program I took a class in which I went into a local High School and brought articles to read with an English and Social Science class, and with my fellow Hutchins students we each lead a group of ten High school students. I remember two of the articles were on differing opinions on gun control, a topic that is relevant today. The idea that conversation can help open minds and help us to see other people's points of view is so important today. This experience helped me to continue doing this kind of learning through many teaching experiences from public schools to private schools to homeschoolers. John Dewey (1938) said that every generation has to discover democracy on its own and indeed seminars and deeper discussions about important topics are one way to bring about a more democratic society. When a person is respected for their thoughts and ideas they start stepping up to this and becoming more thoughtful and aware. The importance of conversations can be seen on a political level as Jonathan Haidt (2012), the social psychologist says, "If you really want to change someone's mind on a moral or political matter, you'll need to see things from that person's angle as well as your own. And if you do truly see it the other person's way— deeply and intuitively—you might even find your own mind opening in response. Empathy is an antidote to righteousness, although it's very difficult to empathize across a moral divide."

Before I decided to become a teacher I was working in a vegetarian, whole wheat Pizza Restaurant that I started with friends. It was during this time that I realized that I wanted to be a teacher. I was reading the writings of Bronson Alcott and how he started a school in the eighteen hundreds that was very different from schools at that time. Part of his school was talking with his students and having discussions about the important things in life. He taught using the Socratic Method and his daughter Louisa May Alcott wrote about him saying, "My father taught in the wise way which unfolds what lies in the child's nature, as a flower blooms rather than crammed it, like a Strasbourg goose, with more than it could digest" (1993). Many of Louisa May Alcott's books express this philosophy of teaching, as well, especially *Eight Cousins*. Robert Maynard Hutchins said, "Education is a kind of continuing dialogue, and a dialogue assumes different points of view" (1952). How often do I and my fellow teachers ask students to be quiet so we can tell them something when we would be better off learning how to facilitate their discussions and learning.

When thinking about some of the most influential educators and what they contributed to teaching, Frederich Froebel (1782-1852) taught about the importance of learning through play, being outdoors, and making it child centered. Bronson Alcott (1799-1888) taught using the Socratic method and having deep discussions with children. John Dewey(1859-1952) focused on the importance of developing curriculum through children's interests and making them project based. Maria Montessori (1870-1952) said that observing children was important for the teacher and having children learning through their senses and at their own pace was crucial. Alexander Sutherland Neill (1883-1973) emphasized freedom for children and the importance of respecting their rights. Caleb Gattegno (1970) emphasized the "most important component of education, the learner" (p. ii), the subordination of teaching to learning, and teaching to inspire not to inform.

A number of years ago, when I was teaching first grade at a local public school, I was doing a language arts teacher training and we were given a year long project to delve into our own ideas on education and create in an innovative way of teaching language arts, which we presented at the at the end of the year to other teachers. I choose teaching my first graders how to seminar with each other by delving into mature and important topics and encouraging them to discuss these more deeply. I let them choose from a number of themes and they picked friendship, death, war, and dreams, among others. I found three different picture books on each theme that I could read to my students and then we discussed them in Hutchins fashion. I was amazed by the depth of conversation I had with my first graders and the conversations that they had with each other. They would break up into groups of about four or five students and discuss the stories while a tape recorder recorded their conversations. I listened to these and took quotes from these discussions and wrote them up on sentence strips that were then read by the class. This helped to deepen the conversations as the year progressed. They got to see examples of reflections, opinions, ideas, and feedback. These examples, from their classmates, helped them by being a model of ways to have more in-depth conversations. When we discussed war we learned that one of the students in class had left his country of Laos on a boat to get to America and about some of his experiences of war. He made me aware that a simple game like Hangman can be a horrifying reminder of war. We changed that game to the Gingerbread Person. As for our discussions about books, the first graders were encouraged to do three things: talk about how this book reminded them about their own life, how the books compared with each other and how these books made them think about the world in a different way.

When discussing the literature we were reading we brought in a number of levels to our discourse from intellectual to social and emotional feelings. This includes the emotion called "elevation" coined by the social psychologist and researcher Jonathan Haidt, who writes "I have defined elevation as a warm, uplifting feeling that people experience when they see unexpected acts of human goodness, kindness, courage, or compassion. It makes a person want to help others and to become a better person himself or herself" (2005). When reading to children through the years it is this feeling that would cause me to tear up and children say "why are you crying?" They would be confused and I would try to explain that I was not crying because I was sad, but because I was so touched and inspired. These are the kinds of books I often read to the children and were part of the discussion groups. A few examples of picture books that have precipitated the elevation feeling are the following: Patricia Polacco, *Mrs. Katz and Tush*; Kirby Larson and Mary Nethery, *Two Bobbies*; Alan Rabinowitz, *The Boy and a Jaguar*: and Deborah L. Rose, *The People Who Hugged the Trees*.

Some examples of picture books we read for different themes on the topic of self-esteem included: Yashima, *Crow Boy*; Haseley, *The Scared One*; and Henkes *Chrysanthemum*. For War we read Mark, *Rose Blanche, Hiroshima, No Pika* and Polacco, *Pink and Say*. When studying about death we read Bunting, *The Wall*; Nobisso, *Grandpa Loved*; Simon, *The Saddest Time*; De Paolo, *Nana Upstairs, Nana Downstairs*; Viorst, *The Tenth Good Thing About Barney*; and Walker, *To Hell with Dying*. When studying Dreams/Hopes we read Ringgold, *Tar Beach*; Zemach, *Awake and Dreaming*; and Polacco *Applemando's Dreams*. An important topic and area of study that I have taught throughout my teaching career has been the environment and for first graders we would read: Luenn, *Mother Earth* and *Song for the Ancient Forest*; Rose, *The People Who Hugged the Trees*; Dr Suess, *The Lorax*; Giono, *The Man Who planted Trees*; Levine, *Pearl Moskowitzs Last Stand*; Bunting, *Someday a Tree*; and Cowcher, *Rainforest*. A teacher named Dyan Pike, who teaches high school in Sonoma County went to the presentation on the thematic reading/seminar groups and she was inspired to organize these books into the different themes. She told me she was using them as an "into" reading experience for her high school students for various novels she had the class read throughout the year.

About five years after teaching first grade I was teaching in a second grade class and introduced reading different books on similar topics and having discussions that were again recorded and particular ideas of the students printed up for the class to listen to in order to model great conversations in action. I did this with a class that was run by another teacher and still the conversations were surprisingly deep and showed students connecting and deepening their thinking. There were, of course silly conversations and off topic discussions, as there was with my first graders, but knowing they were being recorded helped them to stay on the topic and knowing that they might have something they say be written up for the class to read was motivating to them to make their discussions more focused and meaningful. Having their name written next to one of their own quotes was reinforcing and encouraged them to talk with more feeling and depth. I believe that in time the conversations themselves were engaging and motivating on their own.

A wonderful lesson that is great to do before reading a novel, as well as to begin a great discussion, is from the California Literature project called the Tea Party. The teacher chooses various quotes from a text; I used Fleischman, *Seedfolks* that I read with a class of junior high school students. Each person has a quote that they practice reading, asking the teacher if there are any words they do not know how to read or pronounce. Once they are done practicing their line by themselves they start the "tea party". People find a partner to read their quote to as if they are gossiping at a party and they do this in groups of two or three people until everyone has heard everyone's quote. After this we talk about what we think the book will be about and what some of the quotes mean. To give you a taste of this activity here is a sampling of some of the quotes I took from Seedfolks: "He was a salmon traveling upstream through his past"; "The older you are the younger you get when you move to the United States"; "She kept a scrapbook with the obituaries of all the doctors she out lived and could recite the list of names by heart like a chapter out of Genesis"; "That small circle of earth became a second home to both of us"; "The object in America is to avoid contact, to treat all as foes unless they're known to be friends"; "When I heard her words, I realized how useless was all that I'd heard about Poles, how much richness it hid, like the worthless shell around an almond"; "If you're a teenager the whole world hates you"; "I was related to bears, to dinosaurs, to plants, to things that were a million years old"; "My great-grandparents walked all the way from Louisiana to Colorado"; "My father, he always has a smile on his face and plan moving in his head"; "Sometimes I think I've actually had more effect on the world since I retired"; "He was trusted and liked and famous, after his exploit with the pitchfork"; "Pantomime was often required to get over language barriers"; "But the garden's greatest benefit, I feel, was not relief to the eyes, but to make the eyes see our neighbors"; and "I was just a watcher, but I was proud of the garden as if it were mine." The conversation from reading these and more quotes from Seedfolk was amazing. Our minds want to create meaning and love puzzles like this kind of activity to try and figure out what is going on. The class would discuss what they thought the book was about and make a gestalt from this hodgepodge of quotes. When reading the story people in the class were thrilled when their quote was read, for after reading it to thirty-one other students they had it memorized and it was their special place in the book. They also could now see it in context and get a much richer meaning from it.

When I was in high school I began to experience the amazing feeling of synchronicity that would come about when studying something in History class that had to do with something we were studying in both English and Science. These moments when our mind finds connection in learning are precious. As teachers we ideally are creating these moments in the life of our students. When one of my science students exclaimed when we studied something about animals that she had just been talking to her parents about that morning, that was one of those moments. When my class was learning about telomeres I heard that one of my students went to a doctor in San Francisco and the doctor asked what they were learning in science and she told them they were learning about telomeres; he was happy to tell her that he was one of the people who had done research on telomeres and knew the woman who got the Nobel Laureate studying them. Empowering students by teaching them the edge of knowledge, so they can think about this and possibly come up with their own ideas is also another ideal for teaching and learning. Recently when my science class was studying Dark Matter and Dark Energy they got in groups to propose their ideas about what Dark Energy and Dark Matter are. Here are some of the things they said: "It is outside the dimension of Earth"; "Dark Matter is energy that makes everything the same"; "It keeps forming and expanding and pushing everything out"; and "Maybe the edge of the universe is being pulled on by some force." After our discussion one of the students said that maybe someday in the distant future someone would read their quotes and say that the homeschool science class somehow knew what Dark Energy and Dark Matter were before anyone else.

All of this reading, writing and being in seminars with others ideally helps us to change our lives and put forth a more ideal way of living. With all the problems we face in today's world with climate change, humans polluting our biosphere with CO2 emissions, warfare, the larger numbers of poor people, homelessness, racial prejudice, violence, inequality in the treatment of women, horrible treatment of other animals, extinction of species, lack of education, government corruption, lack of food and clean water, and more—there must be something each of us can do. If we use our intelligence towards action that helps turn the tide of any and all of these areas of struggle, we are indeed finding another hidden treasure in our way of living in this world. We do this when we take action by making changes in how we live—be it car free, eating more plant based diets, living in smaller homes, using renewable energy, using public transportation, riding bicycles, walking to do errands, getting fossil fuel out of our homes and investment portfolios, purchasing from reputable businesses, lowering our carbon footprint by flying less, investing money with banks that are not profiting from businesses that are poisoning our planet, and doing work that somehow contributes to a healthier world. We all have ways we can improve how we live, and it is time that we start doing something to make these changes. Being in conversation with others who may not agree with all our ideas, exchanging ideas and thoughts with each other is an important contribution in the process of bringing about positive change.

Recently, my husband and I started a Climate Conversation group of friends in which we read articles, passages from books and listen to Ted Talks or other in-depth talks about climate change. We seminar with each other about the most important issue facing all life on our planet. We started this group after being inspired by a group I was in at the Center for Climate Protection in which eighteen of us came together along with the leaders of the group to learn about climate change and engage with others in ways that we can make a difference for our planet. I thought it was telling that hardly anyone in my group started a group of their own and I think this is because so few of us have experienced the seminar process in-depth. Many people think they have to be an expert on a topic to organize a group about it. That is not the case; the beauty of the seminar is how we teach each other and learn from good readings and the conversations we share with one another.

In my science class, which meets once a week for three hours, we build a community of learners by starting out the year in which they see all the areas of science and the subtopics to give them ideas about what peaks their interest. From this information I create a sample plan for the year, which I run by the class the next week and they tweak this to what they want to learn. Each week I spend hours researching and thinking up lessons that will integrate with many other areas of learning with lots of hands-on lessons, experiments, and a sprinkling of games and movement activities. I also find a book to read to the class that is either science fiction, about animals, or scientists or heroic children and adults doing actions to help our planet. All of this creates a community of learners that spends time each class reflecting on what they liked and learned at the end of class. Throughout the class are times when we stop to discuss a topic or something we learned and reflect on this. A recent example was the announcement in early April, 2018, that scientists had discovered a new organ in our body. We learned about the interstitium and how this organ may help us learn more about how to better take care of our body. Students were fascinated, and their excitement about this and their previous science knowledge helped them to reflect on what a finding like this means. Recently I was talking to someone who said that she did not understand why people get so upset about animals going extinct. My science students would never say that because they have learned about food webs and the importance of all the animals in an ecosystem. I told them about this person's statement and they were as shocked, although perhaps not as upset, as I was when I heard this heartbreaking statement from a person I know. The students have critical thinking skills to take a statement like that and see the problem with that kind of thinking. We need thinkers in this world because there are a lot of changes the Earth is going through due to humans changing our biosphere.

When you start to experience the seminar process in your life, you may find that it works in groups of 12 or fewer people quite nicely, and with two or three people, and surprisingly even with oneself. That is one of the hidden and secret treasures. When studying what makes a healthy person, one of the tenets we discussed was the following: "Learning to see beyond what everyone else believes is to realize what you believe and want in your life." One of the science students responded to this with much enthusiasm and it is the seminars that help nurture this deeper understanding of ourselves and our beliefs. Once you start this process you can't say to others things like "I try not think about... or I would be too upset." When we seminar with ourself, we learn to have the honesty of facing our own flaws and areas to be developed, so that when we look back we see that we are growing throughout our life and that this process never stops. In the words of Robert Maynard Hutchins (1952), "The object of education is to prepare the young to educate themselves throughout their lives."

I hope this chapter inspires those reading it to create seminars in their life whether it is with family, friends, students, colleagues and/or neighbors. With respect for other people's ideas and thoughts we can help each other to be smarter, more caring and aware people on this precious planet. John Taylor Gatto wrote near the end of his book, *A Different Kind of Teacher*, the following: "If you can build a society of emotionally generous, search-for-solution friends who understand and venerate the mystery search as the single most important aspect of intelligent, satisfying life you've found the greatest engine possible to sustain the wonder of childhood for all of a lifetime. Indeed, if you can find two souls whose conversation is sprinkled with insights about mystery, and whose curiosity about your own insights is lively and eager; you own a treasure whose worth is beyond valuation." It is this nonpareil that we are helping our students gain for a lifetime that is the most profound part of seminars; making sure that seminars are a part of education is paramount.

References

Alcott, Louisa May. 1993. Cary Ryan, ed. *Louisa May Alcott: Her Girlhood Diary*. Bridgewater Books.

Dewey, John. 1938. *Experience and Education*. Kappa Delta Pi.

Fleischman, Paul. 1997. *Seedfolks*. HarperCollins.

Gatto, John Taylor. 2002. *A Different Kind of Teacher: Solving the Crisis of American Schooling*. Berkeley Hills Books.

Gattegono, Caleb. 2010 [1970]. *What We Owe Children: The Subordination of Teaching to Learning*. Educational Solutions Inc.

Haidt, Jonathan. 2005. "Wired to Be Inspired." *Greater Good Magazine: Science-Based Insights for a Meaningful Life*. March 1.

2012. *The Righteous Mind: Why Good People are Divided by Politics and Religion*. Vintage.

Hutchins, Robert Maynard. 1952. *The Great Conversation: The Substance of a Liberal Education*. Encyclopaedia Britannica, Inc.

Introduction to Seminaring in Hutchins

Owen Laws

"Wise men characteristically ask interesting questions while experts usually reveal their lack of wisdom by answering them."

~ Joseph W. Meeker

Owen Laws graduated from Hutchins in 1988, having been active in the peace movement during his years at Sonoma State. He wrote this description of the seminar during his senior year, and it is still being used to orient students as they enter the Hutchins program. He went to Sweden in 1986 and remained there as an exchange student every other semester for the next two years, and moved there permanently after graduation. He is a member of the Green Party, and has served in City and County government. He currently owns and operates a cargo bike courier service in Northern Sweden.

A seminar is a contract between people to be prepared – every day – to explore the boundaries of knowledge. A dynamic seminar is one in which the members work together to help each other understand the readings and the questions which develop out of the readings and conversations. There is likely to be nothing more exhilarating in your years of college than the experience of a really good seminar.

The most important part of a seminar is keeping up with, or exceeding, the reading. There is nothing more frustrating than trying to discuss a book in a seminar and realizing that the other members haven't read it.

In order to be able to participate effectively in a seminar, it is important to be aware of several basic seminar skills. If you are reading, come to class, and familiarize yourself with the following seminar skills, you are almost certain to have vibrant, dynamic, and lively seminars:

- You are important to the seminar.

- You are the teacher. What would you like to learn?

- Try to come to class with questions, or thoughts or feelings about the material.

- Don't let the instructor / facilitator answer all of the questions, and don't direct your questions to the facilitator; direct them towards each other.

- Take risks. *Take the initiative.*

- Verbalize incomplete thoughts, feelings, or questions. Try.

- Help your fellow students build on incomplete ideas. Don't leave them hanging when they do take risks.

- Be an active listener. Write thoughts down so you don't forget them. *Ask divergent questions* (questions that permit many answers), and attempt to answer them.

- Often, asking a quiet person a question, or merely giving him or her an opportunity to talk will evoke a really interesting response and lead to good conversation.

- Be compassionate. To have a good seminar you have to make yourself vulnerable. Your feelings are just as important as your thoughts. Often others will feel similarly, and good conversation will ensue.

- Don't be afraid of adding some structure at times. Go-rounds and brainstorms can be useful when conversation is dull or to find out quickly how everyone feels about something.

- Instructors are not perfect. Facilitating a seminar is much harder than giving a lecture. Often instructors will talk too much, either because you *aren't talking,* or because they are really enthusiastic about the material. Help them to be sensitive to your needs.

• Hutchins is an incredibly unique opportunity to learn how to learn.

TAKE ADVANTAGE OF IT!

• Have fun.

Many of the above skills involve some kind of interaction with other people. They are geared towards helping you learn how to develop a line of thought in cooperation with others. The objective is knowledge, not self-gratification. As one Hutchins student said, "The strength of Hutchins is that it teaches you how to express yourself in a safe environment." Hutchins does not supply positive reinforcement for competitiveness.

It is also important to start each seminar in a relaxed way. You might want to give everyone a chance to say how they are feeling, or you might just have casual conversations, whatever it takes to create a safe atmosphere for intensive discussion.

Occasionally certain people will dominate the seminar. Here are some behavioral characteristics to watch out for and avoid, in yourself as well as others (Moyers, 1983).

HOGGING THE SHOW: talking too much, too long, too loudly.

PROBLEM SOLVER: continually giving the answer or solution before others have had much chance to contribute.

SPEAKING IN CAPITAL LETTERS: giving one's own solutions or opinions as the final words on the subject.

NIT-PICKING: pointing out minor flaws in statements of others and stating the exception to every generality.

RESTATING: saying in another way what someone else has just said perfectly clearly (not *always* bad).

SELF-LISTENING: formulating a response after the first few sentences, not listening to anything from that point on, and leaping into at the first pause.

All of the things mentioned in the two lists are important to be aware of, but don't freak out trying to memorize them. The objective of this paper is to facilitate communication by making you aware of the dynamic which will occur in your seminar. By learning to identify various skills and behaviors, you will be better communicators, both in and outside of the seminar.

Ultimately though, as Mervyn Cadwallader suggests, "the essence of good communication (is) trusting and being trusted... trust is at the heart of a program built on a sense of community" and of the seminar (1984, p.356).

References

Cadwallader, Mervyn L. 1984. "Experiment at San Jose" in Richard Jones and Barbara Leigh Smith, eds. *Against the Current: Reform and Experimentation in Higher Education*. Schenkman Pub Co.

Meeker, Joseph W. 1970. "Academic Fields and Other Polluted Environments." Essay presented to the Innovation Conference, March 23.

Moyers, Bill. 1983. "Overcoming Masculine Oppression in Mixed Groups." *The International Day of Nuclear Disarmament: Handbook for Civil Disobedience*. Livermore Action Group.

Creating Queer Spaces in the Hutchins School: Student-Led Interdisciplinary Pedagogy

Dr. Lena McQuade

Lena McQuade joined Hutchins as a Track 1 student during her freshman orientation in 1995. She graduated with a double major in Hutchins and Women's and Gender Studies in 1999. Not done reading or writing, she went right into graduate school and earned her PhD in American Studies and a graduate certificate in Women's and Gender Studies from the University of New Mexico in 2008. She was a dissertation fellow in the UC Santa Barbara Feminist Studies Department for one year before starting her dream job as a professor in the Women's and Gender Studies Department at SSU in 2008. In 2016, she was honored to receive the SSU Excellence in Teaching Award, which she credits in large part to the inspirational professors in Hutchins and WGS who taught her how to teach.

In the Spring of 1999, as an undergraduate double major in Hutchins and Women's and Gender Studies, I was struggling. Struggling, not so much with the academics, but with who I was becoming. I found myself searching for words and representations that would allow me to see myself—as someone who was queer and white and in love across the borders of race, culture, and language. I was straining to find frameworks to understand the overlaps between sexuality, gender, race, love, difference, and most importantly their complicated intersections in my own life. As a Hutchins student, I had been taught methods to approach the complexities of our world. I had learned to read broadly and deeply, consider multiple perspectives, listen carefully, formulate questions, and reexamine previous thoughts. In essence, I had been "learning how to learn" within an academic context. As a senior, I took these Hutchins pedagogical tools, combined with the insights gained through my double major in Women's and Gender Studies that the 'personal was political,' and began a self-initiated investigation into feminist theory, queer theory, and critical race studies. On this intellectual journey of deeper understanding, I found great solace in the words of bell hooks (1991), who wrote: "I came to theory because I was hurting–the pain within me was so intense I could not go on living. I came to theory desperate, wanting to comprehend...I saw in theory a location for healing." Out of the crucible of my own internal struggles around gender, sexuality, and race, tempered through the pedagogical structure of Hutchins, I created and facilitated a class entitled "Contesting Identity: Sexual Orientation and Gender," offered through Hutchins in the Fall of 1999. This essay is an autobiographical account of my experience developing and facilitating a student-led course in the emerging field of queer studies in the late 1990s.

The Hutchins School of Liberal Studies provided a rather unique opportunity for undergraduate students to design and teach their own course. Allowing students to create a class and step into the role of facilitators is very much in line with the educational mission of Hutchins. Founded in 1969, the innovators of the Hutchins School at SSU set out to address the passivity, fragmentation, and alienation they feared was an outcome of traditional academic programs of the time (Olson, 1992). In response, the curriculum of Hutchins centered around core ideas, themes, and enduring questions explored through an interdisciplinary perspective. As former Hutchins faculty member Les Adler (2001) explained, this model of education provides an "'aerial' view of knowledge, looking across, beyond, and through the disciplines to discover and explore the fundamental questions and deepest connections underlying them." Pedagogically, Hutchins operates through small seminars where students are responsible for class discussions, which they prepare for by reading deeply and writing extensively. In Hutchins, students are reconceived, not as passive absorbers of predetermined sets of knowledge, but rather as "the active pattern maker at the center of web, making and applying connections" across interdisciplinary material in class seminars (Adler 2001). As "co-creators" of knowledge among a "community of scholars," students are encouraged to take themselves seriously as intellectuals and conscious actors capable of engaging complex issues in our world (Adler 2001).

Initially, I found this mode of teaching and learning terrifying as a new Hutchins student. My fear reached its peak during the mid-point my first semester when all of my non-Hutchins dorm roommates were flipping through flashcards and highlighting lecture notes preparing for their midterm exams. I clearly remember calling my parents and crying out of gut-wrenching fear that I might be wasting my precious college education because I was not memorizing answers for tests. Instead, I was only asking questions and more questions, which, coming from what Paulo Freire (1970) describes as the "banking" model of education, seemed much less important than amassing memorized facts. Slowly, I began to appreciate that what I was learning to do by asking questions and fumbling around for connections among different readings with other undergraduates in my seminar was actually critical thinking and developing reasoned meanings out of the material we were reading. Learning how to explore complex topics and ask questions rather than just arrive at quick surface answers served me well, not just in the Hutchins seminar, but also in the life I was living outside of the classroom.

In the mid-1990s, the nation was vigorously debating the legal and social position of LGBTQ people. The period was marked by both increasing legal and policy restrictions on homosexuality and a growth in LGBTQ activism and scholarship. Emblematic of the vitriol directed at LGBTQ people during this time, in 1993 Sharon Bottoms Mattes lost custody of her 2-year-old son when Judge Buford Parsons found that her existence as a lesbian was "illegal and immoral and renders her an unfit parent" (Ayres 1993). On the national level, two major pieces of federal policy and legislation—Don't Ask, Don't Tell (1994), which barred openly LGBTQ people from serving in the military, and the Defense of Marriage Act (1996), which federally defined marriage as the union of one man and one woman—not only circumscribed the legal possibilities for LGBTQ people but also sent a strong cultural message that LGBTQ people were excluded from full participation in the social life of the United States. Reflecting this trend towards gay marginalization, a 1996 Gallop poll found that a vast percentage of Americans (68%) thought marriages between homosexuals "should not be recognized by the law as valid." (Baunach, 2011). Then, the 1998 gruesome murder of 21-year-old gay university student Matthew Shepard drew national attention to homophobia and sparked increased LGBTQ activism. As an undergraduate student during this time period, these national events initially sparked fear, outrage, and unease about my own future. But they also ignited my academic curiosity to further understand and contextualize the political forces that were shaping my life.

By my junior year in 1998, I had taken a range of courses across the Hutchins and Women's and Gender Studies departments. But I had yet to take a class organized around what were then the emerging fields of gay and lesbian studies and queer theory. I vividly recall the excitement I felt when I saw the listing for a class on "Androgyny" that would be taught by Professor Susan Barnes. My excitement at the prospect of a semester investigating scholarship that questioned the gender binary was crushed when the class filled to capacity before my registration date. My profound disappointment in not being able to take this class stemmed from a deep sense that this seminar might hold the keys to answer the questions about gender and sexual orientation that constantly swirled through my mind. Paralyzing questions—such as: was I really gay? Was it was possible to be a lesbian and have a viable future?—were a constant feature in my mind. I struggled every day with internalized homophobia, or the ways marginalized people, in the absence of positive reflections of themselves, come to believe and to rehearse readily available negative stereotypes. Feminist philosopher Hilde Lindemann (2001) describes this struggle as one of "infiltrated consciousness" or the internalization of an externally constructed negative subjectivity. I knew that the antidote to the poison of internalized oppression lay in surrounding myself with the narratives and academic perspectives of those who had faced oppression and gained insight through the struggle. Unable to enroll in the classes that might provide the scholarly narratives I sought, I began to think that I might have to do this research on my own.

At the same time that I was grappling with the effects of my own marginalization around sexual orientation, I was also becoming increasingly aware of my racial identity as a white person and of white privilege. These realizations were brought to the forefront of my mind by both the political climate, where I was involved in protesting anti-immigrant and anti-affirmative action ballot initiatives (Propositions 187 and 209), and also through my own relationship at the time. It is hard to describe how powerful and amazing it felt to finally be in a beautiful loving relationship with another queer woman. And in loving her, I witnessed the racism and the combinations of anti-immigrant—homophobic—sexism directed at her on a daily basis. To my horror, I could see how I had internalized the white dominant norms of my society and how these toxins seeped out of me and into my relationship. I saw how I could hurt the person I loved the most through my own stunted understanding about her lived reality as a person of color and my own unexamined assumptions about whiteness as a cultural norm.

Peggy McIntosh (1989) describes some of these white racial dynamics by explaining how white people can linger in a state of racial unconsciousness in part because they are "carefully taught" not to recognize the structural advantages of whiteness that confer unearned racial power. Robin DiAngelo (2011) further theorized this concept of white fragility or how "whites have not had to build the cognitive or affective skills or develop the stamina that would allow for constructive engagement across racial divides." More fully conscious of my own learned racism and the corrosive moral bankruptcy of white superiority, I was driven to move through racial paralysis and guilt towards constructive anti-racist change. I was fortunate to join a local community organizing project of white women who were dedicated to a life-long process of unraveling racism and trying to confront and change their internalized white supremacy. In this group, we read and discussed critical race theory, critical whiteness studies, and autobiographical accounts of racism written by people of color. Through our readings, discussions, and attempts to disrupt the racism within ourselves and our communities, this organizing project gave me a template for how to do engaged scholarship. It was also powerful evidence for me of how complex and intersectional identity, privilege, and oppression could be and how necessary it was to continually refuse "socially taught ignorance."

Emboldened to gain a deeper academic understanding of the complexities of sexual orientation, I began to go to the library every day during the winter break of 1998. I started a tentative search on the topic "gay and lesbian" in the library's Merlin search engine and kept a journal of the sources I was finding. By the late 1990s, the academic fields of gay and lesbian studies and queer theory were growing exponentially. Faculty members at a range of different universities had begun to offer gay and lesbian studies courses and publishers were becoming less reticent to publish on this topic (Heller 1990). The emerging state of the field of gay and lesbian studies was evident in my journal notes where I recorded finding few sources when using a "subject" search, reflecting the newness of "gay and lesbian" as a recognized subject field by the Library of Congress subject headings system. However, when I did a less restrictive "keyword" search that returned any sources mentioning the words "gay and lesbian," I found page after page of sources that I began tracking down and reading. My part-time job as a student employee at the library proved to be both a blessing and a curse. Because of my job training, I was adept at finding sources and I understood how books were organized in the library. I spent hours reading every single title of the books in the HQ 75-76 call number section, where the books on "Homosexuality" and "Lesbianism" were filed (right between "Sexual Deviations" and "Sadism, Masochism, Fetishism, Prostitution, Masturbation, and Emasculation"—cataloguing evidence of the socially negative associations of gays and lesbians). The Sonoma State library had only a handful of the resources I wanted to read, which meant, in the pre-online request era, that I had to personally go to the front desk numerous times and request the titles of books I wanted; books with titles such as "Homophobia: A Weapon of Sexism," "Chicana Lesbians: The Girls Our Mothers

Warned Us About," and "Virtual Equality: The Mainstreaming of Gay and Lesbian Liberation." Despite the challenges of explaining my topic to multiple strangers, my independent research provided me the intellectual sustenance I had been seeking and I began to think about sharing what I was learning with other people.

The interdisciplinary approach of Hutchins became a framework for me to think about how to organize my research. As I searched for sources and read, disciplinary patterns within the material slowly began to emerge. I realized that I had located readings from a range of academic fields including the sciences, anthropology, history, literature, law, education, psychology, and popular culture. I also found theoretical and transdisciplinary sources, especially from the developing field of queer theory, that posed the types of big questions about identity, reality, and power that I was familiar with exploring in my undergraduate Hutchins seminars. As distinguished historian George Chauncey (1998) explained: "At its best, scholarship in gay studies has illuminated fundamental questions that have been central to Western thought... questions about, for example, the malleability of the self and the construction of social categories, the place of sexual regulation in creating social order, and the relationship between a person's private morality and fitness for public responsibilities." Exploring societies' "fundamental questions" is a critical component of the Hutchins major and I began to understand that a class on LGBTQ topics could actually be applicable to a wide range of students.

Beyond finding patterns and connections, this interdisciplinary and theoretical research was also deeply healing. In my journal, I wrote that writers such as Eve Kosofsky Sedgwick, Monique Wittig, bell hooks, Judith Butler, Gloria Anzaldúa, Michel Foucault, and Teresa de Lauretis, became my mentors because what they were writing reflected everything I was experiencing. I fell in love with theory and its emancipatory power to create new worlds of possibility by naming and describing what previously had been left unsaid or underexamined. Through theory I was able to suture some of the shattered parts of myself and find the words to describe who I was becoming. The research process politicized me as I discovered my agency to learn what I needed to know.

This is not to say that I did not struggle to comprehend some of the very abstract theory I was encountering. I stumbled across a reference to the field defining book, *The Gay and Lesbian Studies Reader* (1993). Based on its promising title, I had hoped that it could serve as central text for the class I was envisioning. Sonoma State did not have a copy nor did any of the libraries in its inter-library loan network, so I ordered it through a local bookstore. When it finally arrived, I remember my dismay when I tried to read some of the theoretically sophisticated and very narrowly-focused chapters that were beyond my grasp as an undergraduate. Sometimes theory opened up new windows of thought, and other times, when I could not comprehend what I was trying to read on my own, I would fall into a spiral of doubt.

Around this point in my research process, I began to seriously question if I could actually translate what I was learning into a class that I would somehow manage facilitate. I turned to journal writing as a way to sort out my thoughts. I wrote: "I am up against my wall of knowledge, comfort, and understanding. What does it mean to be a teacher? What if I want to teach but I know about as much as my students? There has to be something more or else I'll just perpetuate stereotypes, myths, and acceptable prejudice. I have to know how to lead the way for others to get up on the ladders of knowledge so we don't just all wallow in the common muck." I continued: "Maybe there isn't anyone else in my immediate circle of contacts who has been down this particular path. This is the struggle to want to learn what no one else is teaching—to see the next step in social progress and have to do it on your own." I followed this journal entry with a cluster brainstorm on the central topic of "fears." Around this word I wrote all my fears at the moment: "That what I teach will be outdated or look ridiculous later," "That I still have too much homophobia in me to teach this," "That I won't be able to handle the questions people ask or know how to effectively combat homophobia or heterosexism," "Coming out in general to everyone who I present this to and all the others involved: parents, library, work, people everywhere," "That I'm not queer enough to teach this or that I'll have to pretend because I don't have any definite answers to anyone's questions let alone my own," "That this is a personal journey and not the appropriate foundation to teach a class from." Then, miraculously, after writing down all these fears, I turned over the page and wrote the first draft my syllabus based on what I did know from all my library research.

In the early spring, I took a draft of my syllabus to Hutchins Professor Debora Hammond. She was supportive of my idea to teach a class and she explained that I would need a class title, to write a short summary of why I wanted to teach this topic, and that it would have to be approved by all the Hutchins faculty. The directions seemed simple enough, but they were like climbing a mountain and it took me several more months to write this one paragraph. Returning to my journal I wrote: "I want to legitimize myself—see me in theory in class—the central focus of discussion not just some sideline or tangent. I want gender and sexual orientation to be the focus. To see all the disciplines, scientists, theorists, and cultural artists grappling with what the nature of these identities are. I want to focus on fluidity, change, multiplicity, and contradiction. I want to honor the cultural workers who are theorizing, performing, and whistle-blowing their way into new space. I want to study this because it's me, it's my work, my identity and the identities of the people around me that I love." I finished this journal entry with the title for the course: "Contesting Identity: Sexual Orientation and Gender."

The outline for this class, that I proposed to the Hutchins faculty, featured an interdisciplinary array of current scholarship and social commentary on gender and sexual orientation. The class began with readings that presented definitions and interrelationships between the concepts of gender, race, sexual orientation, identity fluidity, and queerness. As students in all queer studies classes discover, there are no easy definitions for the term "queer." On the one hand, this formerly (and sometimes currently) derogatory epithet has been reclaimed by some and redefined as a positive descriptor for LGBTQ people. But the term "queer" signifies more than just an identity label, it also functions to critique the process through which some identities and lives are designated normative—or "normal"—often through the exclusion and denigration of groups constructed as "other." The class included readings from the anthology *Homophobia: How it Harms Us All* as a way for all students, regardless of gender or sexual orientation, to consider the negative impacts of oppression on everyone. Following this introduction, the class took up several scientific articles presenting research and debates about the possible existence of a "gay gene" and the supposed biological origins of homosexuality. Since scientific narratives hold a great deal of legitimizing power in our society, these readings provided an opportunity to address connections between scientific scholarship and social power. The course then turned to the sociological book *Coming Out In College* which applied insights from critical postmodernism to study the lives and experiences of out college students. From sociology, the class next investigated historical accounts of LGBTQ lives, with special focus on members of the military and local San Francisco LGBTQ history. The course concluded with an analysis of lesbian representation through the book *Where the Girls Are*. The interdisciplinary range of this course allowed students the opportunity to approach the topic of queer theory and LGBTQ lives from multiple perspectives and disciplines. It was approved by the Hutchins faculty and added as a 2-unit, student-taught, elective course to the Fall 1999 schedule.

Fourteen students signed up to take the Libs 399 seminar, "Contesting Identity: Sexual Orientation and Gender," and they showed up to the first class excited and apprehensive about what was to come. Students reported enrolling in the class for a wide range of reasons. Some reflected sentiments similar to a student who wrote: "When I first saw this class description in the Hutchins schedule, I knew I had to take this course. Here I was, a gay student in a straight college and there was an actual class about the homosexual experience. It was an opportunity that I couldn't pass up." While for other students, even attending the first day this course was quite daunting, as illustrated in the words of one student: "When I walked into the classroom the very first day of class, I thought for sure I signed up for the wrong class. I am not one to listen or even talk about issues pertaining to the gay and lesbian culture. I get shivers down my spine when I think about this subject." Given the range of student exposure and comfort regarding the class topic, we all had to work to develop a sense of trust and a common purpose in this class. In Hutchins learning spaces, which are designed to be discussion-based seminars, students must engage actively and collaboratively with each other. Most Hutchins professors do not lecture; instead they facilitate students to take the lead in analyzing course material. If students do not participate through active listening and talking in the seminar, it is challenging to move the class forward.

To address the disparate degrees of knowledge and familiarity with LGBTQ topics, the class began with discussions about how to even talk about this class. Several students commented that they had never before discussed "gay issues" in their entire lives. For some students, this was the first time they had ever said the words "gay" or "lesbian" out loud in a public space. Compounding some students' reticence, was the fact that the course was taught in a virtual social vacuum of accurate information about homosexuality—the internet was not yet a wide-spread source for information and by 1997 only Ellen had ever come out as gay in a televised episode. No wonder it was hard for some students to talk about the readings; terms like "gay," "queer," and even "homosexual" carried negative connotations. The class literally had to learn how to talk about the subject using words that were hard for some students to get out of their mouths. There were some icebreaking moments in the class when we agreed to not worry—to the point of not talking at all—about getting the words and labels correct. Lots of students laughed in recognition about this point. At another moment early on a heterosexual student who sat, as she described it, "quietly and miserably in the classroom" decided to share about her resistance to learning about this topic. She was surprised when the whole class started applauding after she spoke and assured her that her fear was a "natural step to encounter" in the learning process. These moments of class and individual self-reflexivity were critical in developing a collegial learning community where students could acknowledge their differences while also working towards a common goal of deeper understanding. Furthermore, these reflections were a tangible way for students to grapple with a central insight of queer theory by exposing the power and effects of normative social construction embedded in our understandings about sexual orientation.

Another instructive struggle in this class was the tension between the students who had no prior exposure to gay people and those who were openly gay, lesbian, and bisexual. Some of the queer students had a lifetime of experience with the class topic and were much more likely, because of their outsider status, to have discussed the topics we were studying. Some felt that the class material was not new to them and that it could be "tedious" to talk about topics that much of their life revolved around. On the other hand, students with no prior knowledge or experience with LGBTQ topics were so overwhelmed with new material that they felt they could hardly even speak in class. There was no immediate solution to this wide range of understanding except to talk about why it existed in the first place and what it could mean. Several queer students made an important point, that for the students who could not relate to the material, this experience of not having your life or knowledge centered is how the queer students felt every day in every other class. This helped open up conversations about marginalization and heterosexual privilege.

Out of these hard conversations and through engaging the class reading material, many students developed deeper levels of self-reflexivity about how homophobia (hatred and fear of gays) and heterosexism (belief that heterosexuality is the ideal social norm) formed the socially taught bedrock of their understanding that they were now beginning to see and question. For example, some students who described themselves as having little previous knowledge about LGBTQ people came to realize that they actually had unconsciously absorbed a great deal of negative social messaging about homosexuality. One student explained this realization stating at first: "I never considered homophobia my problem. I didn't know any gays, lesbians, or bisexuals." She then went on to reflect that "homophobia is not usually taught, but rather it is a hate we are steeped in as growing individuals. It [homophobia] is not something that can be eradicated by simply telling you it is wrong. It is something you have to learn." In a similar vein, another student described their awareness process: "Don't get me wrong...I had no problem with gays. I didn't think they were perverted, or morally wrong, or that something was wrong with them. I just felt that their personal lives should be kept to themselves. I wrongly assumed that being homosexual was sexual in nature. When I say I'm heterosexual, I am not having sex or fantasizing about people of the opposite sex. I had my beliefs about homosexuality that I had never thought to question before this class." These reflections illustrate how social privilege is maintained through the false belief that unless one is negatively impacted by a social injustice then it remains not "my problem." Upon deeper reflection and study, many students in this class came to see how social oppressions harm not only targeted groups but also those in the social majority by "steeping" them in pre-conscious hate and restricting their capacity to connect with other people across forms of difference.

The material in this class also provoked deeper levels of analysis for the queer identified students in providing reflections, language, history, and context for their experiences. It also opened up new possibilities for existence and further reflection. One student commented: "I am in the process of coming out. What that means exactly, I am not yet sure. Just knowing that a gay world exists give me the freedom to find my place within it." Also grappling with the complexities of identity, visibility, and difference, a gay male student remarked that for him "Being queer covers all aspects of your life, it becomes your life, and there are moments when I don't want to play that role. I would like to be able to go through one day without feeling alien to the world, to all the people around me, I want one day when I don't feel overwhelmingly different. Yet I want the difference—I want the awareness it provides for me—I like knowing what I know of the world and of myself." Feminist theorist Audre Lorde (1984) provides a helpful framework for thinking about difference. She wrote: "Difference must be not merely tolerated, but seen as a fund of necessary polarities between which our creativity can spark like a dialectic." Through centering and exploring difference, rather than sweeping it away, students in this class were able to have a more honest accounting of who they are and how our social systems operate. As one student concluded about her time in this class: "I was hoping to be presented mirrors of experience to validate myself. To a certain extent, I have. There was such a high level of respect for those with different points of view and different lifestyles that new ideas were able to flow freely, new information transmitted."

Looking back on this class that I taught as an undergraduate student 20 years ago, I am amazed at the willingness of students to show up and to learn about what was still a very socially marginalized topic. There were students in this class that had only been taught homophobic/heterosexist perspectives and others who were silently confronting their own queer desires—the class really could have ground to a halt or imploded, but it did not. I think that the seminar discussion format and the pedagogical culture of Hutchins was an important factor. Students had practice dialoguing, posing informed questions, listening to different points of view, and pondering complex topics. These foundational skills served as the method to approach this controversial topic. The seminar format produced at least 2 streams of knowledge—both the insight derived from reading an interdisciplinary range of scholarship and also from listening to and conversing with people who had different lived experiences and perspectives. Students in this class did learn academic content from historical, biological, anthropological, legal, and religious studies about homosexuality. But they also really learned from hearing each other speak in class. The experience of this course was about more than just learning facts; it was about developing a learning community and a type of praxis for working with and through difference. One student reflecting on the political nature of this class being one of the very first on LGBTQ topics at SSU, explained that doing the work in this course "feels like Hutchins" because we are actively "discovering things" as a class.

Finally, my time as a Hutchins student and the period in which I designed and taught this class transformed me wholeheartedly. Leaning about LGBTQ people, history, and research gave me a much wider horizon of what was possible—one where I felt that all the complexities of my own life could fit. The strength of my internalized fears and prejudices were met and slowly overcome through a steady stream of scholarship from the fields of critical ethnic studies and women's and gender studies, which gave me the language and conceptual frameworks to understand oppression and privilege. Discovering that I could direct my own learning path into the scholarship and writing that I needed to know was revolutionary for me. I found agency in picking up the tools of research, careful reading, ethical witnessing, and community building. Former Hutchins Professor Les Adler (2001) explained that "this program is designed to encourage students to take themselves seriously as readers, writers, and thinkers capable of continuing an educational process throughout their lives." The interdisciplinary and student-led focus of Hutchins provided fertile ground to explore the impact of queer theory across numerous fields and in our own lives. In training undergraduate students to step into the role of intellectual facilitation, the Hutchins program allowed me to create queer spaces full of possibility.

References

Adler, Les K. 2001. "Uncommon Sense: Liberal Education, Learning Communities and the Transformative Quest." In Barbara Leigh Smith and John McCann, eds., *Reinventing Ourselves: Interdisciplinary Education, Collaborative Learning, and Experimentation in Higher Education,* Jossey-Bass. [Reprinted with permission in this anthology]

Ayres, Drummond. 1993. "Gay Woman Loses Custody of Her Son to Her Mother." *The New York Times.* September 8.

Baunach, Dawn Michelle. 2011. "Decomposing Trends in Attitudes Toward Gay Marriage, 1988–2006." *Social Science Quarterly* 92:2.

Chauncey, George. 1998. "The Ridicule of Gay and Lesbian Studies Threatens All Academic Inquiry." *The Chronicle of Higher Education.* July 3.

DiAngelo, Robin. 2011. "White Fragility." *International Journal of Critical Pedagogy* 3:3.

Freire, Paulo. 2000 [1970]. *Pedagogy of the Oppressed.* Continuum.

Heller, Scott. 1990. "Gay and Lesbian Studies Movement Gains Acceptance in Many Areas of Scholarship and Teaching." *The Chronicle of Higher Education*. October 24.

Lindemann, Hilde. 2001. *Damaged Identities, Narrative Repair.* Cornell University Press.

Lorde, Audre. 2007 [1984]. "The Master's Tools Will Never Dismantle the Master's House." *Sister Outsider: Essays and Speeches*. Crossing Press Feminist Series.

hooks, bell. 1991. "Theory as Liberatory Practice." *Yale Journal of Law and Feminism* 4:2.

McIntosh, Peggy. 1989. "White Privilege: Unpacking the Invisible Knapsack." *Peace and Freedom Magazine*, Women's International League for Peace and Freedom. July/August.

Olson, Warren. 1992. "The Origin and Birth of the Hutchins School of Liberal Studies." Unpublished manuscript.

Participate, Own, Connect: An Educator's Retrospective on Hutchins

Kevin Cody

Kevin Cody is the Farmer Training Program Manager at New Entry Sustainable Farming Project where he develops pathways to generate and sustain new and beginning farmers. With a background in sustainable food systems education, his role at New Entry includes overseeing grants, developing curriculum, building strategic regional partnerships, and providing direct technical assistance to participants and instruction in courses on food systems, crop production and business planning.

Prior to New Entry, Kevin was a faculty member in Environmental and Sustainability Studies at the University of Northern Colorado where he ran the student farm and taught a range of courses from Permaculture Design to Sustainability and Capitalism. He received his PhD in Sociology at the University of California, Santa Cruz in 2015 with an emphasis on agrarian political economy and the internationalization of alternative food networks. He graduated from the Hutchins School of Liberal Studies in 2002.

Two decades ago I was a freshman in the Hutchins School of Liberal Studies. For the past twelve years teaching has been my primary occupation, first as a graduate student at UC Santa Cruz and then as a faculty instructor at the University of Northern Colorado. This essay is an account of how Hutchins fundamentally shaped who I am as an educator by modelling a critically engaged pedagogy that is now central to my own teaching philosophy.

When I enrolled in Hutchins in 1998, I had no intention of becoming a teacher. Unlike most of the students in the program at the time who aspired to be K-12 educators, I was content to pursue a liberal arts degree, the track less taken. In my second year, the late and beloved Jeannine Thompson asked me if I had ever considered becoming a university professor. I hadn't, but the question had the air of declaration and suddenly I found myself considering what seemed like an outlandish proposition. I developed and taught my first college level course two years later as a senior in Hutchins. Creating a syllabus, leading discussions, crafting assignments—this work seemed like a natural extension of the preceding years of seminars. But even then, I was more focused on the content than I was on its delivery. I had not yet envisioned teaching as my vocation.

Four years later as a graduate student in Sociology at the University of California, Santa Cruz, I came to appreciate Hutchins' rarified approach to interdisciplinary education and discussion-based seminars. While the discipline of Sociology is broad, it still seemed needlessly confined compared to what I experienced as an undergraduate. Lectures for the classes in which I was a teaching assistant often contained 100 or more students and a professor reading years-old power point slides, a far cry from the dynamic twelve-person seminars to which I was accustomed. Fortunately, I had plenty of opportunities to teach in graduate school where I quickly found myself employing the Socratic method, scaffolding open-ended questions, and encouraging students to make connections among their readings and classes.

In my first faculty position in Environmental and Sustainability Studies at the University of Northern Colorado (UNCO), I came to realize more fully the profound ways that my own beliefs about how to teach were directly attributable to the ethos that permeates the Hutchins community. When designing new syllabi and programs Hutchins was a frequent point of reference and inspiration. I felt emboldened to integrate a diversity of perspectives and disciplines from which to view and analyze topics like food systems, my specialty. When I started a student farm, I did so with attention towards creating a truly interdisciplinary environment to promote experiential learning and community engagement.

In reflecting on the ways that Hutchins influenced my own pedagogy, three key themes emerge—participation, ownership, and connection. I discuss each one below in relation to my experiences in Hutchins and as a university instructor: participation in class discussion is a way of elevating the collective consciousness, taking ownership encourages students to become personally invested in their education, and building connections helps create a personally meaningful interdisciplinary education.

"Participants only. No Spectators."

There is a dictum printed on the ticket granting entry into the famed Burning Man festival. It says simply, "Participants only. No Spectators." Tens of thousands of revelers transform a stark desert landscape into something absurd and outrageous by contributing art, music, knowledge, snow cones, and myriad inconceivable creations and costumes. Absent individual and collective contributions there is nothing, just a vast empty desert lakebed.

The emptiness of that desert lakebed is the sound of silence during a seminar. Anyone who has been in a discussion-based class knows the sound of silence. The challenge of generating lively discussions with full class participation was evident during my own undergraduate experience in Hutchins. In one seminar, I recall asking what I thought was a well-crafted and provocative question about our text, only to have it silently spiral downward from its lofty heights until it landed on the table with an imperceptible thud. After the class, the professor taught me about how to scaffold questions to bring other students along an intellectual journey. Hutchins also introduced me to things like talking tokens, and ways to balance who talks in class to get more voices involved in the discussion. When participation reaches a critical mass, discussions take on a new dimension, with emergent properties, something more than the sum of our collective voices.

What is that special something that is generated through active discussion and participation and why does it matter? For one, when we add more voices to the conversation, those voices can sometimes do more to challenge our beliefs and values than any assigned author. At the University of Northern Colorado, I taught a class called American Environmental Worldviews that started with a section on the Standing Rock protests. Students read about the conflict over the gas pipeline and identified the environmental worldviews of different actors involved. Debates about oil and gas development were familiar to most students in the class. The university is in Greeley, a town surrounded by over 30,000 oil and gas wells. Most students were sympathetic to protesters' environmental and social justice concerns, and their voices generally dominated the conversation.

To make space for divergent perspectives, I asked if anyone had real experience working in the oil fields. Tyler sat in the back of class and rarely spoke up, so it was a surprise to most when he raised his hand. We had spoken previously in office hours about his work in the oil fields in North Dakota, and his unique views on conservation as a hunter. He described to the class the extreme safety measures for installing and managing pipelines and spoke about the diligence and care with which he and his coworkers approached their work. His comments ran counter to the narrative emerging from Standing Rock and those inclined to side with the water defenders, like most of the students in the class. His voice added complexity to a debate in a way no reading ever could. The views of more vocal opponents to the pipeline were chastened by hearing directly from a peer who, it would seem, was not an evil person out to destroy the earth.

Seminars, like Burning Man and democracy, don't function without participation. Encouraging participation in the classroom is not only about generating discussion to help students better understand a text or an issue like oil and gas development. It is about creating space for students to articulate complex ideas, find the confidence to ask a question, voice their opinion, or share their experience. Together we are more than the sum of our parts, and it is our ability to communicate, to have a dialog, to discuss contentious issues, that makes us human. Participation enlivens and enlightens, it is also an essential step towards owning your education.

Owning the Means of Production

Primitive accumulation, the necessary precursor to capitalist accumulation, according to Marx, is "nothing else than the historical process of divorcing the producer from the means of production." This separation sets the stage for class divisions whereby the owners of the means of production extract surplus value from the workers who have nothing left to sell but their labor. Peasants freed from feudal ties are no longer bound to work the land that provides them sustenance and their feudal lords wealth. Of course, this freedom to sell one's labor comes at a cost, such as workers' alienation. Divorced from the means of production they become but a cog in the machine disconnected from the products, processes, and people that constitute their work. Like Charlie Chaplin in Modern Times, workers in a capitalist system become alienated from what it means to be human, what Marx called our "species-being."

Unfortunately, agency and ownership are not often part of the educational process nor the resulting product. In the factory model of education, students entering college are primed to follow a curriculum map with one or two paths leading to the same destination, a degree in some codified discipline. Courses become boxes to check off and exams a means by which to check them.

What does it mean then, in practice, to encourage students to take ownership of their education, especially as universities strive to become more like corporations? Hutchins presented no shortage of opportunities to take ownership of one's education. Take the open-ended essay prompt, for example. I recall times when, after a 15-week semester and nearly as many books, the assignment was to write something like 10 pages using 5 books, that's all. Limitlessness is overwhelming, like the horizon that contains no human-made boundaries marking the limit to nature's expansiveness. In this prompt there are no power lines, no flight plans, just seemingly infinite land and sky, pages and ideas. I've assigned similar essays and, to be honest, I take some joy in hearing about students struggling with where to start. The challenge is to create an assemblage that helps make sense of the world. Ownership comes through making meaning out of the assembled texts and facilitated seminars, and sometimes through reclaiming the original means of production.

At UNCO I had an opportunity to expand our existing food and agriculture related courses by developing a student farm program. Our first season and first farm class were hurriedly put together, filled with setbacks like torrential rain that prevented planting and pests and pathogens that wiped out most of our greenhouse. Despite these challenges, students seemed to genuinely care about their work and saw value in some unexpected places. A key assignment in the class was to keep weekly journal entries to track things like plant growth and personal growth. The farm presented remarkable opportunities for students to own and connect to their education and peers. I'll let them speak for themselves here:

> "That garden has a place in my heart, and it hit me when we left Wise Acres that I'll do whatever it takes to help take care of it this summer."

> "It is the weirdest feeling to be so invested into plants which don't have eyes or thoughts to share with us, yet I feel just as sad for one of them dying as if an animal had died. I feel myself constantly referring to the plants on the farm as 'my babies' to friends that aren't in the class...Seeing them come up from the ground and fruit will quite possibly be the greatest feeling I will have this summer."

> "All of the stuff we got done on Tuesday really reminded me of the value of group work, which I normally don't like...The work was hard, but the fact that a lot of people were doing it and having fun made it surprisingly enjoyable."

> "This class is teaching us about life, how to move through obstacles, as well as how to grow food. This class offers so much to think about, but you must be actively engaged to learn from the experience."

These quotes show how students' sense of ownership influenced how they experienced the work itself, the product of their labors, and the peers they worked alongside.

To own your education is to retake ownership of the means of production—courses and their texts—where the product is not necessarily the degree but rather knowledge and the capacity for critical thinking, communication, and civic engagement. By presenting students with unique opportunities to tailor their education to their emerging interests, you empower them to take a more vested interest in the outcomes. Through the experiential learning opportunity of the farm, students were able to forge connections between their physical work and diverse areas of study and close the gap between their lives inside and outside of the classroom. The significance of these kinds of connections is the theme of the next section.

Making (Food) Connections

After Hutchins I moved to the Sonoma County countryside. In the height of my second season on the goat ranch where I worked and lived, the manure filled garden turned out an incredible abundance of vegetables; the pigs we raised on bread and whey had been slaughtered and filled two chest freezers; the chickens had reached their egg-laying prime; cheese and milk from the dairy were always on hand; and surplus bread from the bakery where I worked was a constant staple. The work I contributed to produce this abundance helped establish a deep connection I felt with the land, the food, and my community.

In graduate school I gravitated towards the study of food and agriculture because of these formative experiences of rural living and farming. I conducted research with beginning farmers to better understand barriers to their long-term viability, and dove enthusiastically into literature on agrarian political economy, alternative food systems, and peasant studies. As much as I enjoyed researching these topics, it wasn't until I began teaching about food systems that I came to appreciate how well food and agriculture lend themselves to a kind of interdisciplinary education that is personally meaningful for students.

What does it mean to provide a personally meaningful interdisciplinary education? I think Hutchins provides some good examples. In addition to the books and insights about pedagogy, I left Hutchins with new neural networks forged by making connections between science and religion, or psychology and biology, that still influence my worldview. The connections I made across subjects were as valuable as the connections I made between those subjects and my life outside of the classroom. Interests in social activism found an outlet during the Iraq war when a group of us formed the Student Activist League and hosted demonstrations on campus. Interests in showcasing the creative talent of Hutchins led me and other students to establish *Zephyr*, the Hutchins literary journal. Finding ways to encourage students to make connections between course material and their personal lives is a major emphasis of my own courses, especially those focused on agri-food systems.

In my Food Systems and Agrarian Change course, students were encouraged not just to think critically across subject areas, but to integrate their understandings of food systems with their lives outside the classroom and in the community. For example, I designed an assignment to examine the complexities of "local" food production and consumption where students conducted interviews with food systems workers within 10 miles of the university. Student-selected interview subjects included small-scale organic farmers, workers at the JBS meatpacking plant, and at Leprino Foods (the world's largest producer of mozzarella cheese), among others. Not only did this class assignment encourage students to problematize the geographic designation of local and the concept of food miles, it required them to interrogate broader claims about the social, economic, and environmental implications of local and organic agri-food systems.

The importance of place and personal relationships are integral to the study of food systems. The JBS Swift slaughterhouse is a major employer in the community surrounding the university and the industrial grain-livestock complex is the dominant agriculture sector.

As a way to encourage students to consider the landscape where they live, we read the book, *Every 12 Seconds,* an ethnography of a slaughterhouse (the title is a reference to how frequently a cow is killed in line for industrialized slaughter). Students also kept a food journal to uncover their own often overlooked relationships to the food they consume and how they consume it, leaving some to make dramatic changes in diet and lifestyle.

Food systems education is increasingly being integrated into liberal arts curriculum across institutions of higher education. As with the student farm, opportunities abound to integrate hands-on learning and diverse subject areas from biology to sociology when teaching about food systems. Food and agriculture are also deeply personal, an area where values and politics intersect with our bodies, households, and communities. Hutchins is where I learned to make the connections that I've come to see as an integral component to a critically engaged pedagogy.

Conclusion

As I write this reflection on how Hutchins influenced my classroom pedagogy and broader trajectory in academia, I am about to embark on a new adventure in adult education, outside of academia. This month I begin work as the manager of a beginning farmer training program with a nonprofit based in Massachusetts called New Entry Sustainable Farming Project. Just as the university teaching experience helped me uncover and integrate knowledge from my time in Hutchins, I'm certain this new position will elicit insights from past experiences in the classroom, on the student farm, and in graduate school. Participate, own, connect—these strategies to promoting critical thinking and engagement are as applicable to undergraduate students as they are to beginning farmers. They transcend academic and traditional classroom learning.

The program to train beginning farmers has elements of a liberal arts education. Participants are required to make connections between biology and economics in the field and in our courses on crop production and business planning. On our incubator farm, participants own the fruits of their labor on land we help them steward. And learning how to farm is about more than gaining technical knowledge. It entails problem solving, critical thinking, and communicating one's social and environmental values to potential customers and the community. I am thrilled to apply the skills and knowledge I've gained in the classroom to the field of beginning farmer education, as these are the individuals that will form the foundation of a more sustainable food system. It will be a big change from the more traditional classroom teaching. But as a friend said to me recently, "There are many ways to be a professor."

I LEARNED TO LISTEN

Finn Menzies

Finn Menzies came to Hutchins as a track 2 student in 2004. He took Hutchins on an independent study of permaculture to New Zealand, and then graduated with a degree in Liberal Studies and a double minor in Gender Studies and English. He was contributor to the *Zephyr* and then followed his love for poetry to receive his M.F.A. in Poetry at Mills College. Now he is an elementary school teacher dedicated to access and equity, a tarot reader, and a poet in Seattle, WA.

I learned to listen
to the stomachs of books
print moving like tide

I learned to listen
to my body's song

I learned
I am a dream &
language will never hold me
my name is salt
through the hands of the divine

I learned
how to weigh our lives
how to save nothing each month
but my dignity

I learned my lineage
is a lineage of terror
and how we will pay

I learned I am a room full of stars
a hunk of mineral
an animal
on my knees

I learned to listen
to my own sin and salvation,
they were always the eyes
of my own waking

I learned to listen
to my own dying
time between rains
between meals
this minute

I learned to listen to you
with my wounds and my birthright
balancing the earth on her pin

I learned to listen
by feeling
palms on the wall
in middle of the night

AMAZING GRACE

AnnMarie Miller

AnnMarie Miller wrote the following Intellectual Autobiography in the spring of 2007 in Francisco Vazquez's section of LIBS 402: Senior Synthesis. LIBS 402 is the culminating course in the Hutchins major; it involves a comprehensive review of the student's entire academic career, in which they are asked to put together a portfolio of their work and reflect on their learning and personal growth through the course of their experience in the Hutchins program. This essay has since been used, with AnnMarie's permission, in several sections of LIBS 302: Introduction to Liberal Studies, to orient students transferring into the Hutchins School in their Junior year. She has also granted permission to include it in this anthology.

After graduating from Hutchins, AnnMarie threw herself into working full time as the operations manager of a local conference center with a history in the human potential movement. When that came to a natural end in 2013, she accepted a position in the wine industry, but fairly quickly learned that position was going to be short lived. Somewhat terrified she signed up for flying trapeze lessons and focused on learning to jump. She soon after enrolled in SSU's Wine EMBA program, graduating in 2016, and is currently the general manager of Herb Lamb Vineyards in St. Helena, CA, and continually looking for ways in which she can contribute positively to her local community.

When I first came to Hutchins, I was frustrated. I had been attending college at SRJC on and off for eight years and was tired of being surrounded by students who I perceived were simply going through the motions, pushed only by their parents to be there in the first place. What I wanted was to be with other serious students and I felt I would find them in Graduate School. I simply wanted to get out of Undergraduate School as quickly as possible. I knew a few people who knew people who had attended Hutchins and everything I was told made it seem like a good fit. My urgency made the fit seem less important, so it was a toss-up between the Art department and Hutchins. Hutchins won simply because it meant one less year to achieve my goal. I literally made my decision knowing very little about the actual Hutchins program. Initially annoyed with the required classes, I figured I'd better look into what I had just committed myself to. What I discovered thrilled me. I felt certain that others interested in this program would be interesting and I could not wait for my first class to begin.

I was utterly disappointed. At SRJC I was continually stifled by teachers who seemed put off by my excited nature and who gave the impression that they had no interest in discussing issues, let alone their interrelatedness. There were some exceptions, but generally it came across to me that they were teaching one subject and that was what I needed to focus on. Above all, there was to be no discussions of politics. I had long ago given up on students who didn't appear interested in any of these things anyway. Here at Hutchins, I foolishly expected students to be somehow drastically different. While I was overjoyed with the teachers I met here and the syllabi of the classes, I found the students to be virtually the same. No one seemed to understand anything. Feeling more knowledgeable than most of my fellow students, I quickly assumed a somewhat superior attitude and stewed in my aggravation. I felt this attitude cement itself when, during a seminar in LIBS 308: The Practice of Culture, one of my fellow students commented: "What Hutchins teaches us is that we're all fucked." If this is what the students at Hutchins felt they were *learning*, there was no hope. It was enough to make me give up.

Instead, I opted for a more proactive attitude. I decided that if I wanted to be with more interesting students, I was responsible for finding something interesting about them. I determined that it was my negativity that was coloring them, preventing me from seeing the value that was actually there. By the end of my second semester, I had accepted the challenge of not simply engaging myself and allowing myself to be frustrated, but instead trying to figure out ways to engage others. I had recognized my complicity in creating my negative perception and I charted a course to change it. I could have easily stagnated, allowing my bitterness to deepen, but instead I chose to embark on a journey that cultured grace.

amazing

The seminar was the easiest place to employ my new attitude and experiment with my challenge. Whereas previously I was very concerned with expressing my opinion because I had one, I now began to ask myself in what ways my opinion might matter to others and what about it might actually be helpful. I soon stopped being so concerned with my opinion, though I still enjoyed expressing it, and instead focused on communicating my *understanding* of the material at hand. This seemed to make a significant difference, even if only to me. I also began to be less concerned with speaking and concentrated on listening to what others had to say. If the seminar is designed so students learn from each other, I needed to pay more attention to what these students *were* saying, instead of just assuming they weren't saying what I thought they should.

how sweet the sound

Attempting to curb my terribly critical nature, I strove to not only listen to others, but also acknowledge when I agreed with someone. More significantly, I tried to let people know when I thought they made an interesting statement, or perceptive observation. This combination, of being less eager to express myself and more attentive to what others had to say, led me to believe that often, even when comments aren't directly related to the material, there were links to be made. For as much as I personally tend to come prepared to discuss the material, I began to find it more interesting to discover these less obvious connections.

how precious did that grace appear
the hour I first believed

Similar to my previous attitude with my fellow students, my attitude with the material assigned in class was initially very limited and it therefore limited my understanding. For as much as I am a careful reader and fairly perceptive, I had a tendency to look at everything through the same lens and therefore always come to similar conclusions. In one of my first Hutchins classes, LIBS 302: Introduction to Liberal Studies, we were asked to view Michael Moore's *Fahrenheit 9/11*. I recall dreading the experience because I had previously seen the film and didn't find it that interesting to begin with. Later in another class, LIBS 320C [A seminar in the Arts and Human Experience], we were asked to view the film yet again. I can still feel the exasperation I initially felt upon reading of the assignment. Resigning myself to not simply view it and write what I already knew about the film, I approached it with as open a mind as I could muster. By the end of the film, I was so excited with what I had previously not seen I was tempted to actually watch it again. Perhaps because this was my first opportunity to have a second chance at the same material, I actually *experienced* looking at the same thing again and seeing something completely different. Understanding different aspects of the same film gave a much greater depth of understanding of the whole film. I always knew that everything is made of multiple layers, but now I felt I actually understood what that meant. I began to wonder what I had missed in all the previous assignments as I felt like the lenses to my eyes had just been cleaned for the first time.

was blind but now I see

I used to like to think that I considered multiple perspectives in everything I did. I realized, in retrospect, that when I began at Hutchins the only perspective I ever really considered was my own. For as much as that perspective may have been colored with other people's experience, it was still *my* perspective and that is what I was bent on expressing. I realized this when I wrote my first research paper. Despite my passion, I didn't feel the paper did the topic justice. The paper was fairly good and I worked really hard at putting it together, but the end result left me wanting something more than what I produced. I wrestled with this for as long as time allowed, but it wasn't until after receiving the paper back and re-reading it that it dawned on me. The paper was intended to present information in such a way that *anyone* who read it would be outraged. But what I felt I produced was a paper that some wouldn't even read. It was written from a perspective so entrenched in outrage it told people *how* to be affected by the situation, rather than inviting them to *be* affected by the situation. Realizing this, I felt I had just been saved. Saved from the lost, rebellious, noisy, brat I had so long loved being, saved from a life frustrated by never feeling understood and saved from the vicious cycle of screaming because of not feeling heard and not being heard because no one wants to listen to screaming.

that saved a wretch like me
I once was lost
but now I am found

As someone who has spent a good deal of her life in pursuit of a liberal education, I find it nearly impossible to stay within a particular discipline and I am not sure I know exactly what that would look like. In fact, I find the thought of limiting oneself to a single discipline troubling, if not almost impossible. I have taken plenty of general education classes within different disciplines, but there are always links to be made to other disciplines. The study of biology, for example, is loaded with comparisons to be made with sociology. I am reminded of an article I recently read in a 2003 issue of *Nature* where scientists "modeled the fitness consequences of two possible decision-making mechanisms: 'despotism' and 'democracy'." Who would initially have thought that biologists would consider such a thing? But that is exactly the point. I believe when I started here at Hutchins, I did not understand just how connected everything really is. Realizing this can be somewhat overwhelming and frightening and yet, understanding this makes the world a much less scary place.

'twas grace that taught my heart to fear
and grace that fear relieved

A good example of interdisciplinary work, as well as creativity and synthesis, is my internship. The path to this project was one of the more interesting in my journey. The internship, a requirement of Track I, was an intimidating endeavor and I did not find relief in the assurance that I could simply use some aspect of my job in place of an actual internship. I spoke with a number of students who had done just that and who described somewhat pointless exercises always quipping, "it was easy." It's not that I like to make things difficult for myself I just detest doing things merely for the sake of doing them. I was facing one of my biggest challenges yet at Hutchins. How do I satisfy the requirement and satisfy myself at the same time? I was dreading the entire experience, but set about attempting to translate my potentially boring responsibility at work into something I, and potentially others, would find interesting. For as difficult as it was initially, I kept telling myself, not that I *had* to do this, but that I *could* do this. This belief in my ability and myself rang true in the end. I created something I could not have been happier with and something I'd never before conceived. It was not confidence that assured my success, but rather my success that bolstered my confidence.

> *through many dangers*
> *toils and snares*
> *I have already come*

When I began at Hutchins, I believed I was a good writer because I could write and I enjoyed writing. Much of the feedback I received on my papers assured me that I was not alone in this belief. But as the semesters went on, I found that when *I* re-read my papers I often found them confusing and difficult to read, not at all what I remembered reading when I first wrote them. I was looking forward to my next opportunity to write a substantial paper and attempt all the improvements I had determined my writing needed. In one of the last legs of this journey I had the opportunity for which I had been waiting. I wrote a paper I was so pleased with I simply could not stop reading it, every time I read it I simply beamed. I thought I was so clever and smart, and I thought what I had written was really good. The day came when we were to receive our papers and, as they often do, our teacher wanted to discuss the papers before handing them back. Looking right at me, he spoke of problem after problem. But they were pretty good he assured us. As I reached for my paper being slid across the table, I could feel the air already starting to leak out of my over inflated balloon-like head. The feedback on this paper was so specific and so unforeseen I took it as an immediate challenge. The final paper I wrote for the class was 'okay', I said to myself shrugging, and didn't let myself think beyond that. This paper was turned in the last day of class before the semester break and I had to wait until the beginning of this semester to get it back. When I did and read the feedback, I felt like I was floating on air. This paper is, I think, one of the best I've ever written. I felt it synthesized, at long last, all that I hope to do in my writing: offer a balanced perspective, communicate coherent points, be enjoyable to read and above all, say something important. I not only felt I had learned something, something I could show because of the improvement between the two papers in this class, but also because I had demonstrated that I had accomplished what was most important to me.

'twas grace that brought me safely thus far
and grace will lead me home

Now that I am arriving at the end of this journey, I am filled with a mixture of exhaustion and exhilaration, but my adventure is far from over. I have learned to let go of a great deal of the baggage I once carried and I know how to make better use of what remains. I began on this path, long ago, wanting to express myself through movement. It seems I have and I will, only with a much more astute awareness of what it means to be graceful. That awareness will forever enlighten my movement. I have learned through my experience here at Hutchins to broaden my understanding of what is possible and see the deeper meaning in what is happening. And I am grateful. I am much less concerned, now, with where my journey will take me as I am, instead, focused on enjoying every step along the way.

and when this heart
and flesh shall fail
and mortal life shall cease
I shall possess
within the vale
a life of joy and peace

Made in the USA
Las Vegas, NV
20 January 2023